English B

for the IB Diploma

2nd Edition

PAT JANNING • PATRICIA MERTIN

Published by Pearson Education Limited, 80 Strand, London, WC2R 0RL

www.pearsonglobalschools.com

Text © Pearson Education Limited 2019
Development edited by Danielle Gee and Ann Arscott
Copy edited by Soo Hamilton
Proofread by Andy Pozzoni and Sarah Wright
Indexed by Georgie Bowden
Theory of knowledge review carried out by Christian Bryan
Designed by © Pearson Education Limited 2019
Typeset by © SPi Global
Original illustrations © Pearson Education Limited 2019
Illustrated by © SPi Global
Cover design by © Pearson Education Limited 2019
Cover images: Front: © **Getty Images:** Busà Photography
Inside front cover: **Shutterstock.com:** Dmitry Lobanov

First published 2019

24 23 22 21 20 19
IMP 10 9 8 7 6 5 4 3 2 1

British Library Cataloguing in Publication Data
A catalogue record for this book is available from the British Library

ISBN 978 1 292 27081 4

Acknowledgements
The authors and publisher would like to thank the following individuals and organisations for their kind permission to reproduce copyright material.

Photographs
(Key: b-bottom; c-centre; l-left; r-right; t-top)

123RF: Ian Allenden FM,10, Zhukovsky 3, Helen Hotson 7, Epicstockmedia 61br, Liubomir Paut-Fluerasu 118, Mark Bowden 132,134,148, Volodymyr Goinyk 179, Joshua Resnick 188, Serezniy 194, Algre 201tl, Rawpixelcl 201cl, Leonid Andronov 201tr; **Alamy Imges**: ImageBROKER/Manfred Bail 9, Hero Images Inc. 22, Matthew Oldfield Editorial Photography 58, Relaximages/MONK 64, Glenstar 98, Aardvark 99, Dpa picture alliance 125, Homer Sykes 128, John Steele 158, Hero Images Inc 162, Michael Wheatley 171, Luciano Mortula 203, A katz 207; **Alexander Biner:** Used with permission of Alexander Biner 163; **Getty Images:** Andriy Onufriyenko 1, Ian Ross Pettigrew 45, Keith Levit/Design Pics 63, FatCamera/iStock 76, Gannet77/iStock 81, FStop Images-Andreas Stamm/Brand X Pictures 89, Campbell Addy/DigitalVision 131, Sandla/iStock 169, Attila Csaszar 173, StockstudioX/iStock 176; **Glasgow Science Center:** Used with permission of Paulina Zurakowska 101, Used with permission of Peter Mackey 104; **NASA**: NASA 223; **Pearson Education Ltd**: Ann Cromack/Ikat Design 107, Drone Explorer 127tl; **Radio New Zealand Limited:** Used with permission of The Plastic Soup Surfer 182; **Shutterstock**: Moomusician 5, Sorang 13, Artem Shadrin 25, Good-Start 24, Rawpixel.com 39, Africa Studio 48, Lakov Filimonov 50, Sue Martin 60, Terry Granger 61tl, Narongsak Nagadhana 61bl, Alex Brylov 65, Oneinchpunch 67, Tommaso79 72, Jan kranendonk 79, Roman Nerud 85bl, 85br, Operation Shooting 94, Pinkyone 109, Gorodenkoff 123, Dpa picture alliance 124, Bartlomiej K. Kwieciszewski 127cl, Victor Maschek 129, Vladimir Konstantinov 144, Marius_Comanescu 160, Philip Bird LRPS CPAGB 168, Richard Whitcombe 174, IM_photo 201cr, Cristi Matei 220, NASA/Jpl/Cornell University 222, Shutterstock 224tc, Fingerhut 224c; **The Plastic Soup Surfer:** Used with permission of The Plastic Soup Surfer 182

All other images © Pearson Education

We are grateful to the following for permission to reproduce copyright material:

Text

P 3, Katee Inghram: Inghram, Katee, What it means to be American, © Katee Inghram. Used with permission; **P 5, Ian Thompson:** Thompson, Ian, What it means to be Scottish, © Ian Thompson. Used with permission; **P 7, Top Five Books LLC:** Conan Doyle, Arthur, The Hound of the Baskervilles, © 2013, Top Five Books LLC; **P 8, Alegria Lores:** What it means to be a Cuban-American-Costa Rican, Submitted by Alegria Lores. © Alegria Lores. Used with permission; **P 13, Michael Bucksmith:** Bucksmith, Michael, Identity and our roots. © Michael Bucksmith. Used with permission; **P 16, 17, E. P. Dutton & Co., Inc.:** Tashlin, Frank, The Bear That Wasn't. © 1946 E. P. Dutton & Co., Inc.; **P 18, 233, Annelies Brabant:** Belonging everywhere and nowhere; living, working, and raising children abroad, by Annelies Brabant, Vitaallestero, 5 June 2016. © 2016 Annelies Brabant; **P 23, Guardian News & Media Limited:** 'The only way you can change anything is in small increments', Interview with Cerys Matthews by Juliana Piskorz., *The Guardian*, 1 July 2018. © 2018, Guardian News & Media Limited; **P 26, Leo Babauta:** The 10 Essential Rules for Slowing Down and Enjoying Life More, By Leo Babauta, zenhabits.net, 11 June, 2009; **P 26, Times Newspapers Limited:** Adapted from Andrew Ellson, Wives lie about being the main breadwinner, © 2018, Times Newspapers Limited; **P 32, Anna Coburn:** "Cull" by Anna Coburn. © Anna Coburn; **P 55, Merriam-Webster, Incorporated:** Happiness. (n.d.) In Merriam-Webster's collegiate dictionary. Retrieved from https://www.merriam-webster.com/dictionary/happiness. © 2019, Merriam-Webster, Incorporated. Used with permission; **P 56, Projets2Coeur:** Pleasure and

Happiness: The Great Mix-up (part 1), By Matthieu Ricard. Blog in www.matthieuricard.org, 3 July, 2018. © 2018, Projets2Coeur; **P 63, PGL Travel Ltd:** PGL, Outdoor Education for Secondary Schools, At PGL Centres in the UK and France. *Mediterranean Watersports.* 2019. © 2019, PGL Travel Ltd; **P 67, Claire Thompson:** How I came to be an opera singer, interview with Claire Thompson. © Claire Thompson. Used with permission; **P 70, ABC-CLIO, LLC:** Stephen D. Krashen, The Power of Reading: Insights from the Research, Ed. 2, Libraries Unlimited, 2004. © 2004, ABC-CLIO, LLC. Used with permission; **P 72, Christian Brown:** Interview with Christian Brown. © Christian Brown. Used with permission; **P 86, Waitrose & Partners:** A pinch of salt by Selin Kiazim, Waitrose Food Magazine, 2018. © 2018, Waitrose & Partners. Used with permission; **P 101, Paulina Weronika Zurakowska:** PAULINA'S DIARY: MY WEEK, Blog in Glasgow Science Centre, posted on 3 Aug 2018. © 2018, Paulina Weronika Zurakowska. Used with permission; **P 104, Peter Mackey:** PETER'S VISIT - GUEST BLOG, Blog in Glasgow Science Centre, posted on 1 May 2018. © 2018, Peter Mackey. Used with permission; **P 107, ICE Scotland:** Heritage Trail, Glasgow's Clyde Bridges, ICE Scotland. © 2019, ICE Scotland; **P 110, History Mystery Ltd:** Top tips for New Escape Gamers, *historymysterygame.com*, 19 Apr 2018. Retrieved from: http://historymysterygame.com/top-tips-new-gamers-2/. © 2019, History Mystery Ltd. Used with permission; **P 111, History Mystery Ltd:** Body of Evidence, *historymysterygame.com*, 19 Apr 2018. Retrieved from: http://historymysterygame.com/escape-games/norwich-guildhall/. © 2019, History Mystery Ltd. Used with permission; **P 111, History Mystery Ltd:** THE MERCHANTS' VAULTS, *historymysterygame.com*, 2018, Retrieved from: http://historymysterygame.com/new-norwich-escape-game-the-merchants-vaults/. © 2019, History Mystery Ltd. Used with permission; **P 111, History Mystery Ltd:** ARCHIVED ALIVE! *historymysterygame.com*, 2018, Retrieved from: https://historymystery.games/escape-games/. © 2019, History Mystery Ltd. Used with permission; **P 113, Telegraph Media Group Limited:** Secondary schools are introducing strict new bans on mobile phones, by Charles Hymas, The *Telegraph*, 24 Jun 2018. © 2018, Telegraph Media Group Limited. Used with permission; **P 114, Telegraph Media Group Limited:** France to impose total ban on mobile phones in schools, By Henry Samuel, *The Telegraph*, 11 Dec 2017. © 2017, Telegraph Media Group Limited. Used with permission; **P 124, Arche Nebra – Die Himmelsscheibe erleben:** Arche Nebra Innen. © 2019, Arche Nebra – Die Himmelsscheibe erleben. Used with permission; **P 126, Telegraph Media Group Limited**: Everything you need to know about visiting Stonehenge, by Sophie Campbell, The Telegraph, 13 Nov 2017. © 2017, Telegraph Media Group Limited. Used with permission; **P 135, The Regents of the University of California:** National Adolescent and Young Adult Health Information Center (2014). Sleep Deprivation in Adolescents and Young Adults. San Francisco: University of California, San Francisco. Retrieved from: http://nahic.ucsf.edu/wp-content/uploads/2014/08/sleep-brief-final. Used with permission; **P 137, 139, The Regents of the University of California:** National Adolescent and Young Adult Health Information Center (2014). Sleep Deprivation in Adolescents and Young Adults. San Francisco: University of California, San Francisco. Retrieved from: http://nahic.ucsf.edu/wp-content/uploads/2014/08/sleep-brief-final. © 2014, The Regents of the University of California; **P 141, 248 Guardian News & Media Limited:** Tablets out, imagination in: the schools that shun technology, by Matthew Jenkin, *The Guardian*, 2 Dec, 2015. © 2015, Guardian News & Media Limited. Used with permission; **P 145, 147, 249, Pearson Plc.:** An Ode to IB, by Catherine Barber, *Pearson International Schools Community*, 26 Jul 2018. © 2018, Pearson Plc. Used with permission; **P 157, Michael Bucksmith:** To what extent is identity linked to where we are from, by Michael Bucksmith. © Michael Bucksmith. Used with permission; **P 165, Alexander Biner:** Interview with Velia. © Alexander Biner. Used with permission; **P 170, 171, George Hinchliffe's Ukulele Orchestra of Great Britain:** George Hinchliffe's, Ukulele Orchestra of Great Britain, 'The Nation's Ukulele Orchestra', BBC News, Radio 4, 23 Sept 2014. © 2014, George Hinchliffe's Ukulele Orchestra of Great Britain. Used with permission; **P 174, 253, Guardian News & Media Limited**: Why fresh water shortages will cause the next great global crisis, by Robin McKie, *The Guardian*, 8 Mar 2015. © 2015, Guardian News & Media Limited. Used with permission; **P 177, WWF-UK:** What is climate change? *wwf.org.uk.* Retrieved from: https://www.wwf.org.uk/climate-change-and-global-warming, © 2018, WWF-UK. Used with permission; **P 179, Guardian News & Media Limited**: Canada's high Arctic glaciers at risk of disappearing completely, study finds, By Ashifa Kassam, *The Guardian*, 17 Jul 2018. © 2018, Guardian News & Media Limited. Used with permission; **P 188, Guardian News & Media Limited:** I rely on plastic straws and baby wipes. I'm disabled – I have no choice, by Penny Pepper, *The Guardian*, 9 Jul 2018. © 2018, Guardian News & Media Limited. Used with permission; **P 191, Narrative Content Group:** Mumbai's Versova Beach is home to the world's biggest beach, by Katherine Martinko, in *TreeHugger*, Jan 26, 2018. © 2018, Narrative Content Group. Used with permission; **P 195, 256, GhulamRabbany:** Md. GhulamRabbany, ENVIRONMENTAL EFFECTS OF TOURISM, American Journal of Environment, Energy and Power Research, Vol. 1, No. 7, September 2013, PP: 117-130, ISSN: 2329-860X. Licensed under a Creative Commons Attribution 4.0 International License; **P 196, CIHEAM:** Sunlu U. Environmental impacts of tourism. In : Camarda D. (ed.), Grassini L. (ed.). Local resources and global trades: Environments and agriculture in the Mediterranean region. Bari: CIHEAM, 2003. p. 263-270 (Options Méditerranéennes : Série A. Séminaires Méditerranéens; n. 57). Retrieved from: http://om.ciheam.org/article.php?IDPDF=4001977. Used with permission; **P 197, Guardian News & Media Limited**: Maasai herders driven off land to make way for luxury safaris, report says, by Jonathan Watts, in *The Guardian*, 10 May 2018. © 2018, Guardian News & Media Limited. Used with permission; **P 199, Telegraph Media Group Limited:** How to be a better tourist, by Gavin Haines, *The Telegraph*, 13 Aug 2018. © 2018, Telegraph Media Group Limited. Used with permission; **P 201, Telegraph Media Group Limited:** Japanese complain of 'tourist pollution' as number of sightseers skyrockets, By Julian Ryall, *The Telegraph*, 10 Sept 2018. © 2018, Telegraph Media Group Limited. Used with permission; **P 204, 258, The Vegan Society:** Definition of veganism, Retrieved from: https://www.vegansociety.com/go-vegan/definition-veganism. © 2018, The Vegan Society. Used with permission; **P 204, 258 The Vegan Society:** Reasons to become a vegan, Retrieved from: https://www.vegansociety.com/go-vegan/why-go-vegan. © 2018, The Vegan Society. Used with permission; **P 205, The Vegan Society:** Why is meat and dairy so bad for the environment? Retrieved from: https://www.vegansociety.com/go-vegan/why-go-vegan.

Dedication

To all the colleagues, friends and students who helped us in the book by sharing their experiences and identities, as well as their ideas about sharing the planet, their social organisations and human ingenuity.

This book is also dedicated to all of the students around the world who are learning English as a second language, and their dedicated teachers who are accompanying them on the journey.

Pat Janning and Patricia Mertin

Contents

Introduction

Welcome to this English B for the IB Diploma textbook, which will accompany you for the next two years.

The book is divided into the five themes to match the curriculum guide – identities, experiences, human ingenuity, social organisation, and sharing the planet. Each theme has a variety of related texts which we hope will encourage you to think about and explore the themes more deeply yourselves.

Accompanying each text are exercises to help you develop your understanding of written English, your ability to demonstrate understanding, and your vocabulary.

We encourage you to explore the topics we have selected in each section more deeply through further discussions, reading related articles, and finding more ideas online.

We hope our choice of topics will inspire you to explore new ideas, to undertake your own research, and to further develop your English language proficiency.

One way which research has shown will help you greatly improve your all-round competency in English is to read more for pleasure. Our section on literature will inspire you to discover new books and new worlds while developing your English proficiency. The books have been chosen to accompany the five themes. The selection represents only a small number of the books available for you to read either in a group or individually. Students and teachers are encouraged to explore reading possibilities together and extend the list.

A note for teachers

Dear colleagues,

Exploring the themes for the new IBDP English B course has been a great adventure and we hope our choice of texts within each theme will encourage you to help your students explore the topics in more depth in the classroom and of course independently.

We sincerely hope that the texts will be sources of inspiration and support in your teaching.

Pat Janning and Patricia Mertin

What this book includes

As you read this textbook, you will encounter numerous boxes containing helpful information and tasks.

Research questions

At the start of each theme you will find research questions to help you focus on the theme and provide inspiration for your own questions.

Research questions

- What make us who we are?
- How do we express who we are?
- Can modern technologies add new dimensions to shaping our identity?

TOK boxes

Questions to help stimulate consideration of knowledge issues as they arise in context.

TOK

To what extent is our use of language determined by our membership of a particular culture?

Objectives

A list some of the tasks and skills you should be able to master as you work through the theme.

Objectives

- To discuss the question 'Who am I?'
- To examine and describe some of the influences which form our identities.
- To evaluate the effectiveness of philosophy lessons for young children and ourselves.
- To outline how the way we project ourselves varies according to the language we are speaking.
- To evaluate how effective the ideas of 'slowing down and enjoying life more' could be.
- To understand and discuss the impact of words on the world around us.
- To understand how the world is changing in the 21st century.

Zoom in on grammar/language

Grammar explanations or reminders.

Zoom in on grammar/language

Phrasal verbs

Many verbs have two parts – a verb followed by a preposition or an adverb – and these are called phrasal verbs, e.g. *look at, think of, break down, put on*.

Some phrasal verbs can take a number of different prepositions or adverbs, with different meanings, e.g. *look in, look out, look after, look for, look round*.

Can you find the four phrasal verbs used in the text *What it means to be Scottish?*

Discussion/presentation task

Ideas for discussions to have in class or presentations that could be prepared and made, that will encourage you to think more deeply about a topic and improve your spoken English.

Discussion/presentation task

Identify the turning points in Martin's story that have influenced his identity. Discuss any turning points in your own lives.

Tip boxes

These boxes point out key features in texts or explain terms that might be unfamiliar to you.

Asking the reader questions helps draw them in.

Language skills objectives

- To think about the use of metaphor.
- To practise interactive oral skills in relation to the identities theme.
- To examine the use of and practise phrasal verbs.
- To examine the function of and practise gerund phrases.
- To understand and practise complex sentences.
- To understand and practise using *instead of* + *-ing* forms.
- To develop writing skills in formal and semi-formal English.

Grammar/language in context

Activities and exercises aimed at reusing a grammar or language point covered in a specific context.

Grammar/language in context

Phrasal verbs

Complete the phrasal verbs in these sentences with the correct preposition or adverb.

1 Many people like best to talk ______ themselves.
2 Can you look ______ my cat while I am on holiday?
3 I'll pick you ______ after work, OK?
4 I'll come ______ after lunch and we'll do our homework together.
5 If you keep ______ interrupting, I shall take you out of the discussion group.

Intercultural activity

Opportunities for you to compare your experiences based on your own cultural background with those of other cultures.

Intercultural activity

Do you know the *Starfish Story*? Research it on the internet and share what you find with your class. Can you find similar stories in other languages?

Tips for writing

For some exercises in which you are asked to write a specific text type, you may find tips to guide you as you plan your writing.

Assessment practice

Throughout each theme you will find examples of the assessments you will encounter in your exams, including the SL Internal assessment, Paper 1, and Paper 2 tasks.

Paper 1 practice task

Now you have read reflections by an American, a Kazakh, a Scot, and an English person. Think about yourself. What is your identity? Write your own reflection piece.

SL students should write 250–400 words. HL students should write 450–600 words.

Internal assessment (SL)

Consider the influence people have on your identity when you join a group or go to another country.

Examine the photograph above and consider the following points:

- What do you see in the picture? Briefly describe the scene.
- Think about the theme of identities. Reflect on the photograph in connection with identities.
- What aspects of identity do you want to focus on?
- Make connections to your own experience and the factors influencing identity.

Using the points above, spend 15 minutes preparing a presentation about the photograph. Use the preparation time to organise your ideas and plan the sequence of what you will talk about.

Your presentation should last 3 to 4 minutes, after which your teacher and other students will have the opportunity to comment or ask questions about what you have said. You must engage in a conversation with them. In total, this task should take approximately 15 minutes.

Exam hints

These boxes give you hints on how to approach your exams.

In the final IB examination written assignment, Standard level students will be required to write 250–400 words and Higher level students will need to write 450–600 words. Try to aim for the appropriate word count in all of your writing assignments as this will help you in the examination situation.

Identities
1

1 Identities

Research questions

- What makes us who we are?
- How do we express who we are?
- Can modern technologies add new dimensions to shaping our identity?

Objectives

- To discuss the question 'Who am I?'
- To examine and describe some of the influences which form our identities.
- To evaluate the effectiveness of philosophy lessons for young children and ourselves.
- To outline how the way we project ourselves varies according to the language we are speaking.
- To evaluate how effective the ideas of 'slowing down and enjoying life more' could be.
- To understand and discuss the impact of words on the world around us.
- To understand how the world is changing in the 21st century.

Language skills objectives

- To practise interactive oral skills in relation to the identities theme.
- To develop writing skills in formal and semi-formal English.
- To think about the use of metaphor.
- To examine the use of and practise phrasal verbs.
- To examine the function of and practise gerund phrases.
- To understand and practise complex sentences.
- To understand and practise using *instead of* + *-ing* forms.

Identity is concerned with the question: 'Who am I?'

Identity is sometimes explained as a sense of belonging to a nation. For example, people talk about 'being proud' of the country they are from. Alternatively, it can be a strong allegiance to a city or an area of a country, such as people living in the mountains of Northern Italy, Austria, and Germany talk of their similar identities all united by the mountain region.

Identity can also be defined by the qualities and beliefs you hold valuable and which dictate the choices you make. Our identities are often passed on to us by our parents.

The different ways of looking at identity also highlight that every individual can have multiple identities, defined not only by place, but also by the group they are in. For example, a person may identify as both a family member and a student in a school. People can choose how they want to define themselves when they answer the question 'Who am I?'

Identity is never final and continues to develop throughout life.

1.1 Nationality and identity

What it means to be. . .

Many people find that their nationality or their homeland influences their identity. The following pages include extracts from people discussing their nationalities and identities.

In the text below, an American international school teacher, who now teaches in China, reflects on American identity.

What it means to be American

by Katee Inghram

For me, to be an American is to understand that we are one, but within that oneness, we are extremely diverse. Because of the country's vast diversity, I think part of being American is less about ethnicity and is more about actions, beliefs, and values. In general, Americans are friendly and talkative and will even talk to and share personal stories with strangers. In my experience, typical Americans believe in and value the ideals of freedom. Many Americans also strongly believe they are the creator of their own destiny. Americans are often thinking of their next move and would rather be their own leader than follow someone else. We very much value individualism and choice. I see the American identity as one that's in a constant state of evolution, especially given that we are a young country compared to the rest of the world. In some ways, I would say Americans are still writing their identity.

Personal – Reflection

Figure 1.1 Americans value individualism

General comprehension

Answer the following questions in complete sentences.

1 How does the writer define being an American? Explain your answer.
2 What does the writer think being American is about?
3 According to the writer, what are Americans generally like?
4 What does the writer say Americans think about freedom and destiny?
5 Why does the writer say Americans are still writing their identity?

Vocabulary

Match the words (1–6) as they are used in the text with their meanings (a–f).

1 vast	a fate
2 diversity	b maker
3 ethnicity	c extremely large
4 freedom	d belonging to a racial group
5 creator	e range of differences
6 destiny	f the right to do what one wants

In this reflection, a student from Kazakhstan shares her thoughts.

What it means to be Kazakh

by Nazym Musin

Personal – Reflection

Kazakhstan is a country in which the majority of citizens are patriotic and proud of being Kazakhstani. I think that many of the fascinating features of our country are yet to be discovered by the rest of the world. That is the impression I get when I talk to people on my travels. Kazakhstan is little known to outsiders.

From childhood, it is considered to be a Kazakh duty to know your family tree and the traditions of the country. Values such as a belief in religion, respect for the individual, and social justice are passed on to us by our parents. We are taught hospitality – to welcome visitors and to care for their comfort. In Kazakh families, a guest is made to feel like a privileged person and is embraced by the family.

We are taught the traditions and history of our country in school. In one lesson, a student talked about attending school ceremonies and said: 'Just seeing that blue flag flying and hearing the Kazakh language is enough to make my skin tingle.'

Being a Kazakh means that our thoughts are the sea and our words are the birds flying over it. It means that we are free under the sky, but united with our people in heart and soul.

General comprehension

Answer the following questions in complete sentences.

1 How do the citizens of Kazakhstan feel about their country?
2 What are two features of Kazakh duty?
3 What does the writer feel is special about the Kazakh attitude to hospitality?
4 According to the writer, in Kazakhstan, what are young people taught by their parents?

Vocabulary

Match the words (1–5) as they are used in the text with their meanings (a–e).

1 hospitality	a treated warmly
2 traditions	b taking part in
3 embraced	c welcoming guests and giving them refreshments
4 attending	d a sensation of pleasure
5 tingle	e long-established customs

Zoom in on language

In the text *What it means to be Kazakh,* Nazym says, 'our thoughts are the sea and our words are the birds flying over it'. Nazym is trying to give the reader a visual picture of the Kazakh people and their feelings about freedom and unity by using a metaphor. When you are reading, always be aware of this aspect of the language and look out for metaphors.

Discussion task

In pairs, look at the two reflections above again. Discuss how American and Kazakh identities are similar and how they are different.

Intercultural activity

In pairs or groups, use research skills to compare the size and location of the USA and Kazakhstan. This knowledge may help to explain the different accounts above. Organise your information so that you can present your findings to other pairs.

In this reflection, Ian Thompson asks how his identity as a Scottish person still functions after many years of living in England and Germany.

Personal – Reflection

What it means to be Scottish

by Ian Thompson

When I say I'm Scottish, I am not talking about my nationality. You can't travel with a Scottish passport. Scotland is part of the United Kingdom of Great Britain and Northern Ireland, so I travel with a British passport.

I call myself a Scot because I was born into a Scottish family in Scotland. I grew up there, went to school there, and lived there until I was 18 years old. Then, like so many other Scots, I left home to seek further education and worked in England and then in Germany.

So how does my identity as a Scottish person still function after so many years of living elsewhere? Those important formative years were spent within Scottish culture, surrounded by its people and its customs, its music and its regional dialects. I have always loved Scotland's landscapes, with the undulating farmland of the south and the east, the mountains and waters of the north and the west, and the endless tundra of the extreme north. The coastline also provides scenic contrasts that are loved by Scots and visitors alike. Scottish cities are popular destinations, renowned for their architecture and the variety of their cultural activities. For example, people come from all over the world for the annual Edinburgh International Festival.

If you visit the city of Glasgow, you will see banners, posters, and stickers telling you that 'People Make Glasgow'. This is something of a trademark for the city, but it does have a basis of truth. Glaswegian people are generally kind, helpful, funny, and memorable in so many ways. I believe these qualities are shown by people all over Scotland, however, not just in Glasgow, and perhaps this is the real reason why I still identify myself as a Scot. Whenever I travel to Scotland, I really feel at home among the people whose values, ideas, attitudes, and customs are so familiar to me.

You can take the lad out of Scotland, but you can't take Scotland out of the lad.

Figure 1.2 People make Glasgow

1

Identities

General comprehension

Answer the following questions in complete sentences.

1 Why did the writer leave Scotland?
2 Which aspects of Scottish culture does he mention?
3 What does the writer love about Scotland?
4 What is the slogan for Glasgow?

Vocabulary

Match the words (1–10) as they are used in the text with their meanings (a–j).

1 formative	a having a strong influence on the development of something
2 surrounded	b male, often young
3 regional	c be all around
4 dialect	d worth remembering
5 undulating	e of an area
6 tundra	f famous
7 scenic	g language used in a particular place
8 renowned	h impressive or beautiful (landscape)
9 memorable	i vast, flat, treeless area
10 lad	j with hills like waves

Zoom in on grammar

Phrasal verbs

Many verbs have two parts – a verb followed by a preposition or an adverb – and these are called phrasal verbs, e.g. *look at, think of, break down, put on.*

Some phrasal verbs can take a number of different prepositions or adverbs, with different meanings, e.g. *look in, look out, look after, look for, look round.*

Can you find the four phrasal verbs used in the text *What it means to be Scottish?*

Grammar in context

Phrasal verbs

Complete the phrasal verbs in these sentences with the correct preposition or adverb.

1 Many people like best to talk ______ themselves.
2 Can you look ______ my cat while I am on holiday?
3 I'll pick you ______ after work, OK?
4 I'll come ______ after lunch and we'll do our homework together.
5 If you keep ______ interrupting, I shall take you out of the discussion group.

In this reflection, Nathan Stiles asks what it means to be English.

What it means to be English

by Nathan Stiles

I was born in Essex and just as I started school my family moved to Lancashire. In those days, people didn't talk about being English, they talked about coming from 'up north' or 'down south'. Depending where you were from, one was better than the other. Obviously, Essex being in the south, I always thought the south was better. As the years passed, the question of national identity became a burning issue and one that everyone these days is scrambling to put their finger on.

The thing is, most of us have multiple identities. We may have a strong sense of belonging to one nation, or perhaps a county or a city. Many people whose parents come from different countries identify equally with both parents' nations. So, the question 'What does it mean to be English?' is an interesting one. Look at my best friend who has lived in London since he was a toddler. He was born in Kingston of Jamaican parents. He has dreadlocks, likes Reggae music, and makes the best callaloo you have ever eaten (have you ever eaten callaloo?), but says he feels English. Feeling English is not a statement about place of birth or ethnicity. It is an attitude, a state of mind, a feeling.

There are those moments when something stirs inside you, a memory, a reverberation of time past. I get that when I pass a schoolyard and see children in their uniforms playing the same games we played: hopscotch, tag, cat's cradle. Or walking down the drinks' aisle in my local supermarket looking for my favourite soft drink. Christmas is an inescapable memory pull: turkey with all the trimmings, wearing those daft hats that are in the crackers, listening to the Queen's speech. Thinking about all those things could bring tears to my eyes, especially when my job meant spending Christmas away from home.

But I identify most with the rural landscape. The years where I spent my youth were defined by the rough moors of the north: windswept, treeless, beautiful. My senses tell me when I am there. It is the colours that change with the seasons – from the purple flowers in spring to the golden dry plants of autumn. The smell of plant life, rich soil, and the feel of the wind on my face. These are the views and smells that trigger my memories, along with long treks with my family, of picnics crouched behind dry-stone walls where boiled eggs and cheese sandwiches were a wonderful feast. The fun of finding the remains of Roman roads and imagining the legions passing in the mists. To know which tracks to avoid because they led to marsh or which to follow to get back home. We would sing as we walked – songs that are still sung in schools and homes. Songs of the lives and loves of the people who have lived and worked in these areas. Songs passed on in the oral tradition from generation to generation.

I remember a line from an Arthur Conan Doyle book when I was at school: 'You never tire of the moor. You cannot think the wonderful secrets which it contains. It is so vast, and so barren, and so mysterious.'

Personal – Reflection

TOK Why is it difficult to define national identity?

Figure 1.3 Moors in northern England

General comprehension

Answer the following questions in complete sentences.

1 According to the writer, what 'triggers' his memories?
2 What do you think 'in the oral tradition' means?
3 According to the text, what kind of countryside is a 'moor'?

Vocabulary

Find words or phrases in the text which match the following meanings.

1 a significant concern
2 more than one
3 rope-like strands of hair
4 a passage between shelves
5 silly

Zoom in on grammar

Gerund phrases

A gerund is the *-ing* form of a verb that functions as a noun. We can use gerunds to form gerund phrases. Look at these examples of gerund phrases as subjects from the text:

- *Feeling English is not a statement about place…*
- *Thinking about all those things could bring tears…*

Grammar in context

Make your own sentences using the following gerund phrases as subjects of sentences.

1 Growing up in a rural community…
2 Meeting new people…
3 Having a big family…
4 Walking the city streets…
5 Looking at the night sky…

In the final IB examination written assignment, Standard level students will be required to write 250–400 words and Higher level students will need to write 450–600 words. Try to aim for the appropriate word count in all of your writing assignments as this will help you in the examination situation.

Paper 1 practice task

Now you have read reflections by an American, a Kazakh, a Scot, and an English person. Think about yourself. What is your identity? Write your own reflection piece.

SL students should write 250–400 words. HL students should write 450–600 words.

Below are the reflections of an educator who now lives in Costa Rica. Do you know where that is? Look online to find the location and see what else you can discover about Costa Rica.

Personal – Reflection

What it means to be Cuban-American-Costa Rican

by Alegría Lores

Answering the question 'What is your native language?' is difficult for me. During my early years, my mother spoke to me in English and my father spoke to me in Spanish. She was from Minnesota, USA, and he was from Cuba. They lived in a Spanish-speaking area of Tangiers, Morocco, but we moved to New York City when I was three. There we lived among Hispanics, but school was in English. When I was nine, my family moved to Costa Rica, where we settled. I married a Costa Rican and eventually adopted the Costa Rican citizenship in addition to my US citizenship.

My life has continued in this fashion, always immersed in a bilingual and bicultural environment. Depending on where it is, I become somewhat more fluent in that language – English or Spanish.

The advantages? Being equally comfortable attending school in either language, being able to translate and interpret in those languages, and the ability to have friends from many countries.

The disadvantages? Not identifying 100 per cent with any one culture, feeling a bit like an outsider wherever I live, and people commenting, 'You have a different accent!'

Would I choose to have it any other way? Absolutely not! I consider myself extremely fortunate to have had the opportunity to live and learn in two cultures and, as a result, be comfortable in both almost effortlessly!

TOK Does language influence the way we think? Read *What it means to be a Cuban-American-Costa Rican* before discussing this with a partner.

Figure 1.4 Costa Rican market

Paper 1 practice task

Write a personal blog reflecting on your first language as it relates to your identity. Think about the following questions, plus any other ideas of your own when writing your blog.

- How does your life compare with Alegría's?
- How many countries have you lived in and how many languages have you learned?
- Do you agree with the advantages and disadvantages Alegría mentions? If not, explain your opinion.

SL students should write 250–400 words. HL students should write 450–600 words.

! You must remember to show your knowledge of English by thinking about your choice of vocabulary and your use of correct grammar.

Tips for writing a blog

- A blog is an online journal or informational website. It is usually started by one person who may then invite others to add their thoughts or comments.
- Before you start writing your blog, decide:
  - why you are writing
  - what you want to say
  - which facts you want to include.
- Organise your ideas into paragraphs with key information and supporting details.
- Give your blog a strong heading and remember that people write blogs because they feel strongly about the topic.
- You can use phrases such as 'I strongly feel. . .' or 'It is my opinion. . .' because the style is often like a newspaper article.

1.2 Identities and change

How is our identity formed?

Internal assessment (SL)

Consider the influence people have on your identity when you join a group or go to another country.

Figure 1.5 Together but different

Examine the photograph above and consider the following points:

- What do you see in the picture? Briefly describe the scene.
- Think about the theme of identities. Reflect on the photograph in connection with identities.
- What aspects of identity do you want to focus on?
- Make connections to your own experience and the factors influencing identity.

Using the points above, spend 15 minutes preparing a presentation about the photograph. Use the preparation time to organise your ideas and plan the sequence of what you will talk about.

Your presentation should last 3 to 4 minutes, after which your teacher and other students will have the opportunity to comment or ask questions about what you have said. You must engage in a conversation with them. In total, this task should take approximately 15 minutes.

Paper 2 practice task (1.1) – Alumni Speech Day

You will hear a speech made by Martin at his old school's Alumni Speech Day. Complete the following gaps. Use no more than three words for each gap.

1 Life in an office working at a desk is now ________.
2 I was shy, physically weak, rather overweight, and ________ any kind of self-confidence.
3 I grew older of course, but that alone wouldn't ________.
4 I would still have been the boy people laughed at, who wasn't ________ anything, and was afraid of everybody.
5 Sport was really popular then, as it is now, but PE classes were ________ to put it mildly.

Listen again and answer the questions.

6 What did Martin do when he first left school?
7 What problems did Martin have as a teenager? List three.
8 What did Martin do to escape his problems?
9 What effect did running have on Martin's self-confidence?
10 What is the real lesson the friend taught Martin?

Select the correct answer from the options.

11 From the speech, we know that Martin is:
 a living in Africa.
 b truly happy in his work.
 c working in an office.
12 Martin's work is:
 a generally abroad.
 b rather tedious.
 c different every day.
13 Martin went for long walks as a teenager to:
 a meet his friends.
 b get away from his mother.
 c lose weight.

Discussion task

Identify the turning points in Martin's story that have influenced his identity. Discuss any turning points in your own lives.

Can you imagine primary school students being encouraged to talk about philosophy? This article reports on some research that was carried out in a London primary school classroom.

Mass media – Article

CHILDREN GIVEN PHILOSOPHY LESSONS TO FACE CHALLENGES OF THE FUTURE

International Baccalaureate students study Theory of Knowledge (TOK) in their final two years of school life, but can you imagine primary school students also being encouraged to talk about philosophy?

How do you think they would manage? Would it be a worthwhile exercise? Philosophy involves thinking about thinking and especially learning to think about tricky questions – for example, *How do I know? What do I know? What is truth?*

Researchers have proposed that if children learn to think about how to think, it may help them face challenging problems in the future in our rapidly changing society. Students in a South London primary school were involved in the pilot scheme and discussed questions such as:

- How do we know something is true?
- Does our identity change as we grow older?
- Is a person the same person at every point in their life?
- Are we still the same person we were last year, or before that?
- Will we still be the same person in 20 years' time?

TOK

How do we know something is true? Which ways of knowing can we use?

To what extent has your identity changed since you were ten years old?

To what extent do you believe you will be the same person you are now in 20 years' time?

The Greek Philosopher, Plutarch, AD 100, asked a similar question in a thought experiment concerning a ship. This experiment was called The Ship of Theseus and his question was:

- If a wooden ship with 30 oars and a crew of young Athenian men goes on a long voyage during which every part of the ship has to be repaired or replaced, will the ship be the same ship at the end of the voyage?

This new research was carried out in a London primary school classroom. The children used a LEGO® model that was passed around the class and each child replaced a LEGO® part of the model.

At first the children said changing the model was like destroying it. But the researcher reported that after some thought, the children decided it still had the same function so it was still the same thing. Then the researcher asked the children if they were still the same person they were as a baby? Did they still have the same functions, were they still made of the same things?

There were 30 children involved in the project and according to the researchers, they all seemed to enjoy it. They learned to think about thinking. The preliminary results of the project were presented at a conference of the Royal College of Psychiatrists. The researchers hope that if children start to think objectively about their own thinking in young years, this will help them guard against depression and other mental problems later in life.

So, what do you think? Are you still the same person you were at five years old? Will you still be the same person when you are 50 years old? Does your identity change? And if so – how do you know?

Asking the reader questions helps draw them in.

General comprehension

Answer the following questions in complete sentences.

1 How do researchers believe learning to think about thinking will help children?
2 What question did Plutarch ask?
3 Why did the children think the LEGO® model had been destroyed?
4 What did they later decide?

State whether the following statements are true or false. Give the phrase from the text that confirms your choice.

5 There have been other projects like this.
6 The children found the experiment too challenging.
7 The results were shared at a teachers' conference.
8 A similar experiment was described many hundreds of years ago.

Paper 1 practice task

Are you still the same person you were at five years old? Will you be the same person when you are 50 years old? Write either a personal blog, an informal letter or email to a friend in response to one of these questions.

SL students should write 250–400 words. HL students should write 450–600 words.

The following text was written by an international school teacher from New Zealand.

Identity and our roots

by Michael Bucksmith

Growing up in a quiet neighbourhood in the capital of Wellington, Aotearoa, we would greet each other with a 'Gidday' or 'How's it going?' as normal. I continued this practice throughout my teens and into my early adulthood. That is when I finally got around to booking my very first international flight, which took me through Australia, India, and on to the much-anticipated United Kingdom. My global journey had begun and I very quickly learned that people greeted each other in all sorts of merry ways around the map. Some of my favourites include 'Alright?', 'Now then', 'Have you eaten?', 'How's everything?', and 'How is your family?'. As much as it meant the world to me to be able to greet people in a way familiar to them, I soon missed my 'Giddays' and savoured the once-in-a-while crossing of paths with a fellow Antipodean.

Figure 1.6 Auckland, New Zealand

Recently I had the pleasure of leading an assembly with a delightfully animated cohort of Grade 5 students. The theme we had was 'Global citizenship' and I wanted to use the opportunity as a chance to challenge some of the traditional, warm, fuzzy ideas that get thrown around from time to time. I knew the children well so we launched into the assembly with gusto. The first question I rhetorically

Mass media – Public commentary

TOK

To what extent is identity connected to where we are from?

offered them was one very commonly heard here in the Gulf where I am based at present: Where are you from?

Seemingly an easy question to answer, I quickly followed it up with the kicker: How do you know?

Responses varied from the predictable: I was born here/there..., My parents are from here/there..., to alternatives like My ID card says..., My ancestors are from..., I speak their language.... I pushed the questioning further with an exaggerated but not impossible example of a New Zealander, born in Shanghai, who grows up to have their own children in the Middle East. Where are those children from?

We had a light argument together and eventually agreed that the discussion is more interesting than the answer, or answers.

One of my sons, who lives in New Zealand, was asked by his teacher to write a piece and submit an accompanying photograph of his happy place. He was born in the Middle East and has travelled reasonably widely for a youngster, including spending time living in South and Central Asia. His happy place is a beach near a town called Bukha, in Musandam, Oman. He holds a New Zealand passport and spoke, until recently, with a clear English accent despite having only native Welsh, Chinese, and Uzbek teachers and North American friends. Where is he from? Is he from the place where he was born? The place he started school? The place on the front of his passport? The place his friends are from? Maybe he is from his happy place? I'll let you ask him that question as I couldn't possibly answer on his behalf. I expect the answer has evolved over time and will continue to do so.

During a parent workshop at school, we discussed identity with parents and it soon became very clear that while there is a deep desire to nurture multiple identities in their children, they didn't want any dilution of their home identity which is deeply embedded in race, religion, culture, family, geography, and nationality. We acknowledged and accepted that allowing our identities to grow and multiply doesn't mean, even for a second, that we let go of that deep sense of identity, belonging, connection, home, peace, and self which grows like an acorn the minute we were conceived and begins to sprout.

We all have many identities (branches) and not just nationalities – our identity is embedded in our roles and relationships with our families, our communities, our social groups – near and far, our online presence, our colleagues, our connection to the past, and to our legacies. It is one of the countless joys of being human, being connected and experiencing this growth in a uniquely personal and satisfying way.

I am very comfortable wandering the alleys of Ho Chi Minh City, or ordering pilaf in Almaty, or a tipple in Budapest, or pizza in Amman, but nothing, nothing beats the flutter I get as the plane touches down in Auckland and I am greeted by immigration staff with a 'Gidday, welcome home'.

General comprehension

Answer the following questions in complete sentences.

1 When did the writer first travel abroad?
2 Which question does the writer say is often asked to people in the Gulf?
3 Why was the teacher's discussion with the students challenging at first?
4 Which was the most interesting part of the discussion?
5 What is the challenge parents have with their children's identities?

Choose the four true statements according to the text.

a The writer enjoys the different ways people greet each other.
b 'Now then' is not a form of greeting.
c The students in assembly were reluctant to answer questions.
d The writer's son has a Welsh accent.
e We have many identities.
f The parents in the workshop wanted their children to feel their real identity.
g The writer's son has not travelled often.
h New Zealanders greet each other by saying 'Gidday'.

Vocabulary

Match the words (1–10) as they are used in the text with their meanings (a–j).

1 anticipated	a recognise
2 savoured	b group
3 animated	c expected
4 cohort	d tremble
5 nurture	e care for
6 dilution	f begin to grow
7 embedded	g enjoyed
8 acknowledge	h watering down
9 sprout	i lively
10 flutter	j fixed

Text handling

Find the correct words from the text to complete the following sentences:

1 For the writer, nothing is better than landing in Auckland and hearing the words ________.
2 Although the writer enjoyed travelling, meeting, and greeting people in different ways, he ________.
3 After some discussion, the teacher and students finally came to the conclusion that ________.

Zoom in on grammar

Complex sentences

A complex sentence is one that contains a main clause and a subordinate clause. A main clause can stand on its own as a sentence. A subordinate clause is attached to a main clause. Complex sentences are a combination of ideas and can add depth to your writing. Look at the following examples:

- ***Although he was over the age of 60,*** *he was still very fit.*
- *You should do more vocabulary work* ***because you need to express yourself better.***

Grammar in context

Focus on complex sentences

The sentence prompts below are taken from the text. Complete them as creatively as you can, as they apply to you.

1 Growing up, we would ________.
2 Recently I had the pleasure ________.
3 I am very comfortable ________.

TOK

To what extent is our identity determined by others? If enough people believe something, does it become true?

The Bear That Wasn't

The Bear That Wasn't was written in 1946 by Frank Tashlin, who was also known as Tish Tash and Frank Tash. His nicknames reflect his fun-loving and humorous nature. Frank Tashlin was born in the USA in 1913 and died in 1972. He was a very talented cartoonist, animator, film director, children's writer, and illustrator. *The Bear That Wasn't* is a cleverly illustrated book with 46 original sketches by the author. It has been reprinted many times. The story relates closely to the theme of identity and is relevant to TOK. We know that every person is an individual with their own character, talents, and values. Sometimes people misunderstand our individual characters but eventually we each think we know who we are, what we believe and how people should behave.

As the *New York Herald Tribune* stated on the cover of the 1995 edition, *The Bear That Wasn't* is 'a fable for grown-ups that will be fun for children. Sit down with the book and get your own bearings.' It tells of a bear whose identity – his character, personality, and talents – were not recognised by humans. As a result of this, he begins to doubt his own identity, leading to the question: To what extent is our identity changed or influenced by the ideas of others?

Think about this while you read the following brief recount of the story and as you follow it up online. This is how the story begins:

Once upon a time, in fact it was on a Tuesday, the Bear stood at the edge of a great forest and gazed up at the sky. Away up high, he saw a flock of geese flying south. Then he gazed up at the trees of the forest. The leaves had turned all yellow and brown and were falling from the branches. He knew that when the geese flew south and the leaves fell from the trees, that winter would soon be here and snow would cover the forest. It was time to go into a cave and hibernate. And that was just what he did.

The bear sleeps throughout the winter, not knowing that above his head men have destroyed the forest and built an industrial complex. When he finally wakes, he gets a huge surprise, as do the factory workers who refuse to believe he is a bear. They tell him repeatedly that he is not a bear. He is a silly man who needs a shave and wears a fur coat.

His identity is not recognised. His special talent of knowing when winter is coming and when it is time to hibernate is not recognised. He is taken to every level of management in the factory right up to the President of the company who says:

'You can't be a Bear. Bears are only in a zoo or a circus. They're never inside a factory and that's where you are; inside a factory. So how can you be a Bear?'

To try and find a solution to the problem, the President takes the Bear to places where other bears could be found. First they go to a zoo and then to a circus, but those bears fail to recognise him as a bear or acknowledge his identity because he is not doing what they do as bears. He is not in a cage at the zoo and he is sitting in a grandstand seat at the circus – so he cannot be a bear.

In the end the Bear is all alone, but winter is coming and so he does what all bears do, as part of their identity, he finds a cosy cave and hibernates. Look for the story online.

TOK

The story raises some interesting TOK questions to consider. In a group or with a partner think about the following and prepare to explain your ideas.

How do we know if something is a bear?

How do we know anything? Do we always need proof, and if so what kind of proof?

If everyone believes the same idea, does that make it true? Why? Why not?

Paper 1 practice task

Imagine you are the foreman who first found the Bear. Write either an informal letter or an email to a friend or family member living far away, describing the event, your thoughts, and what happened next.

SL students should write 250–400 words. HL students should write 450–600 words.

Paper 1 practice task

Consider the following statement as it applies to you. To what extent is our identity changed or influenced by the ideas of others? Write a personal blog, informal email, or informal letter discussing how the statement applies to you.

SL students should write 250–400 words. HL students should write 450–600 words.

How does our identity connect to our roots?

This is an interesting question for many people in the 21st century where global mobility is widespread. One hundred years ago this was much less of an issue, but today it affects many of us. In this blog, Annelies Brabant talks about belonging everywhere and nowhere.

Personal – Blog

Belonging everywhere and nowhere; living, working, and raising children abroad

Posted on 5 June
by Annelies Brabant

Hiraeth (Welsh): Noun. A homesickness for a home to which you cannot return, a home which maybe never was; the yearning, the grief for lost places of your past.

An ongoing issue with living a nomadic life is the inability to provide our children with a home in the traditional sense of the word. I've written about this before, but I have only recently realised that claiming to understand what this meant is actually dishonest because in reality, I did have a home: my parents' hand-crafted house in the south-western United States, where so much of who I am was shaped and nurtured.

Our family 'lived into' this extraordinary house, room by room, as it was built; getting to know every part of it before a new bit was eventually built and lived into. The construction of this house is for me, inseparable from the construction of our family. It grew slowly and lovingly over decades; it seemed to me almost a living thing. This home was built in a secluded place, surrounded by hills and situated alongside stunning natural beauty. This house was the place which allowed our lives to quietly unfold, as they should, providing a sacred space for us just to be. Over the years this house was the backdrop for births, deaths, weddings, heartbreaks, illness, recovery, celebrations. . . all the things in life which give a house a soul; the things that make it 'home'.

This past spring, along with my husband and my dad, I made what may be my last trip to this extraordinary place. Because of the nature of the house which is heated by wood or pellet stoves, has a septic tank, uneven paths between buildings, steep driveways which are sometime impassable in winter, my parents made the decision to move to an easier environment and have rented the house out with the intention of selling it. Thus the purpose of this trip to my childhood home was to sort through layers of my life which had, for various reasons, been boxed up and stored there for over 20 years; things I had, at one point in my life, felt were important enough to save and perhaps pass on to my children.

That night I cried. I felt we were somehow abandoning this member of our family, this holder of memory, this place which stood firm for our family and provided refuge and shaped our family identity for so many years. Like *The Giving Tree*, this house provided us with what we needed to grow up and go away and to live our lives, but now she was to be left without the family who loved and needed her.

Much of my sadness, I know, is that I worry that my children do not and will not have such a place in their own childhoods; there is no family home, no solid anchor, no place to go when life is hard and all they really want to do is to go home. Instead, my children have relationships that have become their homes; family, communities, friendships, and shared experiences... these are the things that build their intangible 'homes'.

And while this is okay (*it has to be, right?*) I can't help but feel that I have robbed them of something critically important. I have prevented them from establishing a sense of belonging in/to a physical place. I have stolen something I feel they are entitled to experience.

Thankfully my heart kindly and lovingly reminds me of this singular truth: what matters most in life is rarely confined to a physical space. So the truth is that home doesn't have to be a physical space. Instead it can be, in the words of Maya Angelou, that 'the ache for home lives in all of us, the safe place we can go, as we are, and not be questioned.' And that is anywhere and everywhere that we are loved.

This way of directing a comment at the reader is called rhetorical speech. It is a technique used to persuade, convince, or influence an audience. With rhetorical speech, a question is often directed at the audience, but the speaker does not expect an answer. Rhetorical speech is typical of blog writing style as it adds a conversational element to the text.

General comprehension

Answer the following questions in complete sentences.

1 What does the writer identify as a problem for people who live nomadic lives?
2 Where was the writer's home?
3 How did the family 'live into' the house?
4 What was special about the environment of the house?
5 Why was the trip described as 'what may be' the last trip to the house?
6 Why did the parents decide to move? Give two reasons.
7 What is the writer's concern for her children?
8 Which factors replace not having a family home for the children in the writer's opinion?

State whether the following statements are true or false. Give the phrase from the text that confirms your answer.

9 The writer never had a real home.
10 The home had little influence on the writer's identity.
11 The construction of the house took many years.
12 Precious possessions had been left in the house by the writer.
13 The writer believes that a home does not have to be just a physical space.

Vocabulary

Match the words (1–10) as they are used in the text with their meanings (a–j).

1 nomadic	a private
2 reality	b extraordinary, amazing
3 secluded	c sloping at a high angle
4 stunning	d travelling
5 backdrop	e what is true
6 steep	f background
7 impassable	g desert
8 abandon	h safe place
9 refuge	i impossible to travel along
10 intangible	j without any physical presence

Text handling

1 Which features of a blog can you identify in this text?
2 Look back at the blog. What are the different ways the writer has started her sentences?
3 Write your own sentences, on any topic, using the following beginnings from the text.
 a An ongoing issue ________.
 b Over the years ________.
 c Thankfully ________.
 d So the truth is ________.

Paper 1 practice task

The writer mentions the story of *The Giving Tree*. If you are not familiar with this story, you can research it on the internet. How does the story connect to the writer's home? Write your own blog about the first home you remember. Use the features of a blog that you have identified above.

SL students should write 250–400 words. HL students should write 450–600 words.

1.3 Identities and language

How we communicate

TOK

Do you feel different when you communicate in your mother tongue? Are you a different person in your mother tongue?

Often students who do not speak the language used in the classroom feel very lonely and even ignored because they have great difficulty communicating with other students and the teachers. Our language and identity are very closely linked, as we know. Without language we cannot express our identity – we cannot explain who we are, where we are from, how we feel, our likes and dislikes, and in the classroom we cannot express our previous knowledge or experiences.

Professor Jim Cummins, a well-known researcher in language acquisition, together with colleagues, began a project to explore how students' identities could be shared even before they had mastered the language of the classroom. This was called the Dual Language project.

Students in first grade created stories in English and illustrated them as they had not yet learned to read and write. They then shared the stories with their parents, older siblings, or other students with the same mother tongue and together they translated the stories into the mother tongue. The stories and illustrations were shared on the Dual Language

Showcase website. As the project developed, new students with other mother tongues told their own stories in their mother tongues and illustrated them and had them translated into English and shared on the website. Involving all students, including their ideas and their languages, increased the students' sense of self and confirmed their identities. Jim Cummins has shown this vital ingredient, identity, is key to successful learning.

Paper 1 practice task

Can you remember when you first started in a school where the language of instruction was not your first language? How did you communicate? How did you feel? Was it easy to make friends? Could your teacher understand you at all? Write a reflection, in the form of a blog, about your experiences as a beginner learning a new language. Write 200–300 words.

Who are you?

We talked to some bilingual students in an international school about identity and asked them to write a personal reflection to a question: 'Who am I?'

Personal – Reflections

A.

Since I was born, the question about who I am has always been with me. This question has confused me for 16 years. This year will probably be the 17th unless I figure out who I am.

I seldom think about it in my busy daily life, but when I am extremely exhausted or depressed, that thoughtful question just comes over me. Who am I? An unimpressive speck of dust in the infinite universe, perhaps nobody knows me except my family, perhaps I am a bit well known, perhaps I am nothing. I am neither like the shining star in the infinite universe that always attracts people's attention nor the food which is able to satisfy people's needs. Actually I never want to be like those things.

My lofty ambition is just to be an ordinary person with nondescript looks, living in a normal place but getting respect from people he knows and people he will meet.

These past 16 years, I have not found what I am looking for, from the beginning to the end. Hopefully this year I will figure it out and be the person I want to be. Then I can say I am the guy who people respect and like.

B.

The biggest thing that ever happened in my life was moving to Germany. This is my fifth year here, but I still can't believe it. I go back to Japan at least once a year and every time I feel like I am 13 years old, the age I was when we left. I thought I would live my whole life there, where I was and with people I knew, but it suddenly stopped. I feel like my life is suspended. I sometimes think about how different my life would be if I was in Japan, but the time I have spent in Germany and the people who are involved in my life are making it worthwhile.

C.

I am the centre, the core, of my world. No one can see what I feel and think except for me. My world is composed of subjectivity and objectivity and sometimes they are in conflict because no one knows my feelings and I don't know theirs. So I have to think about and try to imagine how others feel and act appropriately so that they are more comfortable. That would generate peace in my world. Peace is essential for me to feel happy in my life. Happiness makes me feel I am myself.

D.

I am a learner from a place where everything is constructed of wood. Wood is fragile, weak in the face of fire, water, or vermin. On the other hand, wood can be flexible too. I am a learner from the place of wood, I learn by meeting various identities to become strong, fireproof, water-resistant, and strong against vermin.

E.

I am a terrestrial. I am a human being. I am a student. I am one. There are so many ones around the world and we can communicate.

F.

The son of my parents, the older brother of my brother, a Japanese living in Germany, a human living on earth, a creature of this planet, someone who always desires something, someone who is always asking 'Who am I?'

Figure 1.7 Who are you?

General comprehension

Answer the following questions in complete sentences.

Text A

1 When does the student reflect on the question 'Who am I'?

2 What does the expression 'an unimpressive speck of dust in the infinite universe' tell you about the student's attitude?

3 What is the ambition mentioned and why do you think the student calls it 'lofty'?

Text B

4 How old was the student when he/she left Japan?

5 What is the student's attitude to living away from his/her home country?

Text handling

Text D

1 This student compares his/her environment as made of wood. Which substance would you use to describe your environment and what examples would you use?

Texts E and F

2 These texts are brief and succinct. Consider each text individually. Do you think they are effective? Why or why not?

Discussion task

Read Text C. In groups, take about five minutes to discuss the following questions:

- What kind of person do you think this student is?
- What role do peace and happiness play in your life?

Paper 1 practice task

How would you answer the question, 'Who am I?' Write a blog or reflection of 300–400 words.

1.4 Humans and their choices

Enjoying life more

Part of being human is being able to make choices. We can think through the advantages and disadvantages of decisions we make in a logical way and we often base our decisions on previous experience and on who we are. These decisions can be based on how we see ourselves, how we hope others see us, what we think is important.

In the article below, Cerys Matthews writes about things which are important to her, decision making, and the process of change.

Mass media – Article

THE ONLY WAY YOU CAN CHANGE ANYTHING IS IN SMALL INCREMENTS – an interview with Cerys Matthews

My happiest day would be to find a meadow, light a fire, and cook a big meal. I'd play my guitar or just listen to bird song. Music, food, and good company is, as far as I'm concerned, the elixir of a good life. I don't entertain a lot, but we have a big family and I cook every day. I don't buy pre-made food or takeaways. I'm not into clean eating, but I am interested in trying to reduce my carbon footprint*. We all know how much rubbish we put out every day and we have to start changing the way we live.

I've lived in Ladbroke Grove, London, for 18 years. It's a bit busier than Wales, but it's good to be a small fish in a big pond. My children go to a school where there's at least 75 languages spoken and I like that aspect of it. A lot of interesting minds are drawn to the city and it makes for a culturally rich place to live. I have no romantic illusions about living in the countryside and the public services closing down. As far as I'm concerned, life is about your neighbours and community.

I care about being healthy because it all adds up to, hopefully, staying around a bit longer. I've started cycling and I'm trying this mile-a-day idea, running ten minutes daily. Within days you feel like a different person – I've been doing it for two months.

You can't put off ageing, but you can change your behaviour. Now I embrace it as part of the miracle of life. When you are young, you have the energy to change the world, but when you're older you understand the inevitability of history and conflict. That's why I turn to life in the community. The only way you can change anything is in small increments around you – where you shop, what you buy, and how much you're willing to bring positivity into difficult situations.

*Carbon footprint is the amount of carbon dioxide released into the atmosphere as a result of the activities of a particular individual, organisation, or community.

General comprehension

Answer the following questions in complete sentences.

1 What is the 'elixir of a good life' for Cerys?
2 What does the expression 'being a small fish in a big pond' mean to you?
3 How do we know Cerys leads a healthy life?

Discussion task

In groups, take about five minutes to discuss the following questions:

- What is the elixir of a good life for you?
- What do you think about the idea of running a mile a day?
- Do you agree that 'the only way you can change anything is in small increments'?

Vocabulary

Find these phrases in the text. What do you think they mean?

1 I have no romantic illusions
2 staying around a bit longer
3 inevitability of history and conflict.

Discussion task

The writer raises a number of issues and ideas concerning choices she has made. What choices does she make which we can make for ourselves? What choices will you be able to make in the future? Discuss this with a partner.

Paper 1 practice task

Choose one of the following questions to answer.

1 What has been the happiest day of your life so far?
2 What is one thing in your life that you would like to change? Think about the process of moving forward by small increments as mentioned by Cerys.

Use an appropriate text type – a blog, an informal letter to a friend, or a diary entry – to explain your ideas.

SL students should write 250–400 words. HL students should write 450–600 words.

Tips for writing a diary entry

A diary entry contains comments on a person's individual experience over the course of a day. It will therefore be written largely in the past simple (*I went, we talked*, etc.). It is not intended to be read by other people and this will influence the degree of honesty the writer uses.

- Date your entry.
- Choose a topic to write about and give an opinion.
- Focus on the events on the date of the diary entry.
- Be mindful to include a wide range of vocabulary to show your knowledge of English.
- Diary entries should be informal.
- You may use rhetorical speech, e.g. *Why did she say that?*
- End the diary with a thought or wish for the next day.

Internal assessment (SL)

Figure 1.8 Buying from a farmer's market can reduce your carbon footprint

Examine the photograph above and consider the following points.

- What do you see in the picture? Describe only what you see. Do not give opinions.
- Reflect on the photograph in connection with the theme of the extent to which we all contribute to the global situation.
- What aspects of our carbon footprint do you want to focus on?
- Make connections to the situation in various countries.
- Consider who you are and how important this theme is to you.

Using the points above, spend 15 minutes preparing a presentation about the photograph. Use the preparation time to organise your ideas and plan the sequence of what you will talk about.

Your presentation should last 3 to 4 minutes, after which your teacher and other students will have the opportunity to comment or ask questions about what you have said. You must engage in a conversation with them. In total, this task should take approximately 15 minutes.

In the following blog, Leo Babauta has listed and described ten essential rules for slowing down in modern day life.

How do you know this is a blog? Which features do you notice immediately?

Now follow his advice and read the blog slowly. Concentrate on just reading and understanding it. Take your time.

Mass media – Blog

The ten essential rules for slowing down and enjoying life more

Posted on 20 October
by Leo Babauta

It's an irony of our modern lives that while technology is continually invented that saves us time, we use that time to do more and more things, and so our lives are more fast-paced and hectic than ever.

Life moves at such a fast pace that it seems to pass us by before we can really enjoy it.

However, it doesn't have to be this way. Let's rebel against a hectic lifestyle and slow down to enjoy life.

A slower-paced life means making time to enjoy your mornings, instead of rushing off to work in a frenzy. It means taking time to enjoy whatever you're doing, to appreciate the outdoors, to actually focus on whoever you're talking to or spending time with — instead of always being connected to an iPhone or laptop, instead of always thinking about work tasks and emails. It means single-tasking rather than switching between a multitude of tasks and focusing on none of them.

Slowing down is a conscious choice, and not always an easy one, but it leads to a greater appreciation of life and a greater level of happiness.

Here's how to do it.

1. Do less. It's hard to slow down when you are trying to do a million things. Instead, make the conscious choice to do less. Focus on what's really important, what really needs to be done, and let go of the rest. Put space between tasks and appointments, so you can move through your days at a more leisurely pace.

2. Be present. It's not enough to just slow down — you need to actually be mindful of whatever you're doing at the moment. That means, when you find yourself thinking about something you need to do, or something that's already happened, or something that might happen. . . gently bring yourself back to the present moment. Focus on what's going on right now: on your actions, on your environment, on others around you. This takes practice but is essential.

3. Disconnect. Don't always be connected. If you carry around an iPhone or other mobile device, shut it off. Better yet, learn to leave it behind when possible. If you work on a computer most of the day, have times when you disconnect so you can focus on other things. Being connected all the time means we're subject to interruptions, we're constantly stressed about information coming in, we are at the mercy of the demands of others. It's hard to slow down when you're always checking new messages coming in.

4. Focus on people. Too often we spend time with friends and family, or meet with colleagues, and we're not really there with them. We talk to them but are distracted by devices. We are there, but our minds are on things we need to do. We listen, but we're really thinking about ourselves and what we want to say. None of us are immune to this, but with conscious effort you can shut off the outside world and just be present with the person you're with. This means that just a little time spent with your family and friends can go a long way — a much more effective use of your time, by the way. It means we really connect with people rather than just meeting with them.

5. Appreciate nature. Many of us are shut in our homes and offices and cars and trains most of the time, and rarely do we get the chance to go outside. And often even when people are outside, they're talking on their cell phones. Instead, take the time to go outside and really observe nature, take a deep breath of fresh air, enjoy the serenity of water and greenery. Exercise outdoors when you can, or find other outdoor activities to enjoy such as nature walks, hiking, swimming, etc. Feel the sensations of water and wind and earth against your skin. Try to do this daily – by yourself or with loved ones.

6. Eat slower. Instead of cramming food down our throats as quickly as possible — leading to overeating and a lack of enjoyment of our food — learn to eat slowly. Be mindful of each bite. Appreciate the flavours and textures. Eating slowly has the double benefit of making you fuller on less food and making the food taste better. I suggest learning to eat more real food as well, with some great spices (instead of fat and salt and sugar and frying for flavour).

7. Drive slower. Speedy driving is a pretty prevalent habit in our fast-paced world, but it's also responsible for a lot of traffic accidents, stress, and wasted fuel. Instead, make it a habit to slow down when you drive. Appreciate your surroundings. Make it a peaceful time to contemplate your life, and the things you're passing. Driving will be more enjoyable, and much safer. You'll use less fuel too.

8. Find pleasure in anything. This is related to being present, but taking it a step farther. Whatever you're doing, be fully present. . . and also appreciate every aspect of it, and find the enjoyable aspects. For example, when washing dishes, instead of rushing through it as a boring chore to be finished quickly, really feel the sensations of the water, the suds, the dishes. It can really be an enjoyable task if you learn to see it that way. The same applies to other chores — washing the car, sweeping, dusting, laundry — and anything you do, actually. Life can be so much more enjoyable if you learn this simple habit.

9. Single-tasking. The opposite of multi-tasking. Focus on one thing at a time. When you feel the urge to switch to other tasks, pause, breathe, and pull yourself back.

10. Breathe. When you find yourself speeding up and stressing out, pause, and take a deep breath. Take a couple more. Really feel the air coming into your body, and feel the stress going out. By fully focusing on each breath, you bring yourself back to the present, and slow yourself down. It's also nice to take a deep breath or two — do it now and see what I mean. :)

Text handling

Here are some verbs from the text. What is the noun form of each verb?

1 breathe
2 enjoy
3 connect
4 appreciate
5 suggest
6 contemplate

Zoom in on grammar

instead of

In the text, Leo Babauta uses *instead of* a number of times. He uses it to show that one action replaces another. The action after *instead of* is used in the *-ing* form.

*Make time to enjoy your mornings **instead of rushing** off to work.*

The phrase *instead of* can also be used as a preposition. It shows that one person or thing is preferred to another.

*He takes sweeteners **instead of sugar**.*

On it's own, *instead* can be used as an adverb to indicate an alternative. It usually appears at the beginning or end of a clause and is set off with a comma.

*She didn't go to Greece. **Instead,** she went to America.*

Can you find an example of this use of 'instead' in the text?

Grammar in context

With a partner, use *instead of* + *-ing* to take turns saying sentences with the following prompts.

1 She often goes swimming...
2 My mother went to yoga...
3 Jack wrote me an email...
4 I think I'll go to the gym...

Complete these sentences with *instead of* + *-ing*.

5 Buy the blue notebook ________.
6 I phoned my teacher ________.
7 I'll have water ________.
8 Heather asked Nathan to the party ________.

Discussion task

Leo Babauta presents 'The Ten Essential Rules for Slowing Down and Enjoying Life More'. Work in pairs. Make sure you understand the vocabulary by looking at the context and checking your dictionary if necessary. Summarise each of the ten paragraphs as briefly as possible.

Work in groups and talk about how important (or not) you think Leo's advice is. Would you find it difficult to follow these 'rules'?

Paper 1 practice task

Leo Babauta is coming to your school to talk about his thoughts on how to slow down your pace of life. He is a Zen master. Either design a flyer to distribute around the school to parents and students, or write an article for the school newspaper about Leo's upcoming visit. Write 250–400 words.

Tips for writing an article

- Remember to use an attention-grabbing headline (and sub-headings) as you want people to read your article.
- Have a strong opening sentence and a strong conclusion. See *What it means to be Scottish* for an example of this.
- Use a 'call to action', e.g. *Let's rebel against...*, to further grab the attention of your reader.
- Draw your reader into your argument. For example, add opening phrases such as *Do you agree that...*, *People often feel...*, or *You quickly become aware...*
- Organise your ideas into paragraphs with a clear main idea in each one.

Making choices

In your reading, note or think about the choices characters make. Pay attention to how those choices affect characters' identities and lives.

The books we choose to read are both a reflection of our identity, as well as a step towards the formation of it. Like characters in a book, the choices we make affect our identities and lives.

Intercultural activity

Do you know the *Starfish Story*? Research it on the internet and share what you find with your class. Can you find similar stories in other languages?

You may have read some of the poetry of the American poet, Robert Frost, who lived from 1874–1963. His poems are easy to read but also thought-provoking. Many of his poems are about nature and the countryside, but he also wrote about making choices.

Discussion task

Read Robert Frost's poems 'The Road Not Taken', 'Stopping by Woods on a Snowy Evening', and 'The Armful' and discuss in groups how the poems relate to the theme of making decisions or choices. How does this apply to you? What choices have you faced in your life and how did you make your decision?

1.5 Changing language

The language we speak is closely linked to our own identity, to the way we think, express our ideas, and understand others. We know that language is constantly changing. For example, the English language today is far removed from the language of Shakespeare. If a language is changing, does this mean that the identities of those who speak it are also changing in some way?

The impact of words

Most changes to a language happen slowly and indiscernibly, but sometimes the changes can be abrupt or deliberate. This was the case a few years ago when the publishers of a dictionary for young people announced they were replacing some words related to nature with new words associated with the increased use of technology. The removal of these 'natural' words was met with much protest, but not everybody believed their removal would have a negative effect.

Have a look at three examples of how individuals and groups have responded to this change. The first is an example of a letter written to the editor of a daily newspaper.

Mass media – Reader's letter

14 Apple Street
Coventry
18 September

Dear Sir or Madam,

I have been reading with interest the discussion in your paper following an article on nature words and their removal from a popular children's dictionary.

As the father of two children in primary school, I firmly believe that dictionaries have a vital role to play in the education of young people and the development of their writing skills. However, the English language is widely acclaimed for having more words than any other language. I do not know if that is true, but after a search of the internet, I soon discovered that there are well over 180 000 words in the English language. Obviously no children's dictionary is going to contain that many words – you just have to imagine how big it would need to be. So choices will have to be made.

Dictionaries need to move with the times and reflect our changing world. It is my opinion that the inclusion of words that reflect this process of change are essential.

Formal letters addressed to a person by name, e.g. *Dear Mr Smith*, are finished with the words *Yours sincerely*. However, if the person's name is not known, the letter will start *Dear Sir or Madam*, and finish with the words *Yours faithfully*.

These words are mostly connected to developments in technology. Words such as: blog, broadband, block graph, bullet point, chatroom, cut and paste, and voicemail. I get impatient when I read about people who complain when old-fashioned words are removed from contemporary dictionaries. As the world moves forward, we need language that reflects our changing identity in today's digitised society. Progress in dictionaries is a boon for learning.

Children are curious and embrace new technology much faster than older generations. And they will certainly not stop being interested in nature just because the word 'acorn' is no longer in their dictionary.

Yours faithfully,
John Wainwright

General comprehension

Answer the following questions in complete sentences.

1 What is Mr Wainwright's attitude towards dictionaries?
2 Which words does he believe are essential and need to be included in a dictionary?
3 According to Mr Wainwright, why is it acceptable to remove nature words from a children's dictionary? Give two reasons for your answer.

Vocabulary

Match the words (1–5) as they are used in the text with their meanings (a–h). There are more options than you need.

1 vital	a lively
2 embrace	b accept
3 acclaimed	c accept
4 boon	d declared
5 impatient	e essential
	f irritated
	g praised
	h benefit

Here is a creative reaction to the removal of the nature words. It is a poem entitled 'Cull' by Anna Coburn. Anna is a poet living and writing in Norfolk, England. As a poet, she is aware of the power of vocabulary, but she also lives in a county which is an area of outstanding beauty and with a predominance of rural areas.

Mass media – Poem

'Cull' by Anna Coburn

What **committee** decided?

Bluebell and *buttercup*, *dandelion* and *cowslip*,
heather and *heron* all sent to trash bin?

Only in ancient books of natural law will *kingfishers* flash
their arc of electric blue.

Only in old poems will *larks* rise from cow-trodden *pasture* into a sky of spring.

Only in old tales will lads catch *newts* by the banks of muddy ponds.

Only in old ditties will pale flowers of *cowslip* nod on sunny banks in chill April winds.

In books of ancient customs *conkers* will be pocketed by boys
on their way to school, bright as new-polished boots.

Heads bowed by the light of screen tomorrow's children will
blog their inner thoughts while searching **celebrity chat rooms**
for all the latest gossip.

Mole, water-rat, toad, badger and *otter* will trot beside forgotten banks
of *willow* and *hazel* where the patient *heron* waits and ducks dabble and dive.

General comprehension

Answer the following questions in complete sentences.

1 What aspects of life does Anna feel children are starting to lack in their experience and why?

2 In the poem, where will we be able to find the nature words in the future?

Discussion task

In the poem, the words in *italics* were cut from the new edition of the *Oxford Junior Dictionary* as they were felt to no longer be relevant to modern childhood. The latest additions to the dictionary – the words in **bold** – were felt to be more relevant.

Read the poem 'Cull' again. What is the writer's intention in writing this poem? Do you know the nature words she uses? Look them up and try to identify them. Do these plants or creatures exist where you come from?

The Lost Words

Another reaction to the removal of nature words is the book *The Lost Words* by Robert Macfarlane and Jackie Morris. The book is a collaboration between Macfarlane, who is a nature writer, and Morris, who is an illustrator. They both regretted the loss of the nature words from current dictionaries and hope that the book will reawaken our sensitivity for the magical world of nature.

It is a book for all ages and a glorious tribute to the world of nature we share. It is not only a feast for the eyes, but conjures back to life many words that are fading.

Here is a review of the book written by a member of a book club.

The magical combination of author Robert Macfarlane and illustrator, Jackie Morris, has resulted in a book that is a true delight. *The Lost Words* is a tribute to nature and the language of nature, and in essence has been inspired by the decision of *The Oxford Junior Dictionary* to remove a certain number of nature words, *heron* and *willow*, for example, from their most recent edition, replacing them with words such as *broadband* and *blog*.

The Lost Words is a significant achievement for Macfarlane and Morris. Through the poems in the book, Macfarlane forces us to ask ourselves how well we can experience things we cannot name. Macfarlane, a widely acclaimed travel and nature writer and critic, is most well-known for his book *The Wild Places* published in 2007, which inspired thousands of readers to follow his routes around the British Isles to discover places where nature can still be enjoyed in all its untamed glory. Macfarlane's love of the natural world comes through again in *The Lost Words*.

In addition, the illustrations by Morris show that she is clearly a great observer of nature. Her exquisite hand-painted illustrations are sensitive and meticulous in detail. The colours, warm and vivid, give the book a luxurious feel. And the golden embellishments, are similar to illustrations in mediaeval books, and give the book a feel of something full of knowledge, something historical and ancient. The poems and illustrations blend together magically, making for a delightful and unforgettable reading experience. It is certainly a book to dip into, to talk about, to read aloud. It is a joy to read and will surely inspire young and old alike. And beyond this, Macfarlane and Morris have given a book that is a warning, a wake-up call, and the message is – the threat is real. We have diminished nature and are replacing it with industrial and technological advancements, and are now further reducing the reach of nature by eliminating nature words from a dictionary. Standing against the tide that seems to devalue nature, *The Lost Words* is a testimony to not underestimating the power of words… and of nature.

General comprehension

Answer the following questions in complete sentences.

1 According to the review, what inspired Robert MacFarlane to write the book?
2 What does the reviewer say the book forces the reader to do?
3 What was the focus of McFarlane's book *The Wild Places*?
4 What adjectives does the reviewer use to describe the illustrations in the second paragraph?
5 What does the reviewer mean by 'the threat is real'?

State whether the following sentences are true or false. Justify your answers.

6 Jackie Morris is aware of detail in what she sees.
7 *The Lost Words* is primarily a beautiful book of illustrations.
8 The reviewer says you need to read all of the book to enjoy it.

Paper 2 practice task (1.2) – Reflection on nature

You will hear a reflection by a mother who is speaking about nature. Answer the questions.

1 What time of year is it?
2 What is the name of the flowers the children's mum can see at the bottom of the garden?
3 How does the speaker know the names of the flowers?
4 What do the children mean when they say their aunt lives in 'the back of beyond'?
5 What are the names of the speaker's children?
6 When the speaker and her children went out into the garden, what else did they see apart from the yellow flowers?

Listen again and choose the five true statements.

a Heather and Finn were talking to their friends on their mobile devices.
b Their mum knew she had time for tea because the children were occupied.
c The garden was carefully tended and well organised.
d The speaker lives in Norfolk.
e The cowslips were in flower.
f The children do not think highly of the village where their aunt lives.
g The children bought sweets in the village shop when they visited their aunt.
h Heather thought the flowers in the garden were cowslips.
i The activities of the birds and animals in the garden were a reminder of nature's vulnerability.
j The mum feels the children must reconnect to nature.

Internal assessment (SL)

Figure 1.9 My phone is my dictionary, my thesaurus, and my online teacher!

Examine the photograph above and consider the following points.

- What do you see in the picture? Describe only what you see. Do not give opinions.
- Reflect on the photograph in connection with the above texts on changes in the English language.

- What aspects of the use of the phone do you want to concentrate on?
- How important is your phone to you in school and the learning process?
- What role do you think phones will have in the future?

Using the points above, spend 15 minutes preparing a presentation about the photograph. Use the preparation time to organise your ideas and plan the sequence of what you will talk about.

Your presentation should last 3 to 4 minutes, after which your teacher and other students will have the opportunity to comment or ask questions about what you have said. You must engage in a conversation with them. In total, this task should take approximately 15 minutes.

Paper 1 practice task

Write a blog of 400–500 words putting forward your own response to the removal of nature words from a dictionary. Start the blog with an introduction to the issue. You may include examples from your own experience when referring to nature or technology.

Paper 2 practice task (1.3) – Changing attitudes to language

You will hear a head teacher giving a talk to parents of new children starting school. Complete the following gaps. Use no more than three words per gap.

1 People who only speak one language are ______________ in the world.
2 The development of language ______________ by social pressure and a need to communicate.
3 To understand people and become socially involved with them you have to ______________.
4 Research in countries such as Canada, Sweden, and the UK ______________ the ability of an individual to switch languages.
5 ______________ speakers are better equipped for the demands of the learning world.

Select the correct answer from the options. From the extract, we know that the head teacher:

6 a is able to speak Russian.
b teaches English.
c is not able to speak more than one language.

7 a believes children in school should concentrate on English.
b is in support of bilingual and multilingual speakers.
c thinks speaking more than one language is confusing.

8 a has a friend who can speak Russian.
b has a friend who can speak French and Russian.
c has a friend who is multilingual.

Discussion task

Consider how far your identity is affected by the language you speak and where you learned it. To what extent do you think that learning to speak and think in another language has changed your identity? Do you think differently about aspects of your culture now? How has your identity developed as a result of these experiences?

Note: Before the discussion, make notes and talk with a partner to formulate your ideas. This will make it easier to contribute to a class discussion.

1.6 Our changing world

In the global world of today, where people move rapidly around the world for work and recreation, news and opinions travel even faster. As a consequence of this rapid exchange of information, many established cultural norms are gradually changing in practice. These changes affect our identities and how we define ourselves.

Read the following texts to learn more about these trends.

21st-century life

Mass media – Article

HOW HAVE TRADITIONAL GENDER ROLES CHANGED IN THE 21ST CENTURY?

Not long ago, at least in the Western world, it was considered appropriate for the husband to be the 'breadwinner'. He was the one who earned the money to feed the family. That was his role. At that time, when it was considered by the majority of people to be the man's job to go to work to earn money to feed the family, fewer women went out to work. Wives were expected to stay at home and take care of the family by doing the washing, the cooking, the cleaning. That was their role.

In recent years, however, the situation has changed. The results of a study by the US Census Bureau revealed that many wives not only go out to work, but actually earn more than their husbands. A similar study in Britain showed that of the mothers who go out to work, over 2 million of them earn more than their husbands. The Institute of Public Policy research shows that over the past 15 years there has been a significant increase in the number of wives who earn as much, if not more, than their husbands.

One surprising result from the research, however, was that people still believe that husbands should earn more than their wives. In fact, research revealed that when husbands declared their income for the census, they very often over-reported their earnings while under-reporting the income of their wives. Did the women play down the amount of their income to save embarrassing their husbands? Or did the husbands report higher earnings to save face?

Although women are now reaching equality in the workplace, many people still have this stereotype from decades past in their heads: a good husband must be seen to support the family as the chief breadwinner and the dutiful wife must stay home and take care of the family.

Further results of the US research showed that these opinions are held across the country. Whether people live in rural areas or in the city, the majority of them believe that husbands should be the chief breadwinners.

The Pew Research Center in Washington, D. C. carried out a similar research project which showed that up to 75 per cent of people thought good husbands had to be able to support his families. This seems to indicate that the majority of people still hold the old-fashioned view that men must be the breadwinners, although in actual fact women are equally qualified to bring home a good salary and support the family.

General comprehension

Answer the following questions in complete sentences.

1 What is a 'breadwinner'?
2 According to the text, how did women spend their days in the past?
3 How has the situation changed in recent years?
4 What has not changed?
5 According to the article, why might women under-report their income?
6 How is the old gender stereotype for this situation described in the text?

Paper 1 practice task

In either a blog, an informal letter, or a diary entry, describe your reaction to the report above and explain your personal view of the present situation. Consider how it will affect you personally in the future.

SL students should write 250–400 words. HL students should write 450–600 words.

Mass media – Article

BREATHING NEW LIFE INTO PRINTED BOOKS

Before the advent of television and the internet, many people would enjoy sitting down with a good book to relax after a hard day's work. Reading was a popular hobby for young and old alike. Books were in plentiful supply as most major cities had libraries, and bookshops were popular places to visit on the main shopping streets in most towns.

Now, much of that has changed. Many libraries have closed down as authorities claim they can no longer afford the upkeep. As a result, you will find dedicated local people protesting library closures in towns and cities across the country. This action is often supported by local newspapers and schools. Students, for example, have participated in the protests and have helped raise awareness of the library closures by designing and displaying posters around the affected towns.

As libraries are closing, so are many local bookshops. Much of the market for books has now been taken over by

A city's *infrastructure* is the system or services needed, such as roads, transport, electricity, in order to work effectively.

We use *ambience* to talk about the character of a place, the mood or feeling a place gives.

the internet. We can now download books and read them on our mobile devices, anywhere, anytime. While this of course encourages reading as a hobby it has had a disastrous effect on the business of book printing and publishing, the business of buying and selling books, and, most importantly, the human interactions which take place as a result of reading or sharing a good read.

This situation is similar around the world. To counter this trend, China is taking action to encourage and support more bookshops, using hefty subsidies from tax money.

The Chinese authorities have recognised that bookshops are important. As Mr Zhang Su, deputy director of the Beijing Press Bureau, told *The Times* newspaper reporter: 'Brick-and-mortar bookstores are an important part of a city's infrastructure. They carry the memories of a city; they embody a city's cultural heritage and they affect a city's cultural ambience.'

Although eBooks have taken over the market in China as well, it seems Beijing authorities have several good ideas to counteract this. The city authorities plan to subsidise and increase the number of bookshops in the city. They hope to have a bookshop in every district, in shopping centres, near famous places, and near bus and train stations. They hope the bookshops will stay open late at night, or even 24 hours a day, and they want to incorporate public libraries in the bookshops too.

General comprehension

Answer the following questions in complete sentences.

1 Why are many libraries closing?
2 How are school students raising awareness of library closures?
3 Why do the Beijing authorities think it is important to maintain bookshops in the city?
4 How do the Beijing authorities hope to maintain bookshops?

Discussion task

Work in groups and discuss the question.

What are the advantages and disadvantages of reading on an eBook? Use information from the text as well as your own experience in your answer.

Zoom in on grammar

Reference pronouns such as *that* in paragraph 2, sentence 1 of the text above: 'much of *that* has changed' are used frequently to refer to content in the preceding sentences. In this case, the word *that* refers to the description of towns before the advent of television when reading was a popular hobby and towns had more libraries and bookshops.

There are numerous such reference pronouns, e.g. *whose, which, these.*

Grammar in context

What do the underlined words in these sentences refer to?

1 Paragraph 2: 'Now, much of *that* has changed.'
2 Paragraph 3: 'While *this* of course encourages reading as a hobby...'
3 Paragraph 4: '*This* situation is similar around the world.'
4 Last paragraph: '*They* hope the bookshops will stay open late at night...'

Discussion task

Discuss the following questions with a partner or in a group.

How often do people use the library in your town? When was the last time you used a library? Why? Do you have good bookshops in the town, or do you read eBooks on a device? What about your school library? How well stocked and well advertised is it?

Internal assessment (SL)

Figure 1.10 The best place to get together is the library!

Examine the photograph above and consider the following points.

- What do you see in the picture? Briefly describe the scene.
- Consider the function of libraries in schools and what they can offer.
- What role does a library play in a town or city today?
- What challenges are there to the existence of libraries today?
- Give your own opinion as well as information from the text above.
- Consider how important reading is to you.

Using the points above, spend 15 minutes preparing a presentation about the photograph. Use the preparation time to organise your ideas and plan the sequence of what you will talk about.

Your presentation should last 3 to 4 minutes, after which your teacher and other students will have the opportunity to comment or ask questions about what you have said. You must engage in a conversation with them. In total, this task should take approximately 15 minutes.

In addition to the culture of reading undergoing many changes, people's behaviour in other areas, particularly in public, has also changed.

Why is this?

Has the world we live in become too hectic?

Has the age of instant messaging and instant communication made us too aware of our own needs and our own identity and less aware or respectful of the people around us? Below are some letters which highlight these points and the effect inconsiderate behaviour has on others.

Mass media – Reader's letter

53 Old School Lane
Oldstock, Hampshire
15 June

Dear Sir or Madam,

I read with great interest the recent article in your newspaper about falling standards in the behaviour of theatre audiences. Your Arts Editor has absolutely hit the nail on the head with this criticism of noisy, inconsiderate audience members. I too have recently witnessed intolerable behaviour in theatres, which ruined my enjoyment of a number of live performance.

Just last week, at a performance of the musical *Hamilton*, I was completely distracted from the events on stage by a young woman sitting directly in front of me. She was paying more attention to social networking sites than she was to the performance, and the continual flickering light and clicks from her device were extremely distracting and irritating.

Having spent a considerable amount of money to purchase the tickets and travel quite a distance to the theatre, I was angry that my evening was being spoiled. I even complained to the usher, who sadly, took little action. I returned home feeling upset and very disappointed.

A friend of mine, a fellow theatre enthusiast, told me of a performance he attended recently in London where the events were equally shocking. In the middle of the play, and without stepping outside of his character, an actor was heard to say to a member of the audience whose mobile phone was ringing, 'If you don't get that, I will.'

On top of that, I have heard and read reports of people following football matches on their devices while sitting in the theatre and actually cheering when their team scored. Cheering for football in the middle of a performance! That would have been unimaginable just a few years ago.

What is the solution to this abysmal behaviour? Some friends have told me about theatre attendants who patrol the aisles during performances, especially at concerts, and will rebuke anyone using a mobile device. If the devices are not put away after the first warning, the attendants are entitled to take them away. The could work. Or maybe the solution is to forbid mobile devices in any place of performance. I for one would certainly support that.

I would be interested to hear about other people's experiences in London and provincial theatres recently. Are people better behaved in the provinces I wonder?

Yours faithfully,
Martina Simko

General comprehension

Answer the following questions in complete sentences.

1 The writer has written the letter in response to which article in the newspaper?
2 What do you think the expression 'hit the nail on the head' means?
3 What in particular has irritated the writer?
4 Did anyone help her solve the problem?
5 What do you think the phrase 'without stepping outside of his character' means?
6 The actor says, 'If you don't get that, I will.' What does he mean?
7 According to the writer, what would have been unimaginable a few years ago?

Vocabulary

The writer uses a considerable number of negative words to express her anger and frustration. Look at the words below and find a word in the text that is opposite in meaning. Then use each of the words in a sentence.

1 considerate
2 tolerable
3 inconsiderable
4 imaginable

Explain the following words. Use your dictionary if necessary. Then use each of the words in a sentence.

5 abysmal
6 aisle
7 abomination
8 provincial
9 the provinces

Mass media – Reader's letter

Bach Cottage
Beethoven Road
Brahms
12 July

Dear Sir or Madam,

I was shocked but not surprised to read of the sufferings of your reader during his visits to the theatre. However, I have to say that in the world of classical music, there are an increasing number of audience members who are equally unaware of the accepted standards of good behaviour.

I refer, of course, to the practice of clapping after individual movements of a symphony. This is intolerable and a clear sign of ignorance as the symphony was composed to be heard as one piece, not a series of individual short compositions. These ignorant individuals break the concentration of other audience members. The spontaneous outburst of ill-placed clapping is then usually shortened by their realisation that they are alone in their enthusiasm at that point. It is unfortunate that music lessons in schools, along with other arts subjects, have been so drastically reduced that we are educating a generation of IT experts with little knowledge of culture and artistic appreciation.

Generally, conductors give a clear signal when a piece reaches the end, which should be recognisable for anyone who needs a hint. The conductor can be seen to relax physically and often places the baton on the conductor's pulpit, before turning to face the audience and accept their approval and recognition. Similarly, the orchestra members give clear signals in their body language when the piece is finished.

If only those audience members who are so keen to clap could be a little more aware of body language, to replace their lack of musical knowledge, we could all hear and enjoy a symphony to the end.

Yours faithfully,
Eleanor Elgar

General comprehension

Answer the following questions in complete sentences.

1 What is the writer's complaint?
2 Why is this a problem in the writer's opinion?
3 What solution is suggested?
4 How does the conductor's use of body language signal to the audience that a piece is finished?

Paper 1 practice task

As a young performer or audience member write a letter in response to the complaint above. What advice would you give audience members? How would you suggest dealing with the problem? Is there a solution? Write 300–400 words.

Mass media – Reader's letter

5 Basin Street
The Blues
13 July

Dear Sir or Madam,

Reading the letter in yesterday's paper from a music lover complaining about clapping between symphony movements, I am forced to respond immediately.

Classical music lovers have no inkling of how lucky they are. On a good evening they will probably be obliged to clap just once, or maybe twice, or at a push even three times – in one evening.

Do you have any idea how often we poor jazz enthusiasts are obliged to clap? It depends of course on the size of the band. Luckily we do not have a full orchestra very often, but even with a quartet we are obliged to clap enthusiastically for every solo played by each of the four members. That means within one piece we clap at least four times, imagine that?

In addition, of course, we are called upon to respond to each performer at the end of each set with those words which cause dismay in every audience members' heart – on drums we have... and on the bass... and on piano... and on the triangle... and so on and on.

Enthusiastic clapping is required and expected for each band member.

Tell me, colleagues from the classical world, why do we never hear the words 'and on first violin we have ..... and on the cellos we have...'.

How do you get away with your roles as audience members so lightly?

Yours faithfully,
Benny Tam

General comprehension

Answer the following questions in complete sentences.

1 How would you describe the tone of the letter?
2 Why does the writer think classical music enthusiasts are lucky?
3 When are the jazz fans obliged to clap?

2 Experiences

2 Experiences

Research questions

- To what extent can humans claim to be happy?
- How do we measure the quality of human life?
- What steps could you take to improve the quality of your life?

Objectives

- To identify how individual experiences influence our lives.
- To evaluate the role counsellors may play in our lives.
- To discuss the meaning of happiness.
- To examine the difference between happiness and pleasure.
- To discuss how hobbies can add value to our lives.
- To examine the importance of reading as an experience.

Language skills objectives

- To practise informal writing in emails and diary entries.
- To practise answering questions after listening to dialogues.
- To practise using the structure *not only...*, *but also....*
- To revise the use of prepositions and *-ing* form.
- To understand and practise using number-noun modifiers.
- To practise writing a speech.
- To practise the use of *would* for actions repeated in the past.

From the moment we are born, we start to experience the world and the people surrounding us. Our reactions to our experiences vary and we may feel challenged or confused. Or our experiences may leave us feeling happy and uplifted.

2.1 The happiest days of your life?

Being a teenager is not always easy

In the article below, a student counsellor writes about her work with teenagers in a large international school.

Mass media – Public commentary

Being a teenager is not always easy. That stage of life between being a child and an adult can prove to be a challenge for many young people and can often be equally difficult and frustrating for their parents. Parents may be confused by the sunny young girl or boy they used to know turning into a moody, unresponsive teenager. The teenager is equally confused by their feelings, changing moods, and that awful sense that no one understands them. Teenagers go through emotional, physical, and mental changes as they grow up which affect many aspects of their lives. Friendships, hobbies, school attitude, and performance may all improve or deteriorate as a teenager grows older. As a result, they may feel unhappy, confused, depressed, tired, bored, short tempered, and insecure.

Sound familiar?

In addition, in the 21st century, social media makes the whole process of growing up a great deal more complicated and challenging. As many teenagers spend a lot of time online, this leads them to compare themselves and their lives, often unrealistically, with others. They may feel left out of the activities others post online, or suffer from the feeling of FOMO (fear of missing out). In addition to that, they may have to deal with different levels of cyber-bullying. Finding support when feeling depressed or just upset by the events, comments, and emotions stirred by social media is not easy. Parents often have little idea about the power it exerts over teenagers, because when they were that age, there was no such thing as the internet or social networks. The power and influence of social media is being increasingly recognised by parents, teachers, researchers, and politicians.

But how can the influence of social media be counteracted? What can be done to help?

Some parents may tell their children to 'snap out of it', or suggest they take up sports, join in activities, or just put the phone away, but the reality is that parents find the entire situation just as challenging as teenagers do. It can also be difficult for a teenager to talk about social or emotional problems with their parents. The challenge is not only that the problems are personal and very emotional, but also nowadays a lot of parents go out to work, so they too are kept very busy and the time to sit and chat may be seriously limited. This makes finding the right time and space to talk about personal challenges even more difficult, even when the teenager would be happy to discuss these matters with a parent.

It seems what is needed is an independent, trustworthy, qualified person with time and no distractions, who can listen to problems, who knows how to help and will keep both the conversations and the problems strictly confidential.

TOK How do we know what a teenager is? Is it something that actually exists in the world or is it something westernised humans have constructed between them? Many cultures have no concept of 'being a teenager'. People are either 'children' or 'adults'.

Figure 2.1 A student with a Guidance Counsellor

A lot of schools have counsellors on their staff, some are called Career or Guidance Counsellors, but others are specifically Social Emotional Counsellors. Not every school has someone like this and not every student is willing or happy to talk to a counsellor who is part of the school they attend.

General comprehension

Answer the following questions in complete sentences.

1 According to the text, why is being a teenager in the 21st century particularly challenging?
2 What are three typical problems students face when comparing their lives with others on social media?
3 According to the text, parents are sometimes unable to help their teenage children. Why?
4 What are the qualities a counsellor needs?
5 What does the phrase 'snap out of it' mean in the context of the text?

Discussion task

With a partner, discuss the following question and be prepared to report back to the class about the thoughts and ideas you and your partner had.

'What advice would you give to parents of teenagers who are feeling depressed?'

Zoom in on grammar

not only…, but also…

The connecting structure *not only…, but also…* is usually used in a formal context to connect ideas.

When we set out on the trip, the morning was ***not only*** *dark,* ***but also*** *very cold.*

Find the sentence in the text with this structure.

Grammar in context

Use *not only…, but also…* and the prompts below to make sentences.

1 too much homework/weekly three-hour training sessions
2 never listen/talk too much
3 insect bites/sun burn
4 read the book/write an essay on it
5 never eat meat/not eat dairy products

Paper 1 practice task

A friend of yours is clearly feeling depressed. In an effort to help, write your friend an informal, friendly email offering advice and support.

SL students should write 250–400 write words. HL students should write 450–600 words.

Tips for writing an informal email

- Use an informal register and tone (see below).
- Use paragraphs and structure your work carefully.
- Use descriptive language with a range of vocabulary to make your writing interesting.
- Start and end the email appropriately.
- Use contractions such as *I'm* rather than *I am*.
- Talk about shared experience and knowledge.

Zoom in on language

Register

Register refers to the choice of language and level of formality that you use when writing a text or speaking to people. Register is more than simply using formal or informal language. You will need to consider your relationship to the person and the kind of request or offer you are responding to. Your choice of language must match the situation and the relationship with the person.

For example, when speaking to an adult family member, which of the following would you choose as being appropriate?

- *Would you be so kind as to pass the sugar please?*
- *Could I have the sugar please?*
- *Give me the sugar.*

The correct answer is *Could I have the sugar please?*

Give me the sugar. might be suitable for a sibling, but is too informal for addressing an adult – and, more importantly, the answer might be 'no'.

Would you be so kind as to pass the sugar please? is more suitable for a formal situation with people you do not know, where the aim is to appear as polite as possible.

Language in context

Look at the following situations with a partner. What is an appropriate response for each situation? Think about register.

1 You are in a clothing shop and are asking a shop assistant to try on a pair of jeans.
2 You are talking to your homeroom teacher. You missed the bus and are late for school.
3 You are talking to your swimming coach and asking for ways to improve.
4 You are in an upscale restaurant and are complaining to the manager.

Paper 2 practice task (2.1) – An interview with a counsellor

You will hear an interview with a school Social Emotional Counsellor about her work. Answer the questions.

1 What kind of counsellor is Alice?
2 How did she feel as a teenager?
3 What did she study?
4 What qualities does Alice think a Social Emotional Counsellor needs?
5 What is really rewarding for her?

Listen again and complete the following gaps. Use no more than three words for each gap.

6 To be honest I had ________ and going through my teenage years was not easy for me.
7 I studied psychology with counselling skills ________.
8 In addition, the teacher is often ________ role and responsibilities as a teacher and as a counsellor.

Internal assessment (SL)

Figure 2.2 Alone or lonely?

Examine the photograph above and consider the following points.

- What do you see in the picture? Describe only what you see. Do not give opinions.
- Reflect on the photograph in connection with the theme of experiences.
- What is the difference between 'alone' and 'lonely'?
- What options are open in your school for someone who feels lonely?
- Make connections to your own experience and the experiences of students you know.
- Consider the role of a counsellor.

Using the points above, spend 15 minutes preparing a presentation about the photograph. Use the preparation time to organise your ideas and plan the sequence of what you will talk about.

Your presentation should last 3 to 4 minutes, after which your teacher and other students will have the opportunity to comment or ask questions about what you have said. You must engage in a conversation with them. In total, this task should take approximately 15 minutes.

NEW APP FOR STUDENT COUNSELLING READY TO PROVIDE SUPPORT

For schools that don't have Social Emotional Counsellors, a solution in the form of an app has been created. The app, called Spill, enables anyone who needs someone to talk to about an issue to contact a qualified counsellor. This is even more anonymous and confidential than sitting face to face with a real person. A survey of 500 people by the developers revealed that talking about anxieties with friends was something that the majority of people would rather not do.

A group of fully qualified counsellors, who also give face-to-face counselling, have made their services available online. The counsellors are not only qualified, but also registered with the British Association for Counselling and Psychotherapy. People can contact them and send as many text messages as they want. They are promised two replies each day. The experts say that the app will be especially helpful for people who do not have friends or family to talk to, and in this way at least someone will listen to their problems and offer support. More and more people prefer to talk to others through messaging rather than face-to-face. If we are living in times where digital communication is generally acceptable, why not use it for counselling?

The app offers the possibility for people to ask questions and share their problems in a completely anonymous situation. Users can contact the counsellors at any time through text messages. The counsellors, however, admit that if the problems sound very serious and they realise that the person needs face-to-face therapy, they will then recommend that the person talks to their doctor or to another health specialist.

The app will certainly help some of those who need counselling, but the developers encourage friends to provide support as well. Friends can provide support by making an effort to include anyone who seems down in the dumps in any social activities and by ensuring that no one is excluded in the group. They can also monitor any unkind comments, real or online, and do their best to listen to those who are in need of support.

TOK Are surveys the best way to investigate human experiences? What are the limitations of quantitative data when investigating humans? Is human experience measurable and generaliseable?

General comprehension

Answer the following questions in complete sentences.

1 What is the name of the app?
2 What does the app do?
3 What association are the counsellors registered with?
4 Who will benefit most from the service?
5 How will the counsellors deal with more serious challenges?
6 How can friends provide support?

Vocabulary

Match the words (1–10) as they are used in the text with their meanings (a–j).

1 guidance	a watch over
2 enable	b left out
3 anonymous	c help and advice
4 confidential	d can be obtained
5 acceptable	e secret, private
6 face to face	f unhappy
7 available	g unknown
8 down in the dumps	h allowed, tolerated
9 excluded	i talking to someone in person
10 monitor	j make possible

Zoom in on grammar

Preposition + *-ing*

In the text, there are examples of *-ing* forms after a preposition:

- *by **making** an effort*
- *by **ensuring***

When a verb follows a preposition, we usually use the *-ing* form of the verb.

*You can't make an omelette without **breaking** eggs.* (NOT… *without to break eggs*)

*He improved his English by **taking** an acting class.* (NOT… *by to take an acting class*)

Here are some commonly used phrases with a preposition + *-ing* form:

- *I studied instead of **going** on holiday.*
- *I look forward to **hearing** from you.*

Happiness

Discussion task

How would you describe your feelings right now? Are you happy? What does it mean to be happy? To what extent is it the same for everyone? Discuss in small groups what you think happiness means. Share your thoughts with the class.

How can happiness be measured and compared across countries? The article below describes the findings of a World Happiness Report.

Mass media – Article

In this context, an *index* is a statistic or measure derived from observations.

20 MARCH: INTERNATIONAL DAY OF HAPPINESS

Annually, World Happiness Reports are produced and the Happiness Index reveals which countries have the happiest people. Researchers use a poll in 156 countries to measure the people's level of happiness. Respondents are asked to rate six areas of their lives, referring to the best possible life and worst possible life as their measurement. These six areas are income, health and life expectancy, social support, freedom, trust, and generosity.

The analysis of the results shows that wealth alone does not make a country happy. The economist, Richard Easterlin, has shown in his research that even when a country becomes wealthier, the wealth will be unevenly distributed and does not necessarily lead to greater social equality. So that although a country may be wealthy, if the people are not wealthy then the country's wealth does not contribute to their individual happiness. Your own income makes you happy, if it compares well with others.

For example, in 2018 the United States scored badly on the happiness scale although the country is wealthy. Other factors that played a role in people's perceptions of happiness in the US included poor health and poor life expectancy.

In the 2018 report, three areas of health are specifically mentioned: obesity, depression, and addiction to drugs, none of which increases one's happiness. In fact, everyone of these health issues leads to additional health problems. The report links these poor areas of health to the results of questions in the area of trust, in which the USA also scores poorly. The authors of the report connect this lack of trust to government policies which allow companies to aggressively market prescription drugs and encourage the fast-food industries to produce foods with high levels of sugar, as well as processed foods, both of which are factors in obesity.

The happiest places seem to be the Scandinavian countries, where it is seems that people have more trust in their government's ability to spend money on services such as health and education. In 2018, in the list of the top ten countries for happiness, Finland was first, followed by Norway, Denmark, Iceland, Switzerland, the Netherlands, Canada, New Zealand, Sweden, and Australia. The USA was 18th.

To increase happiness, the report recommends the use of positive psychology strategies. The report states that 'programmes of positive psychology and wellness at schools, workplaces, and in the community can help individuals to change their own behaviours, overcome addictions, and pursue life strategies to bolster their personal well-being and the well-being of friends, family, and community. The evidence is large and growing that such life-changing strategies can be highly effective.'*

**The World Happiness Report 2018.*

TOK Can happiness be measured in an objective way? Or is happiness relative to the individual, time, place and culture? What role does instinct play in helping us to know when we are happy or not?

General comprehension

Answer the following questions in complete sentences.

1 When is the International Day of Happiness?
2 What does the Happiness Index tell us?
3 Which areas of life does the Index focus on?
4 Why doesn't a country's wealth produce happiness?
5 Which areas of life had a negative effect on the happiness results for the USA?
6 Which areas of policy affect the people's trust?

Vocabulary

Match the words (1–8) as they are used in the text with their meanings (a–h).

1 reveal	a in an angry or hostile way
2 respondents	b people who answer questions
3 expectancy	c feeling of anticipation
4 generosity	d show
5 trust	e belief in the reliability of something
6 perception	f kindness
7 aggressively	g awareness
8 strategy	h a plan

Paper 1 practice task

Research your own country's position in the Happiness Index. Write a text referring to this and suggesting ways your country could improve their overall position in the Happiness Index.

Choose from one of the following text types: a blog, a newspaper article, or a letter to your country's leader (Prime Minister, President, etc).

SL students should write 250–400 words. HL students should write 450–600 words.

Tips for writing a newspaper article

- Plan your article by covering these questions: Who was involved? What happened? Where did it happen? Why did it happen? When did it happen? How did it happen? These questions show you that you will write in the past tense.
- Sketch out a plan of your article before you start writing.
- Decide if the information is important, interesting, or unimportant.
- Decide if you will present straight facts, or will you give your opinion?
- Consider your readership – who will be reading this? If your audience is older, you might include different points than if your audience is very young.

Tips for writing a formal letter

- Provide the sender's address at the top, followed by a date, and a salutation, e.g. *Dear Sir, Dear Sirs, Dear Mrs Brown.* If you do not know the name of the recipient, use *Dear Sir or Madam*, or *To whom it may concern.*
- Give the reason for the letter in the first line, e.g. *I am writing because. . ., After reading your article, I would like to. . .*
- Divide the letter into paragraphs and use a new paragraph for a new point or argument.
- End the letter with a formal phrase, e.g. *I look forward to hearing from you.*
- Do not say *Thank you for reading this letter.*
- End the letter with *Yours sincerely*, if you know the name of the person you are writing to. Use *Yours faithfully*, if you do not know the name of the person.

Intercultural activity

How important is it to be happy? How does this vary in different cultures? Work in groups and share your personal experiences. Which specific ideas or events make people happy in your culture?

Matthieu Ricard (born 1946) is a Frenchman who has often been called the happiest man in the world by newspapers. His website describes him as a Buddhist Monk, Photographer, Author, and Humanitarian. Before reading Ricard's blog below entitled 'Pleasure and Happiness: The Great Mix-up', look at the definitions of those two terms.

Merriam-Webster's Learner's Dictionary describes *pleasure* as:

> 1 [noncount]
>
> a : a feeling of happiness, enjoyment, or satisfaction : a pleasant or pleasing feeling
> - I paint for the sheer/pure *pleasure* of it.
> - He smiled with *pleasure*.
>
> b : activity that is done for enjoyment
> - Is this trip for business or *pleasure*?

It describes *happiness* as:

1 [noncount] : the state of being happy : JOY
- They made a toast to long life and *happiness.*
- They found *happiness* together.

2 [count] *somewhat formal* : an experience that makes you happy
- I wish them every *happiness.* [=I hope that they will be very happy.]

It is clear that even dictionaries have not discovered the difference between, happiness and pleasure, which Ricard has determined and describes below. The difference between happiness and pleasure is related to how we reflect on our experiences and how we examine our responses.

Professional – Blog

Pleasure and happiness: the great mix-up

One of the most common errors we make is to confuse pleasure for happiness. According to a Hindu proverb: 'Pleasure is only the shadow of happiness'. Pleasure is the direct result of hedonistic, pleasurable, sensual, aesthetic, or intellectual stimuli. This fleeting experience is dependent upon circumstances, on a specific location, or a moment in time. It is unstable by nature, and the sensation it evokes soon becomes neutral or even unpleasant. When repeated, it may grow insipid or even lead to disgust, like the happiness of eating a cake. It tastes good, but that pleasure ends as soon as we finish it. To prolong this happiness we would have to keep eating more cakes and then, ten cakes later, we might feel nauseous.

Pleasure is exhausted by usage, like a candle consuming itself. It is almost always linked to an activity and naturally leads to boredom by dint of being repeated. Listening rapturously to a Bach prelude requires a focus of attention that, minimal as it is, cannot be maintained indefinitely. After a while, fatigue kicks in and the music loses its charm. If we were forced to listen to the same piece for days on end, it would become unbearable.

Furthermore, pleasure is an individual experience, most often centred on the self, which is why it can easily descend into selfishness and sometimes conflict with the well-being of others. Still, in some rare cases, an individual may derive pleasure from helping, supporting, and doing what's best for others. Such pleasure can transcend the self and contribute to genuine happiness, but only if the individual's motives are truly altruistic and completely focused on the happiness of others.

You can experience pleasure at somebody else's expense, but you can never derive happiness from it. Pleasure can be joined to cruelty, violence, greed, and other mental conditions that are incompatible with true happiness. 'Pleasure is the happiness of madmen, while happiness is the pleasure of sages,' wrote the French novelist and critic Jules Barbey d'Aurevilly.

Some people even enjoy vengeance and torturing other sentient beings. Likewise, a businessman may rejoice in the ruin of a competitor, a thief revel in his booty, a spectator at a bullfight can exult in the bull's death. But these are passing, sometimes morbid, states of elation that, like moments of positive euphoria, have nothing to do with happiness.

More often than not, pleasure does not keep its promises, as poet Robert Burns describes in 'Tam O'Shanter':

But pleasures are like poppies spread,
You seize the flow'r its bloom is shed;
Or like the snow falls in the river,
A moment white – then melts forever.

Genuine happiness may be influenced by circumstances, but, unlike pleasure, does not depend on it. It does not mutate into its opposite, but endures and grows with experience. It imparts a sense of fulfilment that in time becomes second nature.

TOK

To what extent do you believe happiness differs from pleasure? Explain your thinking using examples from your own life.

General comprehension

Answer the following questions in complete sentences.

1 According to the text, what do we often confuse?
2 What does the writer mean by describing pleasure as a 'fleeting experience'?
3 What is the example the writer uses to explain the difference between pleasure and happiness? Explain it in your own words.
4 Which example does the writer give to show that pleasurable activities repeated endlessly lead to boredom?
5 How does the writer show that pleasure can also be selfish?

Text handling

Answer the following questions in complete sentences.

1 What is the idea that the Hindu proverb 'Pleasure is only the shadow of happiness' trying to communicate?
2 How can you express the ideas in Robert Burns' poem very simply?

Vocabulary

Complete the table with the correct verbs, nouns, and adjectives.

Verb	Noun	Adjective
	repetition	repetitive
lose		
	confusion	
exhaust	exhaustion	
		receptive

Ricard uses a wide range of challenging vocabulary in his text. You will be able to understand some of the words by recognising the roots. For example, *pleasurable, sensual, aesthetic,* and *intellectual* can all be understood relatively easily.

Reread the text with a partner and list the new words which you cannot identify. Using a dictionary, work together to understand the words as they are used.

Matthieu Ricard's book, *Happiness: A Guide to Developing Life's Most Important Skill,* is published by Little Brown.

Additional reading (HL)

Robert Burns is not the only writer to have ideas similar to Ricard's ideas. Look up Shakespeare's play *Twelfth Night*, Act 1, Scene 1, and compare Shakespeare's ideas with Ricard's.

Paper 1 practice task

Now that you have read and discussed the difference between happiness and pleasure, write either a blog or an article for the school magazine explaining your own ideas about the difference.

SL students should write 250–400 words. HL students should write 450–600 words.

For tips on how to write a blog, see page 9 of Chapter 1, Identities.

Paper 2 practice task (2.2) – Learning to be happy

You will hear a conversation between three housemates – Bill, Rosemary, and Theresa – about a new course being offered on Happiness. Answer the following questions.

1 Who is making coffee for the three students?
2 What is the popular course called?
3 What is the course about?
4 Which of the three students is not interested in this course?
5 Why does Theresa think the course would be good for Bill?
6 What is the first simple idea recommended?
7 What is the final idea?

Listen again and complete the following gaps. Use no more than three words for each gap.

8 **Bill:** Hey, I have no idea what you ________.
9 **Rosemary:** Talk to someone new every day and take time to ________ someone you care about.
10 **Bill:** I suppose I have to ________ too?

Paper 1 practice task

As Rosemary suggested, write an informal letter of thanks to someone who did something important for you in your life.

SL students should write 250–400 words. HL students should write 450–600 words.

2.2 Experiences can shape our lives

Travel and adventure

More than 2 million Tanzanian children between the ages of 7 and 13 are out-of-school. Girls, the poorest children, and children with disabilities are most likely to drop out of school or never attend school in the first place. The webpage below is the story of one school's commitment to supporting education in Tanzania.

Mass media – Webpage

Supporting students in Tanzania

In 2002, a group of students and teachers from an international school continued the long-standing tradition of travelling to Tanzania to work with students at a secondary school and help them prepare for their state leaving examinations in November. The international school had supported students there for many years. This trip offered their students glimpses into lives which are so much harder than their own, through the experience of living and working in Africa with the Tanzanian students.

Deep friendships have developed over the years between the Tanzanian and the international school students, sustained by 21st-century social media. No student returns from the visit unchanged. International students, teachers, and parents have sponsored the education of Tanzanian students over many years, but the support and sponsorship usually ends when those students graduate from the secondary school.

Figure 2.3 School life in Tanzania

After the summer programme in 2002, two of the students, let's call them Mike and Ben, pulled one of the adult chaperones aside and begged him to sponsor them further. They said if they could not continue their education, they would have to go back to the farm and their lives would forever be dependent on the weather. They said if it rains the crops grow, the cattle thrive, and the family can eat. If it doesn't rain, the crops die, cattle die, and the family starve. The man said he would have to think about it as sponsoring two students through high school and university would be a major financial commitment.

The international students and their chaperones returned home to their normal lives and quickly became accustomed to having a continuous, reliable supply of fresh water on tap at any time and electricity always being available, in contrast to Tanzania. Life became comfortable again.

Unfortunately, three days after their return the chaperone had an accident on the way home from work. This resulted in major surgery, an extended stay in hospital, and rehabilitation which lasted months. After leaving work on that afternoon in August, he didn't return until the following February. He had a lot of time to think and compare the treatment he was receiving, as a matter of course, with conditions in Tanzania. The contrast was dramatic. His decision was made that he would somehow sponsor Mike and Ben to complete their education.

Over the following years, he was greatly helped by colleagues and friends who heard of his project. There was little contact with Mike and Ben in Tanzania, generally only when additional funds were needed or when they shared their examination results and certificates by email. They both worked hard and so he willingly continued to support them. Finally, in 2011, nine years after the visit, they each received their Master's degrees from university and his work was done.

And that was the end of the story.

Coincidentally, a parent from the international school visited the school in Tanzania in 2016. She met Mike by chance at the school and learned that he was instrumental in financing and refurbishing the boys' dormitory, and was sponsoring two students himself. He is now a very successful lawyer in Tanzania. He is married with children of his own, but is still investing time and money in the education of other Tanzanian students. He states quite categorically that he would not be where he is now if it were not for his sponsor. Ben is now a teacher in Dar es Salaam.

The weather in Tanzania has not changed – either it rains or it doesn't. But what could change and needs to change is the possibility for young Tanzanians to be educated and in a position to drive the country forward in the 21st century.

Education is the key, but they can't do it on their own. If you are interested in turning a life round by enabling a student to receive a life-changing education, consider sponsoring a student in a less fortunate position than yourself and make a lasting difference.

General comprehension

Answer the following questions in complete sentences.

1 What did the Tanzanian project offer the international school students?
2 What effect does the visit have on these students?
3 What did Mike and Ben want the chaperone to do?
4 What do Tanzanian farmers depend on (like farmers all over the world)?
5 What comforts did the international school students greatly appreciate when they returned home?
6 How regular was contact between Mike and Ben and the sponsor after his return?
7 Who met with one of the sponsored students some years later?
8 What does Mike do now to support Tanzanian students?
9 What do Mike and Ben now do for work?
10 What has not changed in Tanzania? What needs to change?

Vocabulary

Match the words (1–9) below as they are used in the text to their meanings (a, b, or c). Choose the word which best matches the word from the text.

	a	b	c
1 chaperone	a adult supervisor	b photographer	c older student
2 to thrive	a to live well	b to develop well	c to get rich
3 to starve	a to walk	b to become ill	c to die from hunger
4 commitment	a an obligation	b a friendship	c an instruction
5 reliable	a can be trusted	b supportive	c possible
6 dormitory	a playground	b place to lock up valuables	c large room where several people sleep
7 to refurbish	a to advertise	b to sell	c to redecorate
8 coincidentally	a first of all	b unplanned	c annoyingly
9 categorically	a clearly	b sadly	c simply

Mass media – Travel guide

FIND THE PERFECT ADVENTURE HOLIDAY FOR YOUR FAMILY

Witches and wizards

Drive in the direction of Wiltshire and you will come across the magical stones of the famous Stonehenge near Salisbury. But it is Lacock Abbey where you get the first taste of the world of witches and wizards.

Figure 2.4 The home of witches and wizards?

Only a two-hour drive from London and when you see the stone-slated roofs, twisted chimney stacks, and mullioned windows, you know you are in a magical place. It is the perfect setting to imagine a robed witch or a wizard in a pointed hat coming around a corner. Walk along the cloisters of the abbey and take pictures. You might see families in costumes from the Middle Ages.

In fact, the whole village of Lacock looks like something from a film set for a mediaeval story. Just wander round and soak up the magic!

You can also find lots of other places in the British Isles – from Land's End to John o'Groats – that take you back in time and inspire your imagination, but doing all that in one holiday would be a big tour!

The urban jungle

Robust trainers, a backpack with a giant water bottle, and a mobile phone – that's the gear you need. The list of cities to visit is endless, from Barcelona to Mexico City, but New York must be near the top of anybody's list. Jump aboard a minibus and let yourself be immersed in the world of hip-hop culture. Visit places like Brooklyn or the Bronx that are home to hip-hop mega-icons such as Jay-Z, Biggie, and Nas.

Or you might like a water tour. Take a 19th-century schooner with billowing sails and watch as the crew guide you past the NYC skyline. Lots of pictures for you to take on this tour.

How about the Trapeze School in New York? There are classes and instruction for all age groups. Jump off a platform 20 feet above the ground, safely harnessed into your special gear, and have the time of your life learning the aerial art of flying trapeze. This is the nearest you can get to flying without wings!

Figure 2.5 Trapeze school – the nearest you can get to flying without wings

The mountain trekking experience

Fit enough to trek? The Inca Trail in Peru is one of the world's most famous treks. Try the four-day trek, sleeping in tents at night while enjoying outstanding views of Machu Picchu during the day. See orchids and humming birds along the route, and with the highest point being 4 215 m above sea level, you really feel as if you are on top of the world. Machu Picchu is a symbol of the long-vanished Inca Empire built around 1450 AD and is probably the most visited destination in Peru. In 2007 it was named as one of the New Seven Wonders of the World. You will need to join a guided tour to get the most out of this activity, but it is a never-to-be-forgotten experience for you and the adults you take with you.

Figure 2.6 Machu Picchu – probably the most visited destination in Peru

Need something less strenuous? Try the Dolomites in northern Italy. There are a number of easier routes and one of these is a four-night tour from Corvara to Selva. Mighty mountains, expansive views, Alpine villages, and quirky rifugios or huts where you will spend the night, all make up this breathtakingly gorgeous trek. Although the actual walking is only about four or five hours, the breaks make it a day-long trek. It is well signposted and well walked but is not without dangers and if you have never walked rough paths along steep hillsides you might not find it so easy.

Water worlds

Surfing is a sport with many attractions: it is exciting, teaches you patience, and is an all-body fitness workout. If you join a course, you'll meet lots of other people your age and get to know them quickly while you're all learning together. In Europe there are lots of places to choose from, whether in the Algarve area of Portugal, the Cornish coast of the United Kingdom with the pretty villages of St Ives and Newquay, or Asturias in Spain. All of these places have long coastlines with the all-important waves that you need! Or how about the most famous of all surfing destinations – Australia? New South Wales has enough surf options to accommodate all levels of surfing skill. Ulladulla, south of Sydney is easily accessible. The name is from the Aboriginal language and means 'safe harbour'. It was about 250 years ago that the British explorer and navigator, Captain James Cook, sailed along this coast while he was on his mission to track the course of the planet Venus. He soon found that the region had a lot more to offer than just tracking the planets. He probably didn't do any surfing, although the sport is said to have its origins in the Pacific Ocean regions and it is mentioned in some of the log books of his ships.

Figure 2.7 An all-body workout

General comprehension

Answer the following questions in complete sentences.

Witches and wizards

1 What tourist attraction will you find near Salisbury?
2 What does the writer feel makes the attraction a 'magical place'?

The urban jungle

3 According to the writer, what equipment is essential for the tourist in New York?

4 What kind of transport do you think 'a schooner' is? Give a justification for your answer.

The mountain trekking experience

5 What was the name of the people who built Machu Picchu?

6 What word in this section means 'unusual in an interesting way'?

Water worlds

7 According to the text, why is surfing such a popular sport?

8 What is the connection in the text between Captain Cook and surfing?

Zoom in on grammar

Number-noun modifier

A number and a noun may combine to quantify a characteristic of a noun. There are three examples of number-noun modifiers in the texts. The first one is in the 'Witches and wizards' section: *a **two-hour** drive from London*. Can you find the other two?

Look at these examples:

- *The book has 300 pages. – It is a **300-page** book.*
- *Jack is 17 years old. – He is a **17-year-old** boy.*
- *The run lasted ten minutes. – It was a **ten-minute** run.*
- *The trip lasted five days. – It was a **five-day** trip.*

Notice that when the number and noun function as modifiers, they are singular.

Paper 1 practice task

You recently went with your family on one of the adventure holidays described above. Write an informal email to a friend or a school speech in which you describe what you did, and explain how you felt.

SL students should write 250–400 words. HL students should write 450–600 words.

Tips for writing a speech

- Make sure to use an introduction that catches the attention of the audience. You could use a fact or a quote.
- Always keep your audience in mind as this may influence your choice of anecdotes.
- Give some general information and incorporate an anecdote from your own experience.
- Use rhetorical questions to keep the attention of the audience, e.g. *Would you want this to happen to you? Do you think they like this?*
- Use linking phrases such as *first, second, moreover, I would like to add, finally.*
- End the speech by thanking your audience, e.g. *Thank you for listening.*

There are many organisations that arrange adventure holidays for teenagers. Below is an example of a brochure from one of these organisations.

Mass media – Brochure

AIM HIGHER ACHIEVE MORE

Figure 2.8 A head for heights

Adventures that keep spirits flying high.

Engagement is what we do best.
And learning through adventure is what we're all about.

There are adventures on land and water;
adventures at home and abroad.

Adventures which rely on personal courage;

adventures which need a head for heights;

adventures that require teamwork, cooperation, and leadership.

There are lots of chances to get very, very wet.

There are adrenalin rushes; muddy challenges; initiative exercises requiring thought and care.

All designed to motivate, build confidence, and encourage development in more ways than one.

In the UK, there's a choice of over 50 different adventure activities, all led by skilled instructors who will help your students make the most of the challenges and opportunities each activity presents.

But that's not all. Widen their horizons further with our Watersports and Adventure Programme in France and Spain.

Take on a new environment – explore the rivers and the sea; learn new skills with trained instructors and take a day's excursion to discover new landscapes and cultures.

But the real value, whether at home or abroad, is in the memories, confidence, and newfound enthusiasm they'll bring back.

It's all that learning that happened when they weren't even thinking about it.

In advertising, punctuation rules and conventions are often broken to make a point or to add emphasis.

Mediterranean Watersports

Let the sea inspire

Motivate, engage, and reward your students with a PGL trip to the Med. Enjoy an exciting range of watersports in the clear blue waters of the Mediterranean Sea, and bring home motivated students with new skills and confidence.

New flexible durations from 7 days and the option to fly to your destination mean you can now tailor your trip to suit your own timetable.

Figure 2.9 Learning to surf

How does it work?

All Day on the Water

Your students learn to sail a variety of dinghies plus sit-on-kayaks under the expert tuition of our watersports instructors.

Fun-packed evenings

The fun doesn't stop when the day's activities are over. Our centre teams lead evening entertainment to keep your students occupied, including a nightly disco.

Get out and about

Make the most of your stay with a day or two out and about on an excursion.

From La Fosca

Included in your programme is a day at Water World in Lloret de Mar where you enjoy an exciting range of water attractions including wave pools, slides, and river rafting.

For your excursion day, discover the sights of Barcelona, including the Sagrada Familia, the Nou Camp football stadium, and the famous Las Ramblas Boulevard with its markets and shops.

From Mimosa

Explore the famous mediaeval fortified town of Carcassonne or enjoy the thrills of the Aqualand water park at Cap d'Agde.

Taken from page 20 of the PGL brochure 'Mediterranean Watersports'.

General comprehension

Answer the following questions in complete sentences.

1 Who do you think the advertisement is directed at?
2 What are the three main aims of these holidays?
3 In which countries are the activities located?
4 What do students learn to do while attending the watersports activities?
5 What do the planned excursions in La Fosca and Mimosa offer the students?
6 According to the advertisement students are offered 'learning through adventure'. What can students learn in the adventures they are offered?

Discussion task

In groups of three, take about 10 minutes to talk about your experiences of school trips. Discuss the best and worst school trips you've been on. Give reasons for your answers.

Paper 1 practice task

Based on the information given in the texts, write a diary entry about time spent in either Mimosa or La Fosca. Give your opinion about aspects of the trip such as the people, the activities, the place, and the food. Write 300–450 words.

For tips on how to write a diary entry, see page 25 of Chapter 1, Identities.

Internal assessment (SL)

Figure 2.10 We're all in this together

Examine the photograph above and consider the following points.

- What do you see in the picture? Describe only what you see. Do not give opinions.
- What aspect of group activities do you want to focus on?
- Reflect on how experiences such as adventure holidays can affect you as an individual.

- Give any examples from your own experience.
- Connect the picture to the schools you have experienced and the kinds of activities they offer.

Using the points above, spend 15 minutes preparing a presentation about the photograph. Use the preparation time to organise your ideas and plan the sequence of what you will talk about.

Your presentation should last 3 to 4 minutes, after which your teacher and other students will have the opportunity to comment or ask questions about what you have said. You must engage in a conversation with them. In total, this task should take approximately 15 minutes.

Paper 2 practice task (2.3) – School trip adventures

You will hear a conversation between three students: Annette, Susie, and Bill. Two of them went on a school trip to the Mediterranean to take part in a sailing and kayaking course. Answer the questions.

1 How many weeks were the students on the school trip?
2 What did Susie buy on Las Ramblas Boulevard?
3 Why was Annette so pleased to visit La Sagrada Familia?

Listen again and choose the correct answer.

4 From the conversation, we know that Susie:
  a didn't enjoy snorkelling.
  b prefers paella to pizza.
  c is not fond of visiting buildings of architectural interest.
5 From the conversation, we know that Bill:
  a is an experienced sailor.
  b injured his leg before the school trip.
  c knows a lot about Spanish architecture.

Listen again and choose the five true statements.

a The excursion was to Madrid.
b The girls got suntanned.
c The La Sagrada Familia is an ancient cathedral.
d Susie didn't like snorkelling.
e Annette loved the stained-glass windows in the basilica.
f Susie had pizza for lunch during the excursion.
g Paella contains rice and fish.
h Annette likes cooking.
i Susie and Bill are invited over to Annette's for a meal.

2.3 Hobbies that change our lives

How I came to be. . .

Internal assessment (SL)

Figure 2.11 A teen enjoys his leisure time

Examine the photograph above and consider the following points.

- What do you see in the picture? Describe only what you see. Do not give opinions.
- Reflect on the photograph in connection with the theme of experiences.
- Is this a hobby or is it something more?
- Consider what makes an activity an art form.
- Make connections to other hobbies and activities and the people involved.

Using the points above, spend 15 minutes preparing a presentation about the photograph. Use the preparation time to organise your ideas and plan the sequence of what you will talk about.

Your presentation should last 3 to 4 minutes, after which your teacher and other students will have the opportunity to comment or ask questions about what you have said. You must engage in a conversation with them. In total, this task should take approximately 15 minutes.

A bilingual opera singer

In this interview, one of the authors of this book talked to Claire about how she came to be a successful opera singer.

Professional – Interview

Interviewer: Hello Claire. Thank you for taking time to talk to me today. I know you are a very successful opera singer, but we would love to hear about the experiences which have led you to this point in your career. So to start off, you are bilingual and can speak English and German. Has that been an advantage for you?

Claire: Yes, being bilingual has helped me greatly in almost all facets of my career. English and German are very common languages in opera, oratorio, and songs, and being a native speaker of both languages makes it easier to add nuance to performances. I also live in the UK and often travel to Germany to sing. I did a post-graduate degree in translation after studying music and I have been able to use these skills regularly.

Interviewer: How did your interest in music, and in particular singing, develop?

Claire: I always loved music, and singing especially. I was lucky enough to have a creative and motivating music teacher in elementary school who encouraged me to sing, and I suppose I just never stopped. I started having classical singing lessons in my early teens and each new milestone was more motivation to reach the next.

Interviewer: Lots of young people enjoy singing, but you have taken this a lot further. How did that come about?

Claire: Honestly, not much has changed since I first started. Each new opportunity brings with it chances to learn and grow, and it became a cycle I just couldn't do without. After high school I went to study at the Royal Conservatoire of Scotland. I found that being around lots of people who shared my passion for classical singing and who were launching musical careers in ways I didn't even know existed was very motivating. While I was a student I also learned that I have a great love of teaching and vocal coaching, and this has shaped my career greatly ever since.

Interviewer: It must have been a long and arduous journey requiring real dedication. How did you deal with that?

Claire: Having peers and colleagues all going through the same journey with me made things much easier. At the end of the day, artists do what they do because they love it, so while it takes dedication and there are tough times, the journey is full of amazing moments to make it worthwhile.

Interviewer: Did you, or do you, have a person or an idea which inspires you?

Claire: My greatest motivator has always been the desire to make music, and to help others do the same. There are many great singers and vocal coaches who inspire me, but I have never had one specific goal or idol in mind. I find inspiration in my colleagues every day.

Interviewer: What does a typical working day look like for you?

Claire: Every day is different. Some days I spend teaching singing, which has become a great joy for me. I do this in Glasgow schools, so on those days you might mistake me for a high school teacher. Other days I might have a rehearsal during the day and a concert or a show at night, which is a totally different pace altogether. A recording day is different again, as there is a great deal of time pressure to get things just right. A live audience is quite forgiving if there is a little slip in the performance, as stage presence and charisma can cover things up. In a recording, however, the audience can listen to your mistake over and over again in the comfort of their own home.

Interviewer: Can you describe some of your best moments?

Claire: If the piece or the show is good, the colleagues are good, and I feel I'm in good voice, every moment on stage feels like the best.

Interviewer: I imagine now, as summer is with us, you will have a break from performing. What plans do you have for the autumn?

Claire: Well, artists aren't so good at taking holidays. In this line of work someone is always in the wings waiting to take your place, so taking a break can be scary. The summer time is typically festival and wedding season, so between the two I'll be kept busy. I do have a new project starting in the winter which will take a lot of preparation in the autumn.

Interviewer: And finally, Claire, what advice would you offer to young people listening to this conversation who want to be successful performers in the future?

Claire: My first piece of advice is be punctual and be prepared. If everyone else has to wait for you to get your act together, you will not be asked back, and chances are other producers, conductors, or fixers will have heard about any unprofessional behaviour before the rehearsal period is even done.

My second piece of advice would be to take criticism well. Some criticism is helpful and well meant, and can show where you went wrong and how to correct it. This is incredibly valuable for a musician to continue to develop, and we mustn't waste it by getting defensive or offended. Musicians put themselves in situations with the intention of being critiqued and corrected on a regular basis. In fact, it usually comes with a fee! However, some criticism is unkindly meant and hasn't much to do with the performer at all: it can be very demoralising. Learning to tell the difference is a hard, but invaluable, lesson. Hear the criticism and ask yourself: 'Can I use this to do better, or was this meant to hurt me?' If it is the former, you can decide how, if at all, you will implement this critique into your practice in future. If it is the latter, you can simply wave it goodbye.

Interviewer: Thank you very much indeed, Claire for sharing your insights into the life of an artist and we wish you every success in your chosen path.

General comprehension

Answer the following questions in complete sentences.

1 Why is being bilingual English and German helpful in Claire's chosen career?
2 When did Claire first have singing lessons?
3 Where did she continue her studies after leaving high school?
4 What helped Claire maintain her dedication?
5 What motivates Claire?
6 How does she describe the difference between a live performance and a recording?
7 What does she do during the summer months?
8 What is her first piece of advice to people who would like to perform?
9 What is her second piece of advice?

Vocabulary

Write words that have the same meaning as the underlined words.

1 almost all <u>facets</u> of my career
2 add <u>nuance</u> to the performance
3 my <u>passion</u> for classical music
4 a long and <u>arduous</u> journey
5 you might <u>mistake me for</u> a high school teacher
6 a live audience is quite <u>forgiving</u>
7 a little <u>slip</u> in the performance
8 stage presence and <u>charisma</u>
9 someone is always <u>in the wings</u>
10 to <u>get your act together</u>

Paper 1 practice task

Think about a real or imagined live music performance you have attended. Write a blog to describe the performance and share your appreciation of the event.

Think about the layout and style of your blog.

Remember that you are describing an event for others who were not present, so be sure to include interesting information and details

SL students should write 250–400 words. HL students should write 450–600 words.

The power of reading

Do you want to improve your English and enjoy doing so? You can do this without having extra lessons, without doing grammar exercises or learning lists of vocabulary, but while having fun! There is a very simple way to make your English better and to improve your understanding of written and spoken English language.

Professor Stephen Krashen is Professor Emeritus of Learning and Instruction at the University of Southern California. He is an expert in the field of linguistics, specialising in theories of language acquisition and development. A great deal of Professor Krashen's research focuses on reading and its effects on language acquisition and academic success. He is an internationally known researcher and author. You can listen to him talking about the power of reading on the internet where he has numerous blogs.

The excerpt below is taken from his book *The Power of Reading*.

Mass media – Reference

Chapter 1. The Research

Free voluntary reading (henceforth FVR) means reading because you want to: no book reports, no questions at the end of the chapter. In FVR you don't have to finish the book if you don't like it. FVR is the kind of reading most of us do obsessively all the time.

FVR is one of the most powerful tools we have in language education, and, as I argue in this chapter, FVR is the missing ingredient in first language 'language arts' as well as intermediate second and foreign language instruction. It will not, by itself, produce the highest levels of competence; rather, it provides a foundation so that higher levels of proficiency may be reached. When FVR is missing, these advanced levels are extremely difficult to attain.

In the following section, the evidence for the efficacy of FVR is briefly reviewed. Following this review, I argue that alternative means of promoting language and literacy development are not nearly as effective.

The evidence for FVR

In-school reading programs provide some of the clearest evidence for the power of reading. In these programs, part of the school day is set aside for unrestricted FVR.

Conclusion

In face-to-face comparisons, reading is consistently shown to be more efficient than direct instruction. The conclusion we can draw from these findings can be easily stated: Reading is a powerful means of developing reading comprehension ability, writing style, vocabulary, grammar, and spelling. In addition, evidence shows that it is pleasant, promotes cognitive development, and lowers writing apprehension.

Professor Krashen follows up this introduction with detailed results of a wide range of tests of the effects of different kinds of reading on students' language development. The results demonstrate conclusively that students who read a lot, and read for pleasure, are able to improve their English language proficiency and enjoy the process.

He states, 'In-school reading programs are also effective for vocabulary development, grammar test performance, writing, and oral/aural language ability.'

So how can reading be so powerful? The theory is that while you are reading something that you enjoy, which is not too difficult, you reach the state of 'flow' where you are completely focused on what you are reading and forget the world around you. Reading like this is relaxing, which is why many people read in bed before they go to sleep. There are no book reports to write and no tests afterwards. If you choose a book and then do not enjoy it, change the book. Find something you really enjoy.

Researchers have proved without a shadow of doubt that reading for pleasure in English will steadily improve second language learners of English.

Do try it! Ask some of your friends what they enjoy reading, or ask the librarian, who is the expert after all. Tell them you want to read something that is the right level for you, that is enjoyable, and that you want to read for relaxation. When you find the right books, you will know. Enjoy reading and while you are having fun, enjoy improving your English.

Borrow a book from the library, any book that appeals to you – a graphic novel, a comic, teenage fiction – whatever takes your fancy. You probably won't have time to read in school, but look forward to giving yourself about 20 minutes of 'flow' at the end of a busy school day. If you find you don't like the book, take it back and change it.

Make it a project to read every day for a month, and then see if you notice the difference in class. You will develop your vocabulary, improve your grammar, your understanding, your written ability, and be able to read more fluently and easily. This will help you with all of the classes you take in English.

Recommendations

We have asked a number of teenagers what they enjoy reading for pleasure. Here is one young teenager's response:

I love anything by Michael Morpurgo. He really writes for younger students who are native English speakers, but I find the language is around my level, just not too difficult, but I learn lots of new words. I also find reading books by the same author helpful as I get used to his style of language and that makes it easier for me.

I really enjoyed his book Shadow, *about a boy from Afghanistan and his Springer Spaniel dog, Shadow. I also enjoyed the book* War Horse *which has been made into a play, and I liked* Private Peaceful *about two brothers who were in the First World War. That's another thing – reading his books I learned a lot of history and all about other areas of the world.*

Krashen, S. D. (2004) *The Power of Reading*, Heinemann Press, Portsmouth, NH.

Internal assessment (SL)

Figure 2.12 Reading a novel: relaxing or learning?

Examine the photograph above and consider the following points.

- What do you see in the picture? Describe only what you see. Do not give opinions.
- Reflect on the photograph and caption in connection with what you have read in this chapter about reading.
- What aspects of reading do you want to focus on?
- Make connections between reading and writing.
- Consider the differing reactions of parents and other adults to reading fiction.
- What are your own experiences of reading?

Using the points above, spend 15 minutes preparing a presentation about the photograph. Use the preparation time to organise your ideas and plan the sequence of what you will talk about.

Your presentation should last 3 to 4 minutes, after which your teacher and other students will have the opportunity to comment or ask questions about what you have said. You must engage in a conversation with them. In total, this task should take approximately 15 minutes.

Interview with a librarian

Christian Brown, Librarian at Fakenham Library in Norfolk, UK, took part in this interview which was carried out by the library support group Friends of the Library.

Professional – Interview

1. Tell us a bit about how you came to be a librarian.

My role was born from my love of working with people and helping others. Even as a seven-year-old I set up the 'helpers club' with two other friends to assist my class tutor with any tasks she had. I guess watching my mother assist people as a nurse impressed upon me the need to help others. Then following the birth of my daughter 29 years later, I sought to work closer to home and avoid the 90-mile commute I used to do each day. So I became a Literacy Coordinator for the Norfolk Reading Pathway, which is just two miles from my home.

Even after working with local hostels and the Citizens Advice Bureau, the Reading Pathway was one of the most satisfying and humbling experiences of my working career. Recruiting volunteer coaches to help readers improve their literacy, which in some cases was non-existent, was a great journey. The programme made me appreciate the huge struggle that many of the learners faced each day. It was akin to me going to a country like China, where I could not even identify a single character, and feeling that sense of anxiety or isolation. This role opened my eyes to the library service and supporting learners in literally half of the county. I soon visited and saw the wonderful work that each Norfolk library does. With an opening becoming available at the library in my old hometown, I jumped at the chance. Not only did it enable me to enter a world I loved as a child, but it allowed me to express my creative and supportive side.

The expression 'opened my eyes' means to notice or realise something you had not noticed before.

2. How important have books and reading been to you personally?

I have always found them to be source of strength. Just prior to my teens, my father died due to ill health and I sought comfort in books. I would raid our bookshelves at home and find more and more obscure things to read. I must admit that my interest was always in poetry rather than novels as I never had the patience for the long read. I found that a range of emotions can be conveyed with such grace in less than a page: a range which may take up a chapter in a novel. As a late teen, reading became more intrinsic in my life when reading law at university. I also realised that it was biographies and cookery writing that I really loved as I wanted to know about people and how to choose and prepare food.

3. Libraries have changed tremendously over the past 30 years. Now that technology is so much part of our lives, what do you think the library can offer young people?

I think libraries, certainly in Norfolk which is a rural area, represent the need within our communities. Historically, many libraries have been cold and largely about the written word, but with the advent of the Internet, that has changed. Libraries in modern times are about people and the coming together of ideas and creativity in a community-focused hub. Firstly, a library offers offers an environment where a young person can share an idea with like-minded people, in the real world rather than a virtual one. Our staff represent a diverse array of backgrounds and experience which can be called on. Libraries are always looking for new ways to grow within our communities, hence volunteering or activity participation offers social and intellectual reward. It also allows a person, regardless of age, to be able to develop their interactive skills and confidence. We do embrace technology and use it to make the written word more accessible. Look at free magazine or book downloads, for example, or apps like Libby which enable library users to manage their accounts from their smartphone. Due to our links with the education sector, we can also support any students with our vast array of educational materials.

4. I know that your library is taking part in The Summer Reading Challenge*. Can you tell us what that is?

This year's Summer Reading Challenge is called 'Mischief Makers'. It's being hosted by the chief mischief maker, Dennis the Menace from the comic *The Beano*. There are

---

*The Summer Reading Challenge

In acknowledgement of research carried out by linguists into the role of reading in education, which states that reading for pleasure is more important to children's successes than education or social class, the Reading Agency and UK libraries have set up the joint project Summer Reading Challenge. It aims to get thousands of children into libraries, reading and taking part in a variety of activities during the long summer break.

Children receive a folder and scratch stickers which give off an aroma (not always pleasant) when the surface is scratched. Libraries are also offering interesting activities such as a reading dog. An especially calm and peaceful dog who lies quietly in the library while children take turns reading to him.

three reading challenges for children: from ages 1–5, 5–11, and 11+ . The aim is for students to read six books over the summer holiday and review them. We have scratch and sniff stickers available for each book completed and a certificate and medal awarded to each person who completes the challenge. It starts on the 14th July and runs until the 15th September in every library.

5. What was your favourite book as a teen?

That's easy. It was my father's copy of *John Betjeman: Collected Poems.* Something I could immerse myself in as the mood demanded. I always enjoyed Betjeman's wry humour and social commentary. Even now, reading the opening poems reminds me of the literary awakening I had after moving on from the likes of Spike Milligan, whom I adored as a younger child. But something great always has the power to move you.

6. What are the most popular teen reads at the moment in your library?

These are the top 5 at the moment:

There's *One of Us Is Lying* by Karen M. McManus. It is the story of what happens when five strangers walk into school detention and only four walk out alive. Everyone is a suspect, and everyone has something to hide.

Then there's *The Lie Tree* by Frances Hardinge, which is the story of a 14 year-old-girl in Victorian times when girls had no chance in a male-dominated society. But she wants to follow her father's footsteps and study natural science. It is a detective story with a difference.

There's also *Wonder* by R. J. Palacio. It's the story of a 10-year-old boy with a disfigured face. He is home schooled by his mother but he longs to be normal and go to school. A terrific story about how humans behave.

Another favourite is *La Belle Sauvage* by Philip Pullman, which is the first in a three-part prequel to his bestseller *His Dark Materials.* La Belle Sauvage is the name of a boat. This is one for Philip Pullman lovers.

Lastly, we have *After the Fire* by Will Hill. This is the story of Moonbeam and her life in a strange sect. It is a page-turner, full of suspense and tension. As a reader you want to know more about her secrets.

General comprehension

Answer the following questions in complete sentences.

1 Why did Christian become a librarian?
2 Which types of books did Christian love to read?
3 According to Christian in what ways have libraries changed in the past 30 years?
4 How has technology improved library services?
5 What is the aim of the Summer Reading Challenge?
6 What did Christian like about John Betjeman's poetry?
7 In which books do we know for certain that the main characters are girls?

Vocabulary

Match the words (1–4) as they are used in the text with their meanings. There are more options than you need.

1 improve	a similar
2 hence	b painful
3 intrinsic	c tutor
4 akin	d essential
	e without
	f enhance
	g enchant
	h involved
	i therefore

Choose the word or phrase closest in meaning to the words from the text.

1 commute	a distance	b journey to work	c online task
2 struggle	a difficult challenge	b expense	c workload
3 array	a foreign	b well-trained	c wide variety
4 adored	a read	b greatly admired	c listened to

Zoom in on grammar

would

We use *would* when we look back on the past and remember things that happened repeatedly. Look at this sentence from the interview with Christian talking about the time after his father died:

I would raid our bookshelves at home and find more and more obscure things to read.

The word *would* shows that this action happened in the past on more than one occasion.

Grammar in context

Complete the sentences with *would* and the verbs *go*, *try*, or *visit*.

1 My grandmother was always important to me, as a child I ________ her every weekend.

2 Our sheepdog ________ to round up the children in the park when we went for a walk.

3 When I lived in Frankfurt, I ________ to the flea market every Saturday.

Complete the sentences in your own words.

4 He's a vegan now, but when he was younger ________.

5 When my younger sister was ten years old, she ________.

6 Before computers were widely used, people ________.

Paper 1 practice task

You are having a debating competition at school. You have to choose a position. Either 'Our town needs the library' or 'A library is not necessary in the 21st century'.

SL students should write 250–400 words. HL students should write 450–600 words.

Tips for preparing to speak in a debate

A debate involves two people giving a speech on the same theme – also called 'a motion' – but one person supports and the other is against the motion being debated.

- List the points you need to cover.
- Use short sentences and avoid language your audience might not understand. Make sure to explain the meaning of difficult words or technical terms.
- Begin with an anecdote or fact that grips your audience.
- Check your facts and make sure they are correct.
- Practise what you will say so that you don't need to read it.
- Use cards with key words rather than a sheet of paper to help your memory.
- Look at your audience while you are speaking. Try to look around at all the people and not just at one or two.
- Finish by repeating your main argument.

Mass media – Blog

The success of book clubs

It is difficult to say just how many book clubs exist because they are often informal groups meeting in each other's homes. One estimate in Great Britain says there are as many as 50 000 book clubs. And from places as far apart as the USA and Australia, book clubs are a growing activity for young and old alike. They're really a simple idea: choose a book, everybody gets a copy, reads it within an agreed time – perhaps two weeks or a month – and then they meet up to discuss their reactions to the book.

Figure 2.13 Why are book clubs so popular?

One book club I know takes place once a month in the local library on a Tuesday morning. The books are chosen from a library list which offers multiple copies of books and is absolutely free of charge. There are mostly women in the group, but of the ten members three are male. As it is held in the morning, it also means that most members are retired. In contrast, another book club in a neighbouring town takes place in the evening. There are much younger people there and they usually meet in a restaurant and discuss the book over dinner.

The book club I belong to has only five members and we meet in the evening – we usually drink tea or coffee – and take it in turns to offer our living room as a venue for the discussion. We have a designated 'leader' – he keeps a log of books we have read and regularly asks us for titles we would like to propose to the group for reading. We have been meeting now for nearly two years and I have read books I would never have chosen for myself. The choice of books is eclectic. We have read Jonathan Swift's *Gulliver's Travels*, Kate Atkinson's *Started Early, Took My Dog*, Nathan Filer's *The Shock of the Fall* and Lewis Carroll's *Alice's Adventures in Wonderland*. I think the book I enjoyed most though was Cheryl Strayed's

Wild. It's a book about the Pacific Crest Trail in the United States. I've walked that trail and could relate to challenges she faced even though I didn't walk alone, as she did, but with four other men and an experienced guide. I can honestly say I would never have read these books if I hadn't been asked to read them in the book club.

Why are book clubs so popular? Maybe it is the combination of reading and sharing your ideas with others who have also read the book. You get to hear different reactions an d the most interesting discussions are the ones where we are divided in our opinions. We make notes about characters or events, share sentences or passages that we highlighted, enjoy learning from and talking with each other at our ongoing social encounters.

General comprehension

Answer the following questions in complete sentences.

1 Why is it difficult to calculate how many book clubs exist?
2 How do we know that the majority of members of the library book club are older people?
3 What is the job of the leader in the book club the writer is in?
4 How many people walked the Pacific Crest Trail with the writer?
5 The writer says 'choice of books is eclectic'. What does this mean?
6 What is the writer's favourite book that the group has read and why?

Vocabulary

Find words in the text which match the following meanings.

1 more than one
2 the place where something happens
3 appointed
4 a list
5 drew attention to
6 continuing

Paper 1 practice task

You have decided to have a book club at school. Create a flyer to advertise it. Explain how it will be run. Decide when and where the club will meet and who it is aimed at.

Remember that when you create a flyer, you need to use engaging language and attractive images to appeal to readers.

2.4 Our roots

Have you ever wondered about the generations of your family who lived before you? Where did they live? How did they live? Do you know about the lives of your grandparents or your great-grandparents?

The internet offers numerous possibilities to trace your family tree and even to discover your DNA. All of this costs money, of course, so it is probably better to start off by collecting information from older family members who may well be enthusiastic information sharers.

Personal experiences

Below is the story of Christine, a 72-year-old woman living in Canada who had always been curious about her family history and eventually took steps to find out more. Christine's grandmother, Alice, travelled to Canada from Inverness in Scotland as a young woman in the 1930s. Alice couldn't find work in Scotland and she wanted to see the world, so she took a boat from Glasgow across the Atlantic to Nova Scotia. Alice never returned to Scotland and never saw any of her family again. This is Christine's diary of her experiences of learning more about her grandmother.

Personal – Diary

A diary is a way of exploring your feelings about a topic.

5th April

My father always wanted to visit Scotland, the birthplace of his mother, but he could never afford it and as he died quite young, he missed his chance to do so later in life. He always insisted that he was Scottish, even though he was born in Canada. He used to say, 'If kittens were born in the oven, would that make them cakes?', which was his way of saying the place where you are born is not the decider of who or what you are. But how could he or I be Scottish if we had never even visited the place? How could we know our roots or where we belong if we only knew Canada?

8th April

I have decided to visit Scotland, but I am nervous as I do not know anyone there and I have no idea which relatives might still be living in the village. I don't know how to go about contacting anyone, either. My friend James told me about a website where you can search for your relatives all over the world, and if they are on the website too, you can maybe find them. Imagine my excitement this morning when I was contacted by a cousin of my father who knew there was an aunt who had emigrated to Canada, but had no other information about her. Through the internet I have managed to explore the connection and have discovered that the aunt she had heard of was, in fact, my grandmother, Alice.

15th May

It's now or never! I need to stop dreaming and put my plans into action. So after some serious planning and discussion, my husband and I have booked flights to Scotland, in fact to the capital city, Edinburgh.

21st June

We felt quite nervous as we landed and stepped on Scottish soil for the first time ever. I breathed in deeply and waited for the feeling of coming home, but nothing happened. It was just another airport and another city. What a disappointment.

Neither of us have ever been to Europe so it is a huge adventure, and we have no idea what to expect. A friend told us the Scots weren't so keen on strangers, but I've heard they are friendly. I have to say I'm a bit nervous about the trip, but I'm sure it'll be just fine.

We have planned to stay a few nights in Edinburgh after the long flight so we took a taxi to our hotel in the middle of the city.

22nd June

What a wonderful city, full of history with beautiful old granite town houses and the wonderful castle up on the hill! There's even a park in the middle of the city. We walked up and down Princes Street, pinching ourselves so we would know it was true – we are actually in Scotland!

We were thrilled to hear a piper today in full highland dress, playing the bagpipes in the park. He was very kind and quite happy for my husband to take a photo of me standing beside him. The noise was very powerful, especially when he first filled the bag before starting a new tune. He tried to explain the working of the pipes to me, but it was difficult for me to understand maybe because I'm not a musician. We did learn that it takes a long time to master the instrument and they first practise on a pipe called 'the tranter'. We have often seen pipers in Canada, but somehow it was just not the same as talking to a real Scottish piper on Princes Street in Edinburgh, Scotland.

24th June

This morning we left Edinburgh to travel by train up to Inverness. We passed some of the most beautiful countryside imaginable. We found the other passengers really friendly, especially when they heard our accents. They thought we were American, but were delighted to talk to us, two elderly Canadians. The journey took just over three hours and then we were there.

Figure 2.14 Edinburgh Castle

We have finally arrived in Inverness! We found our hotel and unpacked, and then took a walk down to the River Ness, which flows into the famous loch with the monster, Loch Ness, and had dinner. I have to say the feeling of 'coming home' is still missing. My husband thinks it will hit me when we visit the village where my ancestors were born, lived, and died.

General comprehension

Answer the following questions in complete sentences.

1 Why was the writer nervous about visiting Scotland?
2 How did the writer find more information about her family?
3 In the park in Edinburgh, who did they see? What was he wearing?
4 After Edinburgh, what city did they travel to?
5 How did the writer feel at the end of the last diary entry?

State whether the following sentences are true or false. Give a quote from the text to support your answers.

6 The writer's father visited Scotland regularly.
7 Alice was the name of the writer's aunt.
8 The writer's husband had never been to Europe.
9 The journey on the train took a little more than three hours.

Vocabulary

Find words or phrases in the text which match the following meanings.

1 where someone was born
2 leave your own country and settle permanently in a new country
3 if we don't do it now, it will not happen
4 wanted to continue

Read the diary entries below carefully and note the use of informal language, emotions and personal reflection, notes the writer makes to herself, and how she is looking forward.

Personal – Diary

25th June

I woke up early this morning in our hotel in Inverness and had to pinch myself to realise I am really here! I was dying to get outside, explore, and finally visit the village where my grandmother was born and brought up.
The Scottish breakfast was wonderful except for the black pudding, which was very strange. Whatever was it made of? I hate to think! I'll avoid that tomorrow. Ken wants to see Inverness Castle and the statue of Flora MacDonald looking out to the west where Bonnie Prince Charlie escaped after

being defeated in the Battle of Culloden, so that is what we will do. The words of the song run through my head.

Speed bonnie boat like a bird on the wing
Onward the sailors cry
Carry the lad that's born to be king
Over the sea to Skye.

Oh dear, I want to go to the village and find out about my family, and to Skye and to Culloden; so much to do and so little time. Ken is being very patient, but I am afraid he will get bored!

26th June

Gosh, we slept well here. It must be the fresh sea air. We nearly overslept again! We'd ordered the taxi for 10 o'clock and really had to scramble to be ready in time.

Culloden was interesting, but not as exciting as I had expected as there was a lot to read and a lot of walking around the battlefield too. You had to use your imagination as there didn't seem to be much to actually see. Maybe we just didn't know enough about the place and should have read up on it first at home!

We took a taxi to the village where my grandmother grew up. It seems very small and quiet. There are hardly any shops, but there is a café so we had a drink and chatted to the owner. He didn't know anything about my family but told us about a woman with the same family name who might help. We will go and see if she is home tomorrow.

The village has a lovely shoreline and looks over to Fort George, which is where my great-grandfather was a soldier. It was closed today, but we will definitely try to visit later in the week.

Back to the hotel at last, really tired from so much walking and so many impressions. The plan is set for the morning – back to the village to find the woman and then to Fort George to learn more, especially about great grandfather! How amazing to have this chance. Decided to have dinner in the hotel as we were too tired to go out.

27th June

Another taxi to the village. The woman, Susan, was home and welcomed us into her place, which was rather small but very cosy. The café owner had already told her about us. That was a real surprise, but she said it's like that in a small village.

Mind you, she wasn't much help as she is not very interested in family history and couldn't get her head around the family tree to understand whether she and I are related or not. She didn't have any old photos, either. She thought there must have been some, but she hadn't seen them in a while – so disappointing! I had expected to be welcomed with open arms into the family – but it wasn't like that at all!

Figure 2.15 Fort George

One good thing – Susan told us about another woman in the village who is really interested in ancestry and would love to meet us. So after yet another a cup of tea, she walked us there. That woman, Jane, was fascinating and really excited to meet us, even though we are not in any way related. That was nice, and just how I'd expected Susan to have acted. Jane took us up to the village cemetery. That was a very long walk which felt like it was all uphill, and there was nowhere to buy water or anything on the way, either. We found the family grave and took pictures. My grandmother's name is on the stone, and it even gives the date when she died in Canada so someone in the family must have been in contact with her. What a mystery! Who could that have been?

Jane suggested we should talk to the vicar as he must have church records from the past, but he is only there every third Sunday and we will be gone before that. I'm really disappointed, but Jane has promised to talk to him and see what she can find out for us.

She also mentioned some other places to visit. She said the Black Isle is really beautiful. It is not really an island, just a promontory but with lovely beaches. Most exciting of all, she told us that it's the right time of year to see the dolphins play. Apparently we just drive along the coast (we'll have to find a sympathetic taxi driver) and look for a crowd on the beach. If people are all together watching, that must be where the dolphins are active.

Too late to go to the fort, so that will have to be another day and Ken is excited about seeing the dolphins too.

28th June

An early start again and off to the fort! It was only open for tourists and we had to pay to go in – another surprise! It was quite expensive and really we didn't learn anything new.

We decided to go back to the village for lunch and a walk along the beach before taking a taxi to look for the dolphins.

Walking along the beach, we were totally surprised when a woman greeted us by name. She said 'You must be Christine and Ken from Canada. We've heard all about you. Come and have a sit in the garden, why don't you?'

We were so surprised we didn't know what to say, how did she know who we were? We followed her into her garden anyway – it felt as if she had been waiting for us. This would never happen back home. She was lovely, though – so friendly and warm and so hospitable. We gradually tuned in to her Highland accent, although we had to get her to explain a few words which we didn't know – a bairn, for example, means a child and a burn is a small river. That sounds simple enough, but when they cropped up in the middle of the conversation, both Ken and I had to have a quick think about what these words meant. Sometimes the words we know and use sound different, too, but we are getting used to the accents.

She made us try her homemade cake, but then took us all round the garden telling us about every flower and weed, poor Ken was really exhausted. He is not interested in any gardens – anywhere – ever! But we couldn't stop her and she was so happy to talk to us.

We told her about wanting to see the dolphins and she persuaded us to wait till her husband, Alec, got home and he would take us. He often goes out fishing in the firth and knows best where they are likely to be.

A *firth* is a long, narrow strip of sea reaching into the land.

He came home around 5 p.m., had a sandwich, and we had another cup of tea. Then we all piled into Alec's car and drove to the coast. We drove quite slowly along looking at the beach to see if there was a crowd anywhere.

Lo and behold – a group of people, some with cameras on tripods, others with big cameras, and even some just with their mobile phones – were standing on the beach with their eyes glued to the water. We parked and quickly joined them, then waited patiently for several minutes with nothing happening at all. I could see Ken was getting very bored so suggested he should go and get us an ice cream. I stayed with the crowd and waited patiently.

Then all of a sudden there was a mighty whoosh and a dolphin shot up into the air, twisted, and slid smoothly back into the water. I have never seen anything like it. The crowd uttered 'oooh' in amazement.

And within seconds the next dolphin sprang up and then another and another. With every leap, the crowd ooh-ed and aah-ed and it almost seemed like the dolphins were reacting to the sounds and encouraged to jump farther and higher each time. It was magnificent. I shouted to Ken but he was already there, the camera clicking furiously as he tried to capture every moment. What an experience! Who would have thought our trip to Scotland could have produced moments like these?

This is an example of a rhetorical question, often used in the diary style of writing.

General comprehension

Answer the following questions in complete sentences.

25th June

1 Why does the writer write, 'Ken is being very patient'?

26th June

2 Why was the writer disappointed?
3 What should they have done to prepare better for the visit to Culloden?
4 What were their first impressions of the village where the writer's grandmother grew up?

27th June

5 How did Susan already know about the writer?
6 What is the mystery the writer mentions?
7 Why wasn't Jane's suggestion useful?

28th June

8 What was disappointing at the fort?
9 What happened on the beach?
10 What were the challenges in the conversation for the three people?
11 How would they know where the dolphins could be seen?

Vocabulary

Find words or phrases in the text which mean the same as these words and phrases.

25th June

1 keep away from
2 look around for the first time
3 got away
4 be beaten

26th June

5 really hurry
6 read all about something

27th June

7 understand something
8 a plan of all the relatives past and present
9 took us over on foot

28th June

10 everyone got into the car
11 used our names
12 watching the water carefully

Paper 1 practice task

The text was written as a diary. Look again at the way the text is constructed and laid out. Look carefully at the style of language used.

Now write a diary of your own visit to a place of interest. Start with the planning phase and include the journey, the visit itself, and of course the journey home.

SL students should write 250–400 words. HL students should write 450–600 words.

For tips on how to write a diary entry, see page 25 of Chapter 1, Identities.

Internal assessment (SL)

Figure 2.16 A trip back to your roots: researching your ancestors or just curiosity?

Examine the photographs above and consider the following points.

- Describe the pictures.
- Consider the impact of the internet on research into families.
- Reflect on your own family and what you know about the generations before your parents.
- Does it make any difference to you to know about your family history?
- Are people only looking for positive stories?
- Reflect on the question in connection to what you have read about in this chapter.
- Consider the different arguments for and against researching your ancestry.

Using the points above, spend 15 minutes preparing a presentation about the photograph. Use the preparation time to organise your ideas and plan the sequence of what you will talk about.

Your presentation should last 3 to 4 minutes, after which your teacher and other students will have the opportunity to comment or ask questions about what you have said. You must engage in a conversation with them. In total, this task should take approximately 15 minutes.

Mass media – Article

THAT LAST TOK JOURNAL – EVER

by Tomas Verdant

'At last it's all over.' 'I'll never need that stuff again.' 'What a waste of time!' These are some of the things we have said talking about TOK classes over the last two years. But now looking back over the two years to write this last entry I wonder in retrospect, 'Was the class really that bad?'

If nothing else I learned one thing: never ask yes or no questions. Instead of saying 'Was this class bad?', say 'To what extent has this class been bad?' You can see I understand the essence of the whole TOK course.

At the beginning of the course, I couldn't believe that so many other students got better grades than me on their presentations when all they did was ask questions. My partner and I found answers to everything we questioned. As you can see, it took me a while to figure out what we were supposed to do in this class.

So is TOK really worth teaching? For sure. TOK has actually become part of my life, since everything in my surroundings constantly reminds me of it.

Let me give just one example of an article about a robbery which I just read online. I keep asking myself – did it really happen the way the media portrays it? How do we know? Do we know?

What is truth? Therefore TOK has provided me with an essential ability, unlike normal classes, the gift to question information that I receive rather than just accepting it as a fact. Everything that I think will be useful for me in the future I received from the teacher. The book has been extremely difficult for me to follow, since the English in there is quite challenging. For example, I never did understand how inductive and deductive reasoning work and I can't tell them apart any more. And I still can't believe we spent pages talking about a rainbow.

But most of the time my classmates made up for the parts of the book that were boring for me. We were a very lively bunch, weren't we? We all talked too much, although you always said you wanted us to talk, but also to think deeply and to discuss – so we did! So overall I would not have wanted to have missed any time in our super, amazing TOK class.

Right now I think it has been one of the best experiences in my school life. But then again, how do I know?

General comprehension

Answer the following questions in complete sentences.

1 What did the student learn from TOK classes?
2 What difference have these classes made to him?
3 What has he learned to do?
4 What presented difficulties during the course?
5 Why do you think he ends the article with a question?

Paper 1 practice task

Write a blog about your own experience of TOK during the IB programme. What have you learned? What has been difficult? Which skills will you carry forward in the future?
SL students should write 250–400 words. HL students should write 450–600 words.

Food and experience

This article first appeared in Waitrose *Food* magazine, 2018. The writer describes her connection between her roots, her choice of career, and the person she is today.

Mass media – Article

A PINCH OF SALT BY SELIN KIAZIM

A simple, spiced loaf transports the London chef straight back to the gossip-filled, batch-cooking bliss of her grandmother's kitchen in Cyprus.

I'm a Turkish Cypriot but I was born in Southgate in north London. The whole of the ex-pat Cypriot community seems to have ended up there, so it was a world infused with Cypriot food. There was my Mum's cooking at home and there were the right ingredients available in local supermarkets. And there were restaurants and cafés that did the same dishes. Friends from school would come round and they were often wide-eyed at the food that would be laid out on the table. The barbecue would sizzle with big kebabs. Even a mid-week supper would see a selection of breads and salads, meats and desserts. And every day I would wake up to the smell of onions frying downstairs. While my Dad had a café business, Mum was just always cooking.

But come the summer we would leave north London for the real thing: three weeks at my grandparents' village, Yesihrmak in Cyprus. It was a village by the sea, reached after a drive through lush valleys until we reached those familiar whitewashed houses. Our family out there were farmers. They had vast amounts of land and in their fields grew orchards of citrus fruits and groves of olives, as well as strawberries and watermelons. In the back yard of the house, they had trees heavy with lemons, others with peaches. In the garden they nurtured aubergines and tomatoes. Herbs grew here, there, and everywhere. There were chickens and goats too. My grandfather – who lived until he was a 100 and died only recently – never ate a processed meal in his life.

It was a close community and when there was cooking going on, it wasn't just confined to one kitchen and one person. Everything was done on a grand scale. No one just baked a loaf, or a cake, or a pie; there were always large batches and everyone always shared everything.

During the walnut season, the old ladies picked and candied walnuts until their wrinkly hands were stained black. The men went out to work in the fields and the women cooked. And they swapped and shared and gossiped as regularly and as surely as the sun would rise each morning.

I was too young to get involved in cooking. I was a lucky recipient, along with my two elder sisters. Breakfast was freshly made bread, toasted on an open flame. Once it was charred and dripping with melted butter, we would spread on glorious home-made strawberry jam. Then after a mouthful of the juiciest peach we would head for the beach.

Lunch was grilled meat or fish at a shack and then the evening saw a huge gathering of friends and cousins. There were firin lamb kebabs (cooked slowly in the oven), dolma (stuffed vine leaves), and courgette flowers stuffed with rice, onions, tomatoes, and olive oil, then drenched in lemon juice. There were köftes made with beef and grated potato, fried and crisp. And there was bread.

When I built my first restaurant, Oklava, in London's Shoreditch, I was – almost without realising – recreating my grandmother's kitchen: the open grill and the bread oven. Today, out of that oven comes the Baharat-spiced bread my grandmother made almost every day. As she would, I mix a simple dough of flour, water, yeast, salt, and olive oil, plus a tablespoon of Baharat spice, which is a mixture of allspice berries, cloves, nutmeg, and mahlep (dried cherry seeds). After it has proved, I knock it back, roll it into sausage shapes, and sprinkle over black and white sesame seeds before proving again and baking.

Later, if I dip the crusts into the juices of a salad or aubergine dish, I can sit in my restaurant and imagine I am there in Yesihrmak. It's evening under the hot vines. I'm sipping a glass of my grandmother's cordial and we're having a good old gossip while waiting for the men to come home.

General comprehension

Answer the following questions in complete sentences.

1 How does the reader know that people in the Cypriot village helped each other with the work and cooking? Give two examples.
2 According to the text, what is Baharat?
3 What memories does the writer have when she samples the traditional bread she bakes in her restaurant?
4 When the writer was of school age, why did she wake up every day to the smell of frying onions?
5 The writer's family in Cyprus were farmers. What did they grow?

Vocabulary

Answer the questions.

1 Give a word or phrase from paragraph 2 that means 'the parts of a recipe'.
2 Which phrase from paragraph 3 is a synonym for 'large areas'?

Discussion task

Find the following words in the text and then look them up in your dictionary to find the best definition for them.

an ex-pat *lush* *a processed meal* *batches* *a shack*

Re-read the text with a partner and list any other new words which you cannot identify.

Using a dictionary, work together to understand the words as they are used.

Intercultural activity

How important is cooking, eating, and sharing food with family and friends in your culture and the cultures of your friends?

Paper 1 practice task

Write a diary entry, a blog, or an email to a friend.

Consider your own childhood and your memories of food. In your experience, how important is food to you? What events are associated with memories of certain foods?

SL students should write 250–400 words. HL students should write 450–600 words.

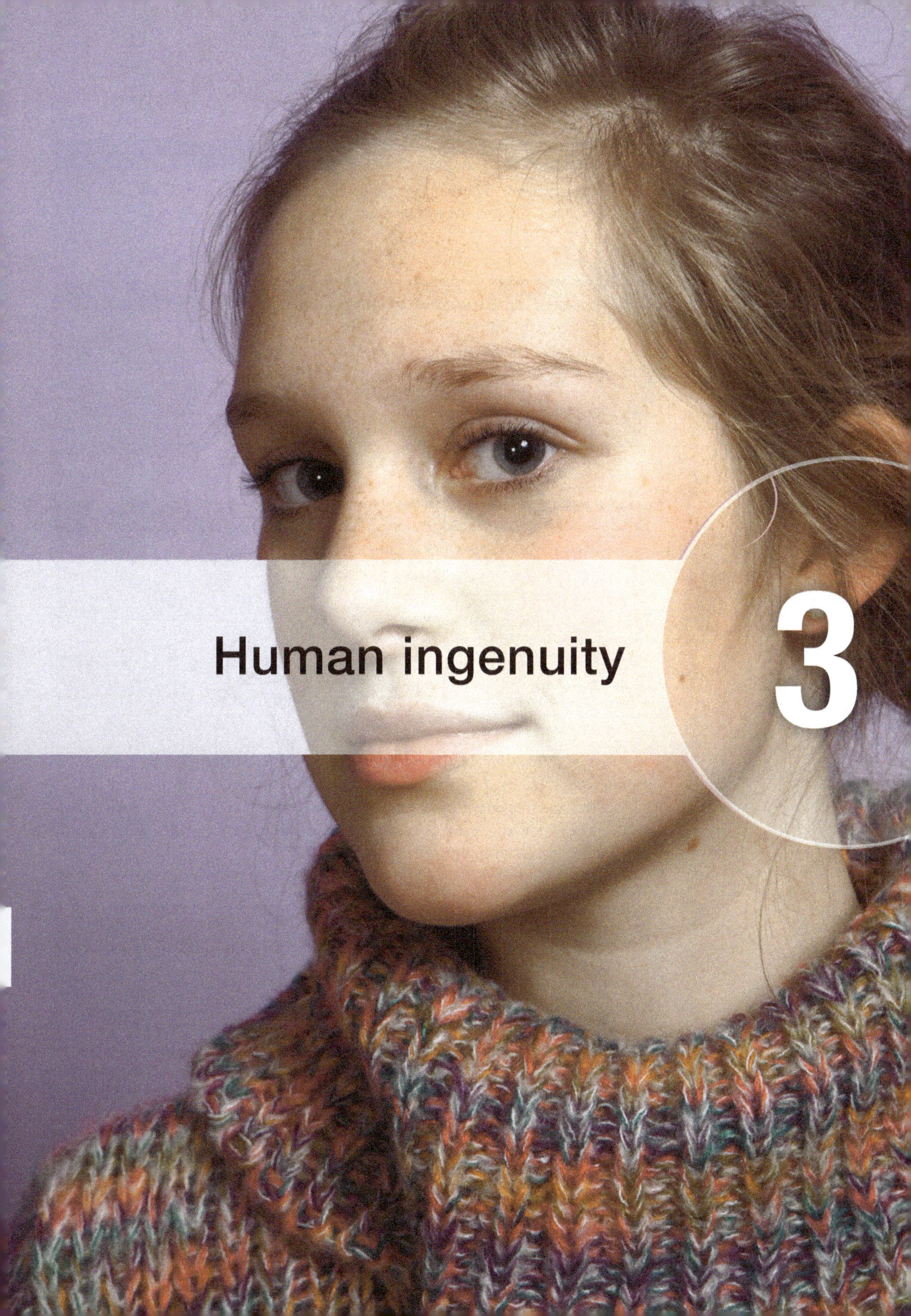

3 Human ingenuity

Research questions

- In what ways does human ingenuity influence our daily lives?
- How can looking at the past tell us more about the present?

Objectives

- To discuss the role of music in our lives.
- To evaluate the extent to which we are dependent on modern technology for communication.
- To analyse the reasons behind moves to ban mobile phones in schools.
- To identify and describe the fascination of ancient sites such as Stonehenge for people today.

Language skills objectives

- To practise interactive oral skills in relation to the human ingenuity theme.
- To examine the use of the passive voice.
- To examine the use of *during* and *while*.
- To examine the use of the zero conditional.
- To look at direct and indirect speech.
- To examine the use of the past perfect tense.
- To examine the use of the imperative.

The ways we think, work, play, conduct our friendships and other relationships, find solutions to problems, change things, and rationalise our world are all influenced by the working and thinking of other human beings. From music to scientific discoveries, and from our knowledge gained of ancient peoples through archaeology, we can see examples of human ingenuity.

3.1 Music as a form of expression

Musical experiences

Mass media – Article

AN EXTREMELY BRIEF WORLD HISTORY OF MUSIC AND MUSICAL INSTRUMENTS

Making noise

Mankind has always been able to make noise. The most obvious instrument is the voice, which can be used in so many different ways, regardless of which languages people speak. Humans can whisper, scream, laugh, wail, and speak, calmly or angrily. Right from the very beginning, babies quickly discover their voices and can cry when they need something, but also laugh and gurgle to show their pleasure.

Every voice is unique and we can recognise the voices of people we know well easily. However, research shows that this ability fades with time if the voice is no longer heard.

Animals too can make their own typical noises: cows moo, dogs bark, lions roar, and mice squeak. But how are these sounds produced?

When we breathe out, the air from our lungs is pushed upwards to force the vocal chords to move closer together and vibrate, and so the sound is produced. However, if the vocal chords are in some way damaged and unable to close or vibrate effectively, the voice quality is greatly reduced or even lost.

In the 21st century, artificial intelligence (AI) has moved into the field of voice communication. Devices have been created which react to the human voice and can carry out numerous tasks to make our lives more comfortable. These devices can understand orders given orally by humans: to wake them up, set the oven, remind them of appointments, and so on. What a long way humans have come from the times when, as far as we know, they only spoke in grunts.

Early instruments

But even then humans enjoyed other ways of making sounds. Just as babies enjoy shaking a rattle or banging two objects together, the earliest forms of music would have developed from similar activities – with the addition of some rhythm. String instruments may owe their existence to the early bows used by hunters. Flutes have been discovered in southern Germany from thousands of years ago. They were made of bird bone and mammoth ivory. Instruments which could be rattled, shaken, or banged together would also have been used. Around the world many different instruments have developed which may be strummed, plucked, banged, shaken, or blown into.

Regional instruments

The maraca is a Caribbean instrument which is like a rattle with a handle, and often the player uses two, one in each hand. The maracas are often made of a dried gourd, filled with beads, beans, or even small stones, with a handle which seals the gourd and keeps the rattle contents safely inside. Maracas are very popular in Latin and South American music, but are also popular in different kinds of lively music in many other countries. The maracas come under the technical name for those percussion instruments where the whole instrument vibrates – idiophones – as do castanets, which are hollowed-out, pear-shaped pieces of hardwood.

African drums and other drums come under the technical term 'membraphone', as it is only the skin which vibrates. African drums are sometimes called 'the heartbeat' of Africa and are used not just for entertainment, but also to communicate, share messages, and express emotions.

One instrument not very often seen or heard outside its home country is the didgeridoo, which has become familiar as an Australian indigenous instrument. It is made of a hollow wooden tube between 1 metre and 3 metres long, and the longer the tube the deeper the sound. In the Alpine regions of Europe there is a similar instrument called the 'Alpine horn', which is in fact even longer. The Alpine horn is carved from soft wood, often spruce or pine. It was used in the past to call the cows home in the evenings or even to calm them during milking. The Alpine horn is a familiar symbol of Switzerland.

TOK

What role does music play in your life and why? Which Ways of Knowing influence your appreciation of music?

A rather different instrument is the ukulele, which fell out of use for some years but is now enjoying a revival. It is a relatively easy instrument to play, usually with four strings, but it can have six or even eight strings. It is plucked or strummed like a guitar. Originally from Hawaii, it was brought over to Madeira by sailors and quickly became popular in the mid-1800s. It has a very special sound. Another guitar-like instrument is the dombra, which is popular in Kazakhstan. It is made of hollow wood, with just two strings which are plucked or strummed.

What a wide range of instruments humans have developed over the centuries across the world! These are true examples of human ingenuity. Music also serves a wide range of purposes in human lives. It soothes a worried child or adult, excites and invigorates when needed, underlines occasions of pomp, great happiness (or great sadness), and enriches our lives on a daily basis.

General comprehension

Answer the following questions in complete sentences.

1 According to the text, what is special about the human voice? How is the sound produced?

2 What can negatively affect the sound of our voice?

Vocabulary

Write definitions and example sentences for the following verbs.

Example:
rattle – to make or cause rapid knocking sounds
The thunder and rain rattled the windows.

1 bang
2 enrich
3 invigorate
4 pluck
5 shake
6 soothe
7 strum

Intercultural activity

In groups, research translations into other languages for the words *whisper, scream, wail, gurgle,* and *grunt.* Is there an element of onomatopoeia (the word being formed from the sound it represents, as in 'cuckoo') about any of these words in English or in other languages? Write sentences for the first line of a story including each of the English words. Which group can write the most interesting first line?

Zoom in on grammar

The passive voice

The passive voice is formed with verb *to be* plus a past participle (object + *to be* + past participle). It is used when we do not know who carried out the action or when we want to emphasise the action.

	Passive	Active
Present simple	*The air from our lungs* ***is pushed out****...*	*We push out the air from our lungs and...*
Past simple	*It* ***was brought over*** *from Hawaii.*	*Sailors brought it over from Hawaii.*
Present perfect	*Devices* ***have been created*** *which react to the human voice.*	*Researchers have created devices which react to the human voice.*

In the passive voice, the person who carried out the action is often not mentioned. For example, in the sentence *Devices* ***have been created*** *which react to the human voice,* we do not know who has created the devices.

Grammar in context

Reread the text above and find three examples of the present simple passive voice and one more example of the present perfect passive. Why was the passive voice used? Rewrite each sentence in the active voice.

Paper 1 practice task

A competition has been announced by a local music company. The prize will be an instrument of the winner's choice to use for a year at no cost. In addition, the winner will receive regular lessons on that instrument.

Entrants are required to write a speech about music in their lives, explaining their choice of instrument and why they deserve to win. You have decided to enter the competition. Write your speech.

SL students should write 250–400 words. HL students should write 450–600 words.

For tips on how to write a speech, see page 62 of Chapter 2, Experiences.

Mass media – Article

THE MUSICAL HUMAN

by musician Ian Thompson

(1) ______________________

Even as a little boy, I knew that music was going to be an important part of my life. I could always get a tune out of musical toys. My family contained no active musicians, but my parents bought me a second-hand accordion and arranged for some lessons from a local player. We later acquired an old piano, which I taught myself to play as a young teenager. My real opportunity came when I went to university to train as a primary school teacher. The head of the music department heard me practising and insisted that I switch from English to music as my choice of principal subject. I had a lot of catching up to do, because I didn't have the background of formal instruction that my student peers had. All went well, however, and I went on to enjoy a long career as a music teacher.

(2) ______________________________

It used to be thought that musical ability was a talent, or a gift, which came from a generous god. Nowadays, we know much more about the human brain. Natural ability in music, and many other activities, depends upon the way in which the brain is configured. I sometimes explain it to students by saying that the brain comes equipped with certain apps, or software, which will enable it to function with a high level of success, as long as the right motivation, experience, and practice are provided along the way. Of course, the human brain is extremely complex, which means that people have an interactive mixture of software on board. Many people are therefore skilled in different activities at various levels. Those who are either exceptionally brilliant or totally unskilled in any one activity are certainly in the minority. I have no doubt that there were musically able people in my own family, but without the necessary encouragement or resources their talents did not come to fruition. My own daughter, however, who grew up in a home filled with music, has become a successful professional musician.

Figure 3.1 A marching band

(3) ______________________________

As far as we know, humans are the only creatures whose brain can process sounds and make sense of them as patterns, ideas, and emotions. From a scientific point of view, music simply consists of sound waves, or bumpy air. The brain software cleverly processes these sound waves in order to access human emotions such as joy, excitement, sadness, or nostalgia. For those who are active in creating music as singers or instrumentalists, success in performance is rewarded with brain chemicals called 'endorphins', which make us feel good.

(4) ______________________________

Music-making is an enjoyable social activity. For example, I play in a marching band which was started by some people in my age-group, hoping to recapture the fun they remembered from their youth. The band has grown over the years, with the addition of many younger players. As well as singing and playing in other ensembles, I also enjoy teaching a number of young music students and, of course, I love going to live music performances. The software in my brain is still functioning, still updating itself, and still confirming my identity as a musical human.

General comprehension

Add the following headings to the article above.

- Music as a social activity
- Early years
- The human brain
- Musical ability

State whether the following sentences are true or false. Justify your answers.

1 The writer came from a musical family.
2 The writer regularly received piano lessons as a boy.
3 The writer trained first to be an English teacher.
4 The writer's peers were all well-trained musicians.
5 Musical ability is a gift from a generous god.
6 Most people are skilled to different levels in different activities.
7 Music consists of sound waves.
8 The writer considers music-making a lonely activity.

Vocabulary

Find words in the text which match the following meanings.

Paragraph 1

1 bought; received as a gift
2 change over
3 main subject

Paragraph 2

4 realisation, fulfilment

Paragraph 3

5 happiness
6 a longing for a time in the past

Paragraph 4

7 groups of musicians

The creation and recording of music continues to develop, led by human ingenuity. Below is one more example of this.

From our arts correspondent

A fascinating evening of lively jazz

The well-known local jazz trio, Bernie and the Boys, gave an enthralled audience a thrilling evening in the community centre last night. The pianist began with a beautiful rendition of 'Starlight', as the band members gradually joined him on stage. To the surprise of many audience members, most of whom are long time jazz enthusiasts and supporters of the trio, the band members appeared without their usual bundles of notes taped together in concertina-style to carry them through the evening.

The band members simply carried in their tablets. The playlist and notes for each piece had been saved and the band members just swiped to turn the page. Are the days of musicians searching for the right page number or of the music score tumbling from the stand in the middle of a piece over?

After this minor distraction, which caused some murmuring amongst the audience members, everyone settled down to enjoy a fine evening of music, which was up to the usual high standard of the band.

General comprehension

Answer the following questions in complete sentences.

1 How has technology caught up with Bernie and the Boys?
2 How does the reporter describe the evening?
3 How does the reporter describe the audience's reaction to the band?
4 Who was the first band member on stage?
5 What was missing as the band appeared on stage?

Vocabulary

Match the words (1–6) as they are used in the text with their meanings (a–j). There are more options than you need.

1 enthralled	a drag from
2 rendition	b falling suddenly
3 enthusiasts	c big surprise
4 tumbling	d speaking quietly
5 distraction	e performance
6 murmuring	f event
	g people keen on something
	h something which takes your attention away
	i fascinated
	j reading silently

Mass media – Reader's letter

25 Trumpet Road
Liverpool
11 November

Dear Sir or Madam,

In response to the article by your arts correspondent in the paper last week, this development does not only apply to jazz band members. While on holiday in Switzerland recently, I had the great pleasure of attending a classical music concert by an internationally acclaimed orchestra. I was surprised, while waiting for the orchestra to enter, to note that there were no orchestra scores on the individual music stands. As the orchestra walked in, during which time there was thunderous applause from the audience, I realised that in addition to their instruments they were each carrying a slim object. These, it transpired were tablets, which were carefully placed on the music stands.

As the music began, I noticed another phenomenon. The days of the violinists at their music stands leaning forward in harmony to turn the pages of the score are over. It now appears to be done by a tap of the foot or some other method which I was frustratingly unable to determine. It is, of course, much easier too for the cellists and double bass players who otherwise have to hold on to their instruments while turning the pages.

However, despite being a true Luddite, in this case I have to admit there is an element of calmness brought in by technology.

Long may this continue, as long as they have enough power in their batteries.

Respectfully,
Angela Dean

This word *Luddite* comes from a reference to a historical event. Do some research and identify its meaning and origin.

Zoom in on grammar

during* and *while

The words *during* and *while* can both be used to talk about activities that happen at the same time.

As *during* is a preposition, it is followed by a noun or a noun phrase.

*People started dancing **during** the concert.*

The word *while* is a conjunction and is usually followed by a clause with a continuous form.

***While** the band was playing, people were dancing.*

Grammar in context

Complete the following sentences with *during* or *while*.

1 I took some photographs ____________ I was waiting for the band to come on.
2 It is necessary for the musicians to turn the page of their music score ____________ the performance.
3 ____________ my holiday in Switzerland, I went to a jazz concert.
4 I find some technology is a real benefit ____________ a concert.
5 ____________ the band was playing, the audience were tapping their feet.

Music and the senses

Shakespeare's famous speech on the role of music and love in our lives

As we know, it is not only recently that people have become preoccupied with the power of music. Shakespeare too was enthusiastic about music, as this speech from *Twelfth Night*, Act 1, Scene 1, reveals.

Duke Orsino is in love with Countess Olivia, but she is not responding in the way he hopes and does not appear to be in love with him. He thinks that maybe too much music might cure his obsession with her and with love, in the same way that eating too much food takes away our appetite for more.

Read the speech carefully and enjoy the beautiful language of Shakespeare.

Mass media – Literature

Duke Orsino: If music be the food of love, play on;
Give me excess of it, that, surfeiting,
The appetite may sicken, and so die.
That strain again! it had a dying fall:
O, it came o'er my ear like the sweet sound,
That breathes upon a bank of violets,
Stealing and giving odour! Enough; no more:
'Tis not so sweet now as it was before.

Internal assessment (SL)

Figure 3.2 Bringing musical scores into the modern world

Examine the photograph above and consider the following points:

- What do you see in the picture? Describe it carefully. Give facts not opinions.
- Reflect on the picture in connection with the theme of human ingenuity.
- How can the musicians benefit from modern technology?
- What other modern developments can be used by musicians?
- Make connections to your own experience and the experiences of students you know.
- Consider classical music performances, for example, a classical pianist or opera singer. Would using a tablet be acceptable?

Using the points above, spend 15 minutes preparing a presentation about the photograph. Use the preparation time to organise your ideas and plan the sequence of what you will talk about.

Your presentation should last 3 to 4 minutes, after which your teacher and other students will have the opportunity to comment or ask questions about what you have said. You must engage in a conversation with them. In total, this task should take approximately 15 minutes.

3.2 Science and technology

Science is a lens through which we can engage with the world. It is as a result of the curiosity of scientists such as Pythagoras and Aristotle in ancient Greece and later scientists such as Newton, Darwin, and Hawking that we have gained knowledge of how and why things happen. A science museum is a paradise for the curious, presenting us not only with answers, but asking questions about things not yet fully understood.

TOK: If the role of science is to uncover truths about the natural world, how can it be that scientific knowledge changes over time?

Glasgow Science Centre

Figure 3.3 Glasgow Science Centre

Interview with Rosie Street, Marketing Manager

Mass media – Interview

In today's interview, I am talking to the Marketing Manager of Glasgow Science Centre (GSC), Rosie Street.

1. When was the science centre started?

GSC was officially opened by HRH the Queen on 5 June 2001.

2. What was the original idea behind the science centre?

The role of the 18 science and discovery centres in the UK was to attract young people to study science, technology, engineering, and maths, and to engage the public with complex scientific issues in a fun and engaging way.

The Millennium Commission allocated capital funding to 18 science and discovery centres across the UK. GSC was the largest funded project in Scotland. The Commission awarded GSC £37 million, half of the capital funding required. Other founding funders included Strathclyde European Partnership with European Regional Development Fund, Scottish Enterprise, Glasgow City Council, the Wellcome Trust, and the Scottish Government.

The Millennium Commission was a United Kingdom public body that was set up to celebrate the turn of the millennium. It used funding raised through the UK National Lottery to assist communities to celebrate the closing of one millennium and the start of the next.

3. Your staff all seem very young and enthusiastic, and the blogs on your website reflect that. Is that a deliberate policy?

GSC staff are our biggest asset. They are enthusiastic, passionate, and believe in GSC's mission to engage people of all ages to discover and enjoy science and understand its relevance to their own lives. This comes across when they engage with our visitors, whether it is a toddler visiting for the first time, a school pupil taking part in our education programme, or an adult attending one of our lectures. They are invested in the mission and their genuine love of science and GSC is obvious when they are interacting with customers.

It is certainly not our policy to have only young staff. We have a range of people working across GSC who vary in age.

4. You are situated right on the bank of the River Clyde. Please tell me a little about the site.

The River Clyde has been a centre for shipbuilding for hundreds of years, with boats being built in the area possibly as early as the 15th century. It was during the 19th century that shipbuilding became a real source of commerce for Glasgow.

However, after the Second World War, the shipping industry went into decline and the once bustling hub on the banks of the Clyde lay dormant.

In 1988, Prince's Dock (once the largest dock on the Clyde) was selected as the site for Glasgow's Garden Festival. Land was reclaimed from the partial filling of the dock's basin.

As part of the regeneration of the River Clyde in the late 1990s, the old Prince's Dock site was chosen as the location of Glasgow Science Centre.

5. It was very busy when I visited. How many people visit on an average day?

Visitor numbers fluctuate depending on the time of year. For general visitors, peak times are during school holidays: Easter, summer, and half-term breaks. For education numbers, our busiest month is June before the school academic year finishes.

We have had a record-breaking number of visitors for the last few years. In the 2017–18 financial year, we had 422 990 visitors.

6. How would you describe your role in the science centre?

As Marketing Manager, I help to market everything Glasgow Science Centre does. I tell people about the events and exciting activities they can take part in if they visit, support our corporate events team, and advertise our educational offer to schools around the country.

It's very varied and I get to work across the whole of the business, which I enjoy. No two days are ever the same at Glasgow Science Centre.

7. What is the most satisfying part of your job?

Working with an incredible team of people here at GSC, who all care very much about the place and what goes on here. Everyone works hard, pulls together, and does everything they can to make this the best place it can be. To work somewhere where people all care about what they do is very rewarding.

If I go out onto the floors and see children and adults having fun and enjoying the exhibits, it reminds me every day why I do what I do.

General comprehension

Answer the following questions in complete sentences.

1 How long has Glasgow Science Centre existed?
2 What was the aim of Glasgow Science Centre?
3 Are the staff all young? How do you know?
4 What was the main industry in Glasgow in the 19th century?
5 What happened to the industry after the Second World War?
6 When is the science centre busiest?
7 What does a Marketing Manager do?
8 What does she find most satisfying about her job?

Vocabulary

Find words in the text which match the following meanings.

Paragraph 2

1 gave

Paragraph 3

2 a small child

Paragraph 4

3 become weaker or smaller

Paragraph 5

4 rise and fall regularly

Paper 1 practice task

After reading about Glasgow Science Centre, you believe that this would be a very worthwhile and inspiring trip for your class. To encourage others to support this idea, write a formal letter to the head of your school, an article for the school magazine, or a blog to encourage your friends to support you. Outline the ideas and the benefits that would be gained from such a visit. You may want to research the website of Glasgow Science Centre.

SL students should write 250–400 words. HL students should write 450–600 words.

For tips on writing formal letters or articles, see page 54 of Chapter 2, Experiences.

Mass media – Blog

Paulina's blog: my week

Posted on 3 August

Figure 3.4 Paulina Zurakowska and two members of the communications team at Glasgow Science Centre

A bit about me. . .

My name is Paulina Zurakowska and I'm 17 years old. Soon, I will be beginning my sixth and final year in secondary school, before hopefully going to university. I am originally from Poland but moved to Scotland when I was only five. In order to improve my English, my parents took me to the library throughout my childhood, which is where my love of reading and writing stemmed from. Since then, I have been avidly reading and writing as a hobby and passion, and now aspire to study English literature and hopefully work in the publishing industry.

My week. . .

When I received an email from the SMF* offering me an internship placement at Glasgow Science Centre, I was initially ecstatic, but I was also a little confused. I was an aspiring publisher, a humanities pupil through and through, so I was intrigued to see what an internship at a science centre, with its communications team, would have in store for me.

My week began on Monday at six o'clock in the morning, which to me, after three weeks of dozing off to la-la land until two o'clock in the afternoon, seemed unfathomable. But yet here I was, proud of my accomplishment of waking up (after two cups of coffee), even though I realised that I desperately needed to sort out my sleeping schedule. I managed to get myself ready, still half-asleep, before leaving my house, ready to start my week as an intern at Glasgow Science Centre, a place I couldn't remember last visiting.

My first day was a perfect taster of what I had ahead of me – it was absolutely terrific! I had the opportunity to explore the environment I was going to work in with a lovely supervisor, Rosie, and as I wandered around the centre, I began to recognise the majority of the building, little fragments of memories being pieced together, one by one like a puzzle.

My most outstanding memory was of my trip to the planetarium. When I was told I could go to as many shows as I wanted, I felt like a giddy eight-year-old again, and it wasn't for nought. As always, GSC delivered a spectacular show capturing the enthralling magic of the planetarium, which I was allowed to write about throughout my week.

I also had the opportunity to have a talk with another member of the communications team, to find out more about PR (public relations). I found I had a lot in common with Sharon, who had shared a similar experience of trying to figure out a career path with English. We had a long talk about the different routes one can take with languages and writing, which, admittedly, did open my eyes. I hadn't expected to find anybody at GSC that I could relate to, and yet here I was, not only being encouraged to keep following my aspirations, but also being enlightened by the different career paths I could pursue.

I got to do a PR taster task. Although this was something different to what I was used to and the writing style was different to the one that I usually practised, I was surprised to admit that I had enjoyed it!

Moreover, I had also been tasked with some admin work. I learned to use software that I had never used before and I noticed I became far more confident in myself and with my computer skills as I completed the tasks set out for me. In addition, I gradually began to feel more accustomed to the workplace, having never worked in an office setting before.

My week at GSC was absolutely remarkable and enriching. I have gained knowledge about the workplace that I would never have acquired anywhere else. I met some lovely people and have definitely grown as a person. I now feel more confident reaching out to strangers and handling tasks on my own, while also realising that it's alright to ask for help when you need it.

I now understand why I was offered this placement, and firmly believe that Glasgow Science Centre is for people from all walks of life, with many different interests. The whole experience has really broadened my mind.

I would just like to say thank you to the communications team for all the help, advice, and support you offered throughout. I have been pleasantly surprised to be able to do what I love in a place that is dedicated to a sector that is completely different to mine, but which I also appreciated.

My week was absolutely fantastic.

---

*The Social Mobility Foundation – a programme I have been involved with for a few months now.

General comprehension

Answer the following questions in complete sentences.

1 According to the introduction to her blog, who is Paulina?
2 Why does the offer of an internship at the Glasgow Science Centre surprise her?
3 What did she have in common with Sharon?
4 What were the two tasks Paulina wrote about?
5 How was Paulina enriched during her week?

Paper 1 practice task

Have you thought about undertaking an internship before you begin your university or other studies? What kind of internship do you think would be helpful for you? Write an official letter of application to a place or business of your choice explaining why you think an internship there would be of benefit to the company and to yourself.

SL students should write 250–400 words. HL students should write 450–600 words.

Tips for writing a letter of application

- Write an engaging first paragraph. Say why you want this internship.
- State where you found out about the position for which you are applying.
- Explain why hiring you will benefit the employer.
- Briefly summarise your strengths, qualifications, and experience.
- Say something about yourself that's not on your CV. It could be charity work, hobbies, after-school activities, etc.
- Make sure to use a formal register and avoid the use of contractions such as *I'm*.
- Close the letter with these words: *I look forward to hearing from you at your earliest convenience.*
- Sign off with *Yours faithfully* if you do not know the name of the person you are writing to. Use *Yours sincerely* if you know the name of the person.

Mass media – Blog

Peter's visit – guest blog

Posted on 1 May

Figure 3.5 Peter Mackey at Glasgow Science Centre

Hello, my name is Peter Mackey and I am nine years old. I am very proud to be able to write a blog for Glasgow Science Centre. I was given a Science Passport as a Christmas present, which is great, because it means I can go to the Science Centre as often as I want, which is a lot! There are so many amazing activities and exhibits to try out and they change all the time, so it never gets boring. I do not like queuing, so when you go in to the Science Centre there are lots of interesting facts to read while you wait, which makes it easier. You will also be given a map, and you can look at the 'What's On' board to help you plan what you are going to do. If you are not able to queue, there are lots of activities at the side you can join in with.

The first places I usually go to are the illusions and special effects rooms, which are cool. We always go to the Live Science shows, where the scientists do loads of amazing experiments and sometimes ask for volunteers from the audience to come down and try them out. I have just been to the Pure Random Science show, which has loads of cool experiments that involve fire, gas, liquid, bubbles, and lots more. There was a spinning wheel with numbers on it, which told the scientists what experiments they were going to do next. The scientist who presented the show that I saw was called Jennifer, and she was funny. There is a gigantic planetarium on the first floor, where you can watch documentaries about space and see Glasgow's sky at night. If you tell the presenters your favourite planet, they zoom into it and tell you facts about it. The planetarium is brilliant in many ways, but most of all because it makes what you see look 3D.

The second floor is about technology and engineering. There is a dance floor that always cheers people up (as they have to dance to make it work), a hurricane tube, and solar panel and energy activities, and you can build a water dam with blocks. I have just done the Egg Drop challenge, where you were asked to make a safety container to protect an egg, and drop it from the top of the stairs. It was really fun. Unfortunately, I got scrambled egg, but I'm going to go again and try and make a better design. There is a 'Think-It' ideas wall for kids and adults to tell the staff their ideas, to make the Science Centre an even more brilliant experience. They really do listen to your ideas – they did to mine!

The third floor is one of my favourite floors because it is the BodyWorks level, which tells you about your senses, what your body can do, and what it looks like inside your body. There is a giant pinboard which you can make body shapes on and there are lots of activities that can make you fit, like a giant hamster wheel, a bar holding test, a sprint timer, and a Hit the Button challenge. Sometimes they have a live lab where the scientists cut up organs, which is yucky and interesting at the same time, but there are gloves and hand gel so it's fine.

I have high-functioning autism. The Science Centre runs autism-friendly hours where it's much quieter, the music is turned down, and the lights get dimmed, which I think is important. There are quiet spaces too that have sensory boxes if people feel stressed or overstimulated. The boxes have sensory things in them like fidget spinners.

If you are hungry, you can go to the Taste Café. It's really cool as you can see the Glasgow Tower, the SEC Armadillo, the Waverley, and the Clyde. There are lots of different things you can eat. I get a lunch box, where you can choose five things to eat or drink. There are lots of different types of food you can choose, so that's good.

Just outside the Science Centre is the IMAX cinema which has the biggest screen in Scotland. I have seen nature documentaries and films there in 3D, which is fantastic.

General comprehension

Answer the following questions in complete sentences.

1 Why is the Science Centre so exciting for Peter?
2 Why does he say queuing is never boring?
3 Where does he usually go first and why?
4 What is the best feature of the planetarium according to Peter?
5 What activity on the second floor cheers people up?
6 What does he use the word 'yucky' to talk about the third floor?
7 Peter has high-functioning autism. What does the Science Centre offer for people with this condition?
8 Peter is obviously very enthusiastic about Glasgow Science Centre and this comes through in his writing. Read the text again. What are some of the positive words he uses to express his enthusiasm?

Zoom in on grammar

The zero conditional

The zero conditional is used when one thing always follows automatically after another. It is formed in this way:

If + present simple + present simple OR present simple + *if* + present simple

***If** you **tell** the presenters your favourite planet, they **zoom** into it, and **tell** you facts about it.*

*There **are** quiet spaces with sensory boxes **if** people **feel** stressed or overstimulated.*

We can also use *can* with the zero conditional.

***If** you **are** hungry, you **can go** to the Taste Café.*

Grammar in context

Complete the sentences about Glasgow Science Centre using the zero conditional.

1 If you want to learn about the five senses, __________.
2 If you have an idea, __________.
3 __________ if you go to the IMAX cinema.

Discussion task

Peter mentions sensory boxes and fidget spinners in his blog. Think of examples of human ingenuity that help people with additional needs and discuss with a partner.

THE RIVER CLYDE IN GLASGOW

Figure 3.6 River Clyde bridge

The story of Glasgow

The story of Glasgow's Clyde bridges in many ways reflects the development of Glasgow. Glasgow may not have grown beyond a quiet monastery town had it not also been the lowest fordable point on the Clyde. As the city flourished in the 18th and 19th centuries, the demand for better communications resulted in bridges being built, which, in turn, encouraged further trade and prosperity. So bridges both nurtured and reflected the growth of the city.

Transportation

The story of Glasgow's bridges also reflects the story of transportation, from the pedestrian and horse traffic of the middle ages, through the railway mania in the 19th century, the 20th-century age of the motor car, and onwards now in the 21st century.

Civil engineering

Glasgow's bridges also reflect the story of civil engineering. Developments in engineering materials and knowledge can be traced in the techniques used to construct the Clyde bridges. Timber and stone, cast iron, wrought iron, and reinforced steel, and pre-stressed concrete were all used in Glasgow's Clyde bridges. Virtually all bridge types are represented on the Clyde. A walk from the Millennium Bridge to the Dalmarnock Bridge will take you past exhibits of more than 150 years of bridge engineering history.

General comprehension

Answer the following questions in complete sentences.

1 What feature of Glasgow's position on the River Clyde contributed to the city growing steadily?
2 Why were bridges built in the 18th and 19th century?
3 What effect did the bridges have on the city?

Vocabulary

Match the words (1–8) as they are used in the text with their meanings (a–h).

1 monastery	a strong enthusiasm
2 flourish	b encourage development of
3 trade	c build
4 prosperity	d show
5 reflect	e grow, develop, thrive
6 nurture	f a place where monks live together
7 mania	g activity of buying or selling goods
8 construct	h economic growth, wealth

Text handling

Complete the table with the correct verbs, nouns, and adjectives.

Verb	Noun	Adjective
balance		balanced
communicate		
		contributed
exhibit		
	reflection	
	suspension	

Intercultural activity

What roles do the rivers play in your home country? How are they different from the River Clyde?

Internal assessment (SL)

Examine the photograph above and consider the following points:

- What do you see in the picture? Describe only what you see. Do not give opinions.
- Reflect on the picture in connection with modern developments in equipment in the kitchen.
- What are some of the most significant inventions for the kitchen from the last 60 years?
- What could be the next development?
- Consider the role of computers.

Using the points above, spend 15 minutes preparing a presentation about the photograph. Use the preparation time to organise your ideas and plan the sequence of what you will talk about.

Your presentation should last 3 to 4 minutes, after which your teacher and other students will have the opportunity to comment or ask questions about what you have said. You must engage in a conversation with them. In total, this task should take approximately 15 minutes.

Figure 3.7 What was it like in your grandfather's day?

3.3 Playing and talking

Escape rooms

The game that is sweeping the world!

Escape rooms are a fast-growing entertainment trend based on the digital escape games found in mobile app stores. But instead of playing alone and in isolation, you play in the real world. It is physical and you are socially interactive. You book your game, get instructions from the Game Master, and then you and your team are 'locked' in the room with a set time to work out how to escape. These are games for two to ten players and success depends on working together.

It is a puzzle-solving activity that demands concentration, communication, and an ability to work out things by applying logical thinking. Although players are told they are locked in the room, or rooms, they are never completely alone because what they are doing is monitored on hidden cameras and communication can be made by loudspeaker. If the team has not successfully solved the problem in the set time, the door automatically opens, but they have lost the game. Rooms are created at different levels of difficulty, from beginners to advanced. However, play is generally not considered suitable for those under 12 years of age, and all those under 18 must be accompanied by an adult.

Mass media – Webpage

Top tips for new escape gamers

There is a lot to take in on your first game. Often you stand there for a while contemplating where to start! Precious time starts slipping away in what is going to seem like the fastest of hour of your life. We're finding that there are a number of phrases we're using all the time when chatting to teams. So we thought we'd share these with you, and if you remember these while you play, we think you'll smash the clock!

Tip #1 – 'It's not someone's front room…' So don't be afraid to look behind things, under things, or search the room thoroughly. Clues could be hidden anywhere. Don't be polite – the room is set up for your enjoyment and your mum isn't here to tell you off for the mess you make!

Tip #2 – 'You might want to try that lock again…' OK, so everyone thinks they know how to use a padlock, right? Well, let us tell you that they are notoriously fickle beasts, especially when that clock is ticking. Always line up numbers carefully or ask a teammate to check it. We are nice and tell you if you have the right code in the right lock if you give up, but other Game Masters might not be so forgiving!

Tip #3 – 'Where did you find that…?' Many things are strategically placed. Keep a track of what you have and haven't used and where you found as it could be useful. Don't wander off looking for something you don't have if you have something you can already use. Generally, if you've been made to work hard to find something, chances are that it's important, so prioritise its use ahead of things you've found easily.

Tip #4 – 'Work as a team. Communication is key to winning the game…' It doesn't matter whether you are a team of two or ten, good communication is going to win you the game. Talk about what you've found and where you found it. Working as a team doesn't mean staying together, though. A good use of time is to split off around the room, try locks, and thoroughly search the room. But keep talking – preferably about what you are doing!

Tip #5 – 'You'll play differently next time…' We guarantee that after your game you'll be talking about it for hours. Who found what where, exclaiming 'Oh of course!', laughing about who had the code all along and didn't try the lock they were standing right next to, etc. You'll be dreaming about codes and locks for weeks. But the next time you play, you'll definitely do something different, and your time and understanding of how games work will improve.

Tip #6 – 'Warning: escape games are addictive…' When our team played their first game, they were straight online to book another for the next day!

And, you know what? Even if you forget all of the above and don't manage to win the game, we guarantee you'll still have an hour of immense fun trying!

Vocabulary

Find the following phrases in the text. By looking at the context, or using a dictionary, use your own words to say what they mean.

1 smash the clock
2 padlocks are fickle beasts
3 the clock is ticking
4 chances are
5 immense fun

Here are three escape rooms to choose from in the city of Norwich, Norfolk.

Mass media – Webpage

Norwich escape rooms

BODY OF EVIDENCE

Ghastly discoveries on the streets of Victorian Norwich spark a murder hunt. In the historic cell block under the Guildhall, where the gruesome evidence was collected, you're under suspicion for the crime. Can you piece together the clues to identify the body, convict the murderer, and find justice for the victim? This real-life murder case lay unsolved for 18 years – you have just one hour!

Please note: This game takes place in real gaol cells that held real prisoners who left behind graffiti using explicit and violent language that is not for the easily offended.

A DARK AND INTENSE TRUE CRIME ESCAPE GAME

THE MERCHANTS' VAULTS

You're trapped in the past with no money, facing the horrors of debtors' prison. In Norwich's largest medieval undercroft, or underground room, you and your team have exactly one hour to discover the secrets of the city's prosperity and build your riches to survive the past and make it back to the present!

The Merchants' Vaults is unusual among escape games as Jenny Caynes, Curator at the Museum of Norwich, explains: 'While there are plenty of games which use historical settings, what makes the Merchants' Vaults unusual is that heritage interpretation experts have teamed up with curators and collections to create not just an exciting game, but one that is historically accurate.

A UNIQUE ESCAPE GAME EXPERIENCE UNLIKE ANY OTHER

ARCHIVED ALIVE!

The City Historian is trapped in the archive vault and he's getting desperate. The poor fellow has locked himself in the secure archive vault. He ate his last fluff-covered boiled sweet from his pocket hours ago and his cup of tea didn't last beyond the first day.

Crammed full of puzzles, curios, stories, and surprises, his office contains clues to unlock the vault. Can you decipher the trail of clues and save him before he becomes part of history himself?

HIGHLY RECOMMENDED FOR FIRST-TIME PLAYERS

General comprehension

Answer the following questions.

1 Which game involves the team gathering together money and goods?
2 Which game asks the team to save somebody's life?
3 Which of the games is set in the time when Queen Victoria was on the throne?

Vocabulary

Match the words (1–6) as they are used in the text with their meanings (a–j). There are more options than you need.

1 ghastly	a a person who owes money
2 decipher	b a prison
3 spark	c an underground room with an arched ceiling
4 debtor	d frightful
5 heritage	e a person who is scary
6 vault	f work something out, usually a code
	g jump over something
	h cause the start of something
	i history
	j start a fire

Paper 2 practice task (3.1) – Escape rooms

You will hear a conversation between three friends talking about escape rooms. Answer the question.

1 From the conversation, you know that Jack:
   a has been observed in a game.
   b has no experience of escape rooms.
   c is not keen on participating.

Listen again and choose five true statements according to the conversation.

a Oliver prefers Ed Sheeran's music.
b Chloe's brother went to Berlin a short time ago.
c Jack went to Manchester for the weekend.
d Chloe's cousin is a boy.
e All three friends have been to escape rooms.
f Chloe and her friends always put their clues in the middle of the room.
g Chloe's cousin played a game called 'Robbery in a campsite'.
h In escape rooms, there is often a box or a safe that needs opening.
i Oliver has been to an escape room in Norwich.

The mobile phone – the greatest invention of all time?

If you want to know what life would be like without a mobile phone, ask your grandparents, or even your parents and teachers. Mobile telephones started to become popular in the mid to late 1990s, less than 30 years ago. Before that, communication was on a completely different level.

The use of mobile phones has now become so widespread that the majority of teachers feel they interfere with the functioning of the school. In many countries, from Australia to the UK, school authorities are now thinking of banning them from classrooms, play areas, and even school buildings.

Discussion task

Before you read the texts, get into groups of three and talk about how much you use your mobile phones and about any conflicts you may have with your parents and teachers about using them. In the introduction, it says that before the mid 1990s 'communication was on a completely different level'. Discuss what this meant for young people and adults. Does the idea of banning phones in schools surprise you? Why do you think schools in so many countries are considering banning mobiles? Be prepared to share your thoughts with the class.

TOK On what basis should the rights of the individual be mitigated against the rights of the group? Are all opinions equally valid? How do we know who is morally right and who is morally wrong?

Mass media – Article

SECONDARY SCHOOLS ARE INTRODUCING NEW BANS ON MOBILE PHONES

Secondary schools are now introducing new bans on mobile phones. All pupils aged up to 16 must lock them away for the entire day. Research has shown that doing this makes children more alert, sociable, and active.

From September, pupils aged 11 to 16 who own phones will be required either to hand them in or keep them in their lockers when they arrive at school. At the end of the school day, the phones will be returned to students.

The change in approach coincides with an appeal last week by culture secretary Matthew Hancock in *The Daily Telegraph* for schools to ban smartphones during the school day. It comes as many government officials feel it is a legal duty to protect children from digital harms.

Typical is Latymer Upper School in west London. After its success in restricting access to phones for younger pupils, its ban on phones is to be extended to all children up to the end of their GCSE years.

The independent school said its ban on mobile phones for pupils aged 11 to 13 had been 'incredibly positive' with an increase in children playing outside, attending clubs and societies and socialising with each other.

From September, all pupils from 11 to 16 will have to switch off their phones

Figure 3.8 A box for students' mobile phones

and put them in their lockers from 8.25 a.m. to 4.00 p.m. Parents will be told they should ring the school if they need to contact their sons or daughters.

Assistant head Marlene Chataway said: 'It's not a question of taking a device away from students, but rather giving them back time, the opportunity to try new activities, and the chance to take a break from social media.'

The phenomenal pull of mobile phones has been demonstrated in a study by *Harvard Business Review* which found people's concentration could be disrupted even by the presence of a switched-off phone on their desks.

'The mere presence of our smartphones is like the sound of our names – they are constantly calling to us, exerting a gravitational pull on our attention,' they said.

General comprehension

Answer the following questions in complete sentences.

1 What age pupils does the Latymer School mobile phone ban apply to?
2 What were the positive effects that Latymer School reported as a result of the mobile phone ban?
3 What is Marlene Chataway's attitude is to the ban? Explain in your own words.

Zoom in on grammar

Direct and indirect speech (reported speech)

In direct speech, we report the actual words of the speaker. The speaker's words go in inverted commas.

Lila said, 'I've lost my phone.'

In indirect speech, we report what a speaker says. We usually use reporting verbs like *say* or *tell*, and change the pronouns and verb tenses.

Lila said (that) she had lost her phone. Lila told me she had lost her phone.

Grammar in context

Find two examples in the text of direct speech and rewrite them as indirect speech. Also find an example of reported speech and rewrite it as direct speech. When do we use reported speech? Which text types make use of reported speech?

Mass media – Article

FRANCE TO IMPOSE BAN ON MOBILE PHONES IN SCHOOLS

France is to impose a ban (1)______ pupils using mobile phones in primary and secondary schools starting in September 2018, its education minister has confirmed. Phones are already forbidden in French classrooms, but starting next school year, pupils will be barred (2)______ taking them out at breaks, lunch times, and between lessons.

Teachers and parents are divided (3)______ the ban, however, with some parents saying children must be able to 'live in their time'. In France, some 93 per cent of 12- to 17-year-olds own mobile phones.

'These days the children don't play (4)______ break time anymore, they are just all in front of their smartphones and from an educational point of view that's a problem,' said Jean-Michel Blanquer, the French education minister.

'This is about ensuring the rules and the law are respected. The use of telephones is banned in class. With headmasters, teachers and parents, we must come up with a way of protecting pupils from loss (5)______ concentration via screens and phones,' he said.

Studies suggest that a significant number of pupils continue to use their mobiles in class and receive or send calls or text messages.

Up to 40 per cent of punishments are mobile-related, according to Philippe Tournier, a Paris headmaster with the SNPDEN-UNSA Teaching Union. But he said it was tricky to know how to clamp down on the practice without being able to search pupils' bags.

It remains unclear how the ban would work. Mr Blanquer had previously suggested that schools would have to provide lockers for pupils to store the phones during school hours.

'We are currently working on this, and it could work in various ways,' said Mr Blanquer. 'Phones may be needed for teaching purposes or in cases of emergency so mobile phones will have to be locked away.'

General comprehension

Answer the following questions in complete sentences.

1 How do parents feel about the ban on mobile phones?
2 When students have mobile phones in classrooms, what are the two main concerns?

Text handling

Complete the text using the words below. There are more words than you need. When you have finished, compare your answers with a partner.

at	by	from	of
on	over	to	while

Professional – Formal letter

Dear parents and guardians,

At the end of the first week of the new term, I would like to thank everyone for a good start to the new year. A main focus for all teachers here at Chatsworth School has been how to create the optimum learning environment. To further this aim, we have taken the decision to ban all mobile phones on the premises. This decision was taken after lengthy discussion and an examination of current research into learning and mental health.

The mobile phone is a ubiquitous device in this country and over 90 per cent of children are said to have their own phone. Research into the widespread use of mobile phones has shown that in 2001 there were no schools that banned mobile phones. However, six years later, this had changed dramatically with over 50 per cent of schools instituting such a ban. This became even more startling in 2012 when 98 per cent of schools had created regulations about bringing and using mobile phones at schools.

Following the trend, we have decided to say 'no phones at Chatsworth'. To those who feel mobile phones aid learning, I can only say that last term we carried out an experiment asking half the pupils in a tenth grade class to take notes in humanities class on their phone, and the other half to use pen and paper. The teacher identified that those using pen and paper had written down 50 per cent more information.

I trust you will speak to your child about these new measures and support us in our work.

Yours sincerely,
Robert Greenwood
School Principal

Discussion task

How might your parents or guardians react if they received this letter? Discuss with a partner or in groups.

General comprehension

Answer the following questions in complete sentences.

1 When did the principal write the letter?
2 What is the main reason given for the banning of mobile phones?
3 The principal says, 'The mobile phone is a ubiquitous device'. What does this mean?
4 In which time span did banning phones in schools jump from 0 to 50 per cent?
5 What argument does the principal give to support the opinion that mobile phones do not aid classroom work?

Dear Mr Greenwood,

I am writing this letter to you today because I feel something needs to be said about this unreasonable decision to ban mobile phones from school starting this September. I feel very strongly about this.

My son is 10 years old and I need to know that he has arrived safely at school in the morning after he sets off across town. In addition, he needs to be able to let me know if he is in any difficulties or needs picking up unexpectedly. During the day he can let me know how he is getting on in school and tell me if there are any problems with the playground bullies. Believe me, Mr Greenwood, your pupils are not all as kind and helpful as you seem to think they are.

I have installed a tracking app on my son's phone so that I can stay informed about not only where he is, but also where my daughter and husband are. This is the way the modern world works and you need to step into the 21st century if you think differently.

As for working in the classroom, I do believe that the mobile phone should not be used when the teacher is talking to the class. If the pupils are asked to turn off their phones in class, this would be a reasonable solution.

I do hope you will rethink your school's policy regarding mobile phones. I'm sure many other parents have concerns similar to mine.

Yours sincerely,
Mrs Samantha Burberry

Paper 1 practice task

Write a formal letter in response to the letter from Samantha Burberry. Write your letter from the point of view of another parent. You can choose to agree or disagree with the opinions of Mrs Burberry. Take her points and give an opinion. The response should be polite and formal. You can include further reasons of your own as to why banning mobile phones could be either unacceptable or worthwhile.

SL students should write 250–400 words. HL students should write 450–600 words.

For tips on how to write a formal letter, see page 54 of Chapter 2, Experiences.

TOK

On what basis should emotions be used to influence knowledge? Is knowledge based on emotion more or less valid than knowledge based on more rational processes? What is the relationship between emotion and reason?

If Alexander Graham Bell hadn't invented the telephone in 1876, there would never have been telephone boxes.

Mass media – Webpage

The history of the telephone

Although the Scottish inventor Alexander Graham Bell is generally acknowledged to be the inventor of the telephone while he was working in the United States of America, there were other scientists who were on the verge of a similar breakthrough at the time. The self-educated German physicist, Philip Reis, demonstrated the use of his invention in 1861. He could have become more famous than Bell, but his work had several shortcomings. Similarly, Italian emigrant Antonio Meucci, who lived in America in the latter part of the 19th century, patented a telephone in 1871 but failed to find a commercial backer for his invention.

However, probably the most famous story about the race to the patent office is the one between Elisha Gray and Alexander Graham Bell. Gray also lived in America and he had been working on a similar telephone device at the same time as Bell. In 1876, Gray sent his lawyer to the patent office to register his device, but Bell's lawyer had arrived there just hours before.

The iconic red telephone box was the result of a competition in 1924 to design a 'kiosk' that would be acceptable on the streets of London after the first concrete boxes of 1920 were considered old-fashioned. Sir Giles Gilbert Scott was chosen as the winner and his mainly cast-iron design was accepted. However, his choice of colour was not accepted. He had proposed silvery green but red was considered to be more noticeable.

Figure 3.9 The iconic red telephone box in London

In 1925 the system of operating the telephone was the coin box – the Button A and Button B prepayment equipment, which users had been familiar with for over 25 years. To make a call, users inserted the appropriate fee, which prepared the circuit for dialling. The caller then dialled the number and pressed Button A. This allowed the coins to be deposited into the cash box and the call to be transmitted. If a call could not be connected for some reason, or if there was no reply, Button B was depressed, the line was disconnected after 5 to 7 seconds, and all the coins were returned to the caller.

Today, mobile phones are making the telephone box obsolete. Tourists in London still take photographs of themselves standing next to or inside the boxes, but these days there are probably only very few people who know how to operate one.

General comprehension

Answer the following questions.

1 Who are the four scientists named as all working on the development of the telephone at the same time?
2 What was the name of the winner of the 1924 competition?
3 What colour was suggested for the first telephone boxes?
4 What colour was finally chosen and why?

Text handling

Match the beginnings of the sentences (1–5) taken from the text and the introduction with endings (a–e) to make new meaningful sentences.

1 The self-educated German physicist
2 Italian emigrant Antonio Meucci
3 The iconic red telephone box
4 In 1925 the system of operating a telephone
5 If Alexander Graham Bell hadn't invented the telephone,

a was originally designed to be a different colour.
b did not become famous because his work was flawed.
c was only possible if you had coins.
d then Elisha Gray would probably be famous.
e was unable to find a sponsor for his idea.

Zoom in on grammar

The past perfect

The past perfect is used when referring to an action that happened before another action in the past.

Gray sent his lawyer to the patent office to register his device, but Bell's lawyer ***had arrived*** *there just hours before.*

He ***had proposed*** *silvery green but red was considered to be more noticeable.*

Think about other examples in which you would use the past perfect tense.

Grammar in context

Complete the following sentences with a verb in the past perfect tense.

1 I thought I __________ the teacher my homework, but he said he didn't have it.
2 After Ms Brown __________ the art classroom, she went to lunch.
3 During the presentation, I didn't say anything until my friend __________ speaking.

Mum, give me the cornflakes!

Read the letter below, written by a parent to the local newspaper about the use of voice control devices and the issue of politeness.

Mass media – Public commentary

Dear Sir,

Voice command devices (VCDs) are revolutionising our homes. As with all new gadgets, there can be disadvantages that might not be immediately noticeable. In our home, our VCD is a whizz at playing all our favourite music, whether it is Rag'n'Bone Man for our daughter when she comes in from school or Ed Sheeran for me when I'm relaxing. My partner uses our VCD to remind him of things in his diary for the next day, and I use it to keep my 'to do' list up to date. All these functions are incredibly useful and a true enrichment to our daily lives.

However, it's how we use it that is starting to bother me. Make no mistake. Our VCD is definitely not a person so when we ask it to do something, we use the imperative. 'Play Ed Sheeran's latest album' or 'Put tomatoes on my shopping list'. There is no need to ask nicely, to be polite, or to use any of those phrases that we learned from our parents to make social interaction a much less confrontational situation. So, when my daughter said, 'Mum, give me the cornflakes!' alarm bells started ringing!

Will the use of voice control devices change the way we talk to each other? Are we heading for a future where nobody says 'please' or 'thank you' any more? Do we need to worry about this? When I was a child, if I asked for something and didn't say 'please' my mother used to say, 'What's the magic word?' That implied that there was a value in politeness and that it was there

TOK

How do we know what it is to be human? When artificial intelligence becomes as complex as human intelligence, how will we know what moral rights other beings may be entitled to?

for a reason. It was how you got things done in the grown-up's world. As our school becomes more digitised, do we need to introduce a new subject to the curriculum perhaps called 'Being polite'?

I'd like to hear what other parents think.

Yours faithfully,
Jane Grenville

The letters below are three responses to Jane's letter.

Dear Sir,

In reply to Jane Grenville's letter, I can only say that it is surely the parents' responsibility to teach the social skills of politeness. I do not have much understanding for the kind of thinking that demands that schools fill the gaps which parents are neglecting.

Robert Jones

Mass media – Public commentary

Sirs,

I agree with Jane Grenville. It is becoming a nightmare listening to my kids demanding all sorts of things from me and my husband, without any care about being polite. Surely this is something the school should address.

Molly Garner

Mass media – Public commentary

Dear Mrs Grenville,

You are writing your letter to the wrong people. You should write to the manufacturers and tell them what you recommend. However, I think you'll find that they are already on to this and there is an adaptation feature called 'Magic Word' which they are setting up.

Spike

Mass media – Public commentary

General comprehension

Answer the following questions in complete sentences.

1 What does Mrs Grenville think about the voice control device?
2 What does she think might be a solution to the problem she sees?
3 There are three letters in response to Mrs Grenville. Which of the three writers agrees with her?

Text handling

Complete the table with the correct noun forms. Can you think of more words to add to the table?

Verb	Noun
revolutionise	
function	
imply	
introduce	
recommend	
agree	

Zoom in on grammar

The imperative

The title of the text is *Mum, give me the cornflakes!* This is an example of the imperative. For the positive form of the imperative, we use the base form of the verb, e.g. *give, take, stand up*. These are called imperative verbs.

Imperative verbs are used to tell people what to do and to give advice. Negative forms of the imperative are constructed with don't, e.g. ***Don't walk** on the grass.* ***Don't feed** the fish.*

Imperatives may also be used in a set of instructions and introduced by bullet points, e.g.

- **Take** the phone out of the box.
- **Attach** the power cable.
- **Plug** it into the charger. **Charge** for 12 hours.

Grammar in context

Complete the following sentences with an imperative verb. The verbs can be positive or negative.

1 ________________ your examination booklet until instructed.
2 If you want to use the computers in the library, ________________ the librarian.
3 ________________ the oven to 190 degrees before you put in the pizza.
4 ________________ the windows if it is too cold.
5 ________________ French fries. They aren't healthy.

Paper 1 practice task

Write an email to a friend of yours and tell them about your voice control device. Tell them what it is used for and what different members of the family think about it. You can use ideas from the letters or your own ideas. Make your own point of view clear.

Write between 250 and 400 words.

An email is written in informal or semi-formal English. You can use expressions such as 'Hi' and 'How are you doing?' but remember to use a good range of vocabulary and grammar to show your knowledge of English.

For tips on how to write an informal email, see page 49 of Chapter 2, Experiences.

Research and presentation task

In pairs, take some time to research current developments in devices to improve daily life. Perhaps self-driven vacuum cleaners, lawn mowers, or drones. There are many ideas you could explore. Collect your information and be ready to present your findings to the class.

Presentation tips:

- Divide the information so you both have a chance to speak.
- Introduce yourselves and your chosen topic of research.
- Describe the device, where it originated, and its function.
- Give personal opinions about the value of the device and its future applications.
- When the presentation is over, signal this to your audience by saying, 'Thank you for listening'.

Internal assessment (SL)

Figure 3.10 Phones should be banned in school!

Examine the photograph above and consider the following points:

- What do you see in the picture? Describe only what you see. Do not give opinions.
- Reflect on the picture in connection with the theme of the advantages and disadvantages of using phones in school.
- Can we guarantee that students will use phones only for work?
- What options are open to schools if phones are disturbing class work?
- Make connections to your own experience and the experiences of students you know.
- Consider the role of electronic devices in schools.

Using the points above, spend 15 minutes preparing a presentation about the photograph. Use the preparation time to organise your ideas and plan the sequence of what you will talk about.

Your presentation should last 3 to 4 minutes, after which your teacher and other students will have the opportunity to comment or ask questions about what you have said. You must engage in a conversation with them. In total, this task should take approximately 15 minutes.

3.4 Ancient wisdom

Nebra, Stonehenge, and Seahenge

Mass media – Leaflet

NEBRA

Nebra is a small, sleepy town in the east of Germany. It lies between Weimar and Leipzig, both of which you may have heard of through their connections to the famous German poets Goethe and Schiller. However, the story of Nebra over the past few years reads like a crime novel. This little town in a rural area of forests, small hills, farms, and a nature reserve is close to the Unstrut River, which is famous in these parts for the winemaking that takes place on the hillsides along its banks. The population of Nebra is just over 3000 people.

The story begins in 1999 when two men were illegally searching for treasure using metal detectors in the hills near Nebra. They discovered the *Himmelsscheibe*, which means 'a slice of heaven'. In English, it is referred to as the 'Nebra Sky Disc', which you can see in the picture. At the same time, they discovered two very clearly antique, highly decorated swords, two ancient forms of hatchets, a chisel, and some pieces of spiral bracelets from armour.

Figure 3.11 Nebra Sky Disc

All of these treasures were clearly very old, but the two men had no intention of handing them over to the authorities. They were after a quick profit, so without having any idea of the value of their treasures, they sold them to other equally unscrupulous dealers. As time passed, the treasures were sold on in a chain of dealers who were willing to pay thousands of deutschmarks, before finally being offered to an archaeologist who immediately recognised their importance. In a police-led raid, the dealers were captured and the treasures secured in a hotel in Basel, Switzerland. The original thieves were eventually identified and given suspended jail sentences of six months and 12 months respectively.

The Nebra Sky Disc is a bronze disc, 30 centimetres in diameter, weighing 2.2 kilogrammes. It is thought to have been buried around 1600 BC. Archaeologists estimate it was made up to 150 years earlier. It is around 3600 years old. The sky disc is inlaid with gold and depicts astronomical positions and religious symbols. Archaeologists consider it to be one of the most important artefacts of the Bronze Age ever discovered.

Figure 3.12 Nebra Ark visitor centre

General comprehension

Answer the following questions in complete sentences.

1 Where is Nebra?
2 What is the area around the Unstrut River famous for?
3 Did the two men who found the treasures first have permission to use metal detectors to find treasures?
4 What did they find with the Nebra Sky Disc?
5 Why did the men decide not to hand their findings over to the authorities?
6 What did they do with their finds?
7 Were the dealers who bought and sold the treasures honest?
8 Who finally recognised the true value of these items?
9 What happened in the hotel in Basel?
10 What happened to the original thieves?

State whether the following statements are true or false. Correct the false statements.

11 Nebra is a major city in Germany.
12 The area around the Unstrut River is famous for wine.
13 The Nebra Sky Disc was first found hundreds of years ago.
14 There were other treasures found with the sky disc.
15 The men who found the treasures were famous archaeologists.
16 The men decided not to tell the authorities about the treasures they had found.

17 The Nebra Sky Disc and other treasures were bought and sold for huge amounts of money.
18 The police caught some of the criminals in a hotel in Germany.
19 The original thieves were never caught.
20 The Nebra Sky Disc is made of gold.

Paper 2 practice task (3.2) – Nebra Ark audio guide

You will hear an audio guide to the Nebra Ark. State whether the following statements are true or false.

1 The Ark points north to where the Nebra Sky Disc was found.
2 There is no planetarium in the Nebra Ark.
3 There is a puppet theatre in the visitor centre.
4 The summer solstices were not important for the early farming people.
5 The sky disc is very easy to understand.

Listen again and complete the following gaps. Use no more than three words for each gap.

6 You probably had a good view of the Nebra Ark ____________ position on the slopes above the Unstrut River.
7 Now you can ____________ an exciting tour of the Nebra Ark.
8 For early farming people, the summer and winter solstices were ____________ in their annual calendar.
9 The Nebra Sky Disc is the world's ____________ representation of the cosmos.
10 Don't worry though, our exhibition will ____________.

Mass media – Travel guide

STONEHENGE

Everything you need to know about visiting Stonehenge

by Sophie Campbell, travel writer

1. Cremation ground? Sun worship site? Alien landing pad? The sight of Stonehenge with its broken circle of stones and mighty central trilithons standing in apparent isolation on Salisbury Plain has been mesmerising travellers for centuries.

2. In recent years, however, it has been enjoying a renaissance, partly because its 1960s concrete excrescences have been swept away and replaced with an airy visitor centre a mile down the road. The stones have been returned to their full glory and what is known of their story is explained, while new finds and interpretations are announced as they arise. In 2015, for example, the discovery of a massive and previously unknown palisaded enclosure beneath the banks of Durrington Walls, a couple of miles away, reinforces the idea that Stonehenge is one component of a planned Neolithic landscape on a vast scale.

3. How to get there

Public transport

Green Traveller has made a video on getting to Stonehenge without using a car, including by bike.

Vehicle

The visitor centre and car park (free for ticketholders) sit to the north of the A303, where the A360 and B3086 meet at Airman's Corner. In summer, traffic can back up to the Countess Roundabout on the A303 in both directions. It may be worth taking the back route via the B3086 and the Packway south to Airman's Corner.

4. Highlights for adults

Getting off the shuttle halfway, at Fargo Plantation, and wandering through the trees to see the mysterious – and much older – oblong ditch known as the Cursus, before approaching the stones on foot, as they should be approached (if possible).

Figure 3.13 Stonehenge

5. Highlights for children

Seeing the recreated face of a 5000-year-old Neolithic man in the visitor centre and then being able to play in his house (the Neolithic village outside is based on remains found at Durrington Walls and often has re-enactors and demonstrations).

6. Best time to visit

Winter. At the end of the day, to catch the sun going down behind the stones to the southwest – even better if it's frosty. And, of course, the winter and summer solstices, when entrance is free, but you have to contend with mighty crowds.

7. Best view

Pass the entrance to the stones and follow the fence round to the north, veering down the faint parallel lines in the grass known as the Avenue. About 100 yards downhill, turn and look back to see the stones silhouetted against the sky.

General comprehension

Answer the following questions in complete sentences.

1 According to the text, is it known what Stonehenge was used for?
2 What two reasons are given for the renewed popularity of Stonehenge?
3 Where in England is Stonehenge?
4 At what times of the year is entrance free?

Vocabulary

Match the words (1–9) as they are used in the text with their meanings (a–p). There are more options than you need.

Paragraph 1

1 cremation ground
2 trilithons
3 mesmerising travellers

Paragraph 2

4 renaissance
5 airy
6 palisaded enclosure

Paragraph 6

7 winter solstice
8 summer solstice
9 mighty crowds

a confusing the people who visit
b a place where dead people were burned
c fascinating the people who visit
d a construction made with three stones
e aliens
f renovation
g an area surrounded by wooden posts
h a reawakening of interest
i having lots of space and light
j an area surrounded by a modern fence
k strong people
l coldest day of the year
m day with the shortest period of daylight
n large numbers of people
o day with the longest period of daylight
p holiday time

Mass media – Webpage

Seahenge

Figure 3.14 Seahenge in Norfolk

Seahenge is a name coined by the media to describe the circle of timber posts surrounding a huge tree, buried upside-down with its roots clearly visible in the air, discovered at Holme beach in the British county of Norfolk in 1998.

The name makes a connection to Stonehenge, the circle of stones in Wiltshire in the south of England. Archaeologists use the word 'henge' to classify a circular or oval construction of stones or timber.

There is a lot of speculation about the function of Seahenge. Proposals include a place of worship, a burial site or other ritual activity. Its location, when it was constructed over 4000 years ago, during the Bronze Age, would not have been on the beach. Over the past 4000 years, the sea has moved forward, eroding the land in the process.

The henge was removed from its location on the beach and transported to the nearby city of King's Lynn, where it was reconstructed in the museum and can be visited today. Removing the henge was considered the best way of preserving it from deterioration due to the effects of sea and air after its exposure to stormy weather.

The removal of the henge was controversial, with some people believing it should stay in its ancient location. This opinion was held by many local people who had known of the presence of the henge for decades before archaeologists discovered it.

TOK

What is the role of language in creating knowledge in history? Can language mislead? On what basis should labels and terms in history be decided?

TOK

To what extent are the Nebra Sky Disc, Stonehenge, Seahenge, or other artefacts from the distant past, relevant to our lives?

General comprehension

Answer the following questions in complete sentences.

1 Who gave the structure the name 'Seahenge'?
2 According to the text, what was the purpose of Seahenge?
3 Where can the henge currently be seen?
4 Why do you think some people wanted to keep Seahenge in its original location?

State whether the following statements are true or false. Give a reason for your answers.

5 Seahenge is made of the same kind of material as Stonehenge.
6 Seahenge was constructed on the beach in Norfolk.
7 Nobody knew the henge was there before its discovery in 1998.
8 The henge was transported to the museum to prevent it from rotting away.
9 The word 'henge' is a technical term used to describe similar constructions.

Internal assessment (SL)

Figure 3.15 Just a heap of stones?

Examine the photograph above and consider the following points:

- What do you see in the picture? Describe only what you see. Do not give opinions.
- Consider the knowledge that we can gain from examining things from the past.
- What can these stones tell us about people who had no written documents?
- What do you think these stones were put there for?
- Make connections to your own experience of visiting historical sites.

Using the points above, spend 15 minutes preparing a presentation about the photograph. Use the preparation time to organise your ideas and plan the sequence of what you will talk about.

Your presentation should last 3 to 4 minutes, after which your teacher and other students will have the opportunity to comment or ask questions about what you have said. You must engage in a conversation with them. In total, this task should take approximately 15 minutes.

Paper 1 practice task

In pairs, research Stonehenge or Seahenge. Use your research findings and the information above to create your own flyer for visitors. Be prepared to share your flyers with the class.

Tips for creating a flyer

- Remember that a flyer is a form of advertising. Make sure to consider your audience, e.g. young families, senior citizens.
- Give examples of activities your audience would enjoy.
- Use illustrations and bullet points to make it easier for your readers to take in information.
- Include important information and facts about the site.

4 Social organisation

4 Social organisation

Research questions

- What groups and organisations are reflected in society?
- How are individuals able to influence the social group they are in?

Objectives

- To compare different stages of education.
- To evaluate the role of school rules.
- To discuss the importance of sleep for adolescents.
- To examine how life has changed in the past 100 years.
- To evaluate the effect of a range of communities.

Language skills objectives

- To practise interactive oral skills in relation to the social organisation theme.
- To revise the use of the imperative.
- To examine idiomatic language.
- To practise forming nouns from verbs.
- To focus on the use of *should* and *ought to*.
- To revise the use of the passive voice.

TOK What are the best methods to study human social organisation? How does studying humans as group members help and hinder our understanding of what it is to be human? Can the 'individual' ever be a unit of study in the human sciences?

We all live in societies, in social groups within social systems. Our lives are organised and structured to maintain stability for the good of everyone. We go to school, join clubs, study, and follow the rules of the groups we are in. In all societies, work is the basis of human existence for young people and adults, and following work we need to relax and regenerate. In the following chapter, you can consider communities such as schools, villages, and clubs, and examine their structures, the ways of bringing people together, and how problems are dealt with.

4.1 Schools around the world

School – the best time of your life?

Mass media – Webpage

School communities

Regardless of which country you live in or which languages you speak, one thing is certain – your school is your social organisation and from day one you belong to that special social group.

Figure 4.1 Enthusiastic kindergarten students

The early years

Do you remember your first day in kindergarten? Were you in the Green group, or the Robin group, or maybe the Buttercup group? Did your group have a special name? The group names are chosen from areas which are familiar to small children: colours, birds, flowers, and others. Very young children who spend their mornings, and often even longer, away from their parents need to have a special feeling of belonging, being safe and protected, loved and surrounded by friends. During their years in kindergarten children learn a lot. Their language develops and they learn colours, numbers, rhymes, and songs, and most importantly how to get along with others who are not family members. They learn to play together, to share and cooperate. The teacher and assistants remain with the same group of children over a long period of time. It is a busy, important phase of learning.

The next stage

In primary school the group system continues.

Class groups tend to move up through the school together, therefore many long-term friendships are formed during the primary years. The children have the same teacher for nearly all of the subjects over the school year. In some schools, the same teacher leads the children through all of the primary years. The learning goals continue to develop age-appropriately and the first homework will be assigned, the first tests given, and the first report cards sent home. During this period, the teachers carefully monitor students' learning and often encourage students to be independent learners. It is an exciting stage of life full of new discoveries.

The secondary stage

This is the time you are in now. The system and schedule gradually become more complex as the students no longer study the same subjects at the same levels. The bigger the school, the more choices there are available. The teachers are subject specialists, and as a result, students and teachers deal with a wide range of people for short periods on a daily basis. Students are expected to manage their own learning and take responsibility for it.

Organisation and discipline

In kindergarten, the rules for the children tend to be expressed verbally. Any written rules are more often given to the parents of kindergarten children who are required to bring and collect their children at set times and be sure they have indoor shoes and a change of clothes amongst other things. As students get older and become young adults, there is a need for clear guidelines for behaviour and rules concerning what is allowed or forbidden: rules governing plagiarism, bullying, and unexplained absence from school and the ensuing sanctions. Such discipline ensures that the community works well together and each individual is considered.

In primary school, rules are usually basic and focus on respect for each other. This situation changes in secondary school where the rules become more detailed and much more prescriptive.

Figure 4.2 Secondary students participating in class

Secondary school rules generally focus on attendance, dress style, what is allowed or not allowed, behaviour guidelines which must be followed, and rules concerning alcohol and drugs. In addition, schools now have guidelines concerning the use of technology, such as whether or not mobile phones are permitted in the classroom. Most schools provide new secondary students with a *Student Handbook* or similar so that the students have the rules in writing and cannot claim that they are unaware of them.

Zoom in on grammar

The imperative

In Chapter 3, we learned how to use the imperative to tell people what to do, give advice and instructions. We can also use the imperative to give commands or orders.

In the event of fire, ***close*** *doors and windows,* ***follow*** *the teacher's instructions, and* ***exit*** *the building silently.*

Can you remember how to form a negative imperative?

Discussion task

Kindergarten years

Did you stay in the same group and the same room for all of your kindergarten years? Think back to your kindergarten days. What do you remember? Talk to a partner about it and then write a short personal reflection to share with your group.

Primary school

How much do you remember of your primary school years? Share your memories in conversations with a partner or group.

Paper 1 practice task

Secondary school

Imagine you have been asked to rewrite your school's *Code of Conduct and School Rules*. Think about how your school, the classes, and the social groups are organised. Write a description using the headings in the webpage above, but include more detail as the systems may change across the grades.

Write so that the reader will clearly understand the system and rules in your school.

Here are some examples of school rules to help you.

- Students and teachers will treat each other with respect at all times.
- Students must arrive at school punctually and be ready to work.
- There will be no running or loitering in the corridors.
- Students must always wear the correct school uniform, as described in the parent-student handbook.
- Girls may not wear make-up or any kind of jewellery.
- Piercings and tattoos are strictly forbidden for all students.
- All students must keep their hair tidy and clean. Girls' long hair should be tied back from the face. Boys' hair may not be longer than collar length, or cover the face, and should be conservative in style.
- PE uniform may only be worn during PE classes.
- Students may not bring scooters or skateboards to school.
- Chewing gum is forbidden.
- Students may not bring cigarettes or any other smoking equipment, alcohol, or any other kinds of drugs to school. Breaking this rule will lead to an immediate suspension from school.
- Mobile phones may be brought to school, but may only be used in mobile phone areas at times determined by teachers. Any other use of mobile phones will lead to immediate confiscation.

Professional – Report

Sleep deprivation in adolescents and young adults

Sleep: How does it affect adolescents and young adults?

Sleep is essential to the healthy development of adolescents and young adults, as well as for their success at school and in the workplace. Two-thirds of adolescents report insufficient sleep, as do one-third of young adults. In adolescence, insufficient sleep, inadequate sleep quality, and irregular sleep patterns are associated with daytime sleepiness, negative moods, increased likelihood of stimulant use, higher levels of risk-taking behaviours, poor school performance, and increased risk of unintentional injuries. Over a quarter of high school students report falling asleep in class at least once weekly.

In young adulthood, a lack of sufficient sleep has been linked to poor self-rated health and psychological distress.

The growing evidence supporting the importance of sleep and the negative impact of sleep deprivation has brought the issue to the attention of public health professionals. Healthy People 2020, which sets the nation's public health agenda, has included 'sleep health' as a topic area, and developed objectives for sleep health, including: (1) increase the proportion of students in grades 9 to 12 who get sufficient sleep; (2) increase the proportion of adults who get sufficient sleep.

In this information brief, we discuss the definition of sufficient sleep, barriers to adequate sleep, ways to recognise sleep deprivation, and efforts to promote healthy sleep in adolescents and young adults.

TOK Studies suggest the average school day does not suit the adolescent sleep pattern. It might be better to start and finish later with nap time in the middle, but this might not suit wider society. How might the rights and needs of one group be mitigated against the rights and needs of another? On what basis can social groups be ranked according to importance?

General comprehension

Answer the following questions in complete sentences.

1 What proportion of young adults admit to not getting enough sleep?
2 What effects does lack of sleep have on adolescents?
3 What proportion of students admit to falling asleep during classes? How often does this happen?
4 What has brought this to the attention of public health professionals?
5 Which objectives for sleep health have been developed by Healthy People 2020?

Vocabulary

Find words or phrases in the text which match the following meanings.

1 very important
2 not enough in quantity
3 lack of something considered necessary
4 not regular
5 accidental

Professional – Report

How many hours are 'sufficient' for adolescents and young adults?

Ages 12–17: 8 or more hours
Ages 18–21: 8 or more hours
Ages 22+: 7 or more hours

What are the signs of sleep deprivation?

The effects of ongoing sleep deprivation may include:

- concentration difficulties
- mentally 'drifting off' in class
- shortened attention span
- memory impairment
- poor decision making
- lack of enthusiasm
- moodiness and aggression
- depression
- risk-taking behaviour
- slower physical reflexes
- clumsiness, which may result in physical injuries
- reduced sporting performance
- reduced academic performance
- more 'sick days' from school because of tiredness
- truancy

Vocabulary

Find words or phrases in the text which match the following descriptions.

1 forgetting things
2 being bad tempered
3 dropping things and knocking things down
4 skipping school
5 not able to concentrate for long

Discussion task

How many hours of sleep are 'sufficient' for your age group? Do you get that many hours of sleep? How rested do you feel in the morning? What are ways to make sure you get enough sleep? Discuss with a partner or in groups.

Before reading the text below, have you ever heard the expression 'circadian rhythm'? It sounds complicated but is really quite simple. The National Sleep Foundation defines 'circadian rhythm' as a 24-hour internal clock running in the background of your brain that cycles between sleepiness and alertness at regular intervals. It is also known as your sleep/wake cycle.

Professional – Report

Why don't teenagers and young adults regularly get enough sleep?
Several factors contribute to lack of sleep in adolescence and young adulthood. Insufficient sleep during this critical growth period arises from physiological, behavioural, sociocultural, and environmental changes. Little is known about the influences on sleep among young adults. Factors known to affect adolescents often occur simultaneously, and include:

- (1) ________________________________
  In early adolescence, teens experience a shift in their circadian rhythms, causing the peak production of melatonin, a sleep-inducing hormone, to occur later in the evening, from around 11.00 p.m. to 8.00 a.m.
- (2) ________________________________
  The change in normal sleep cycles is further complicated by school schedules. Forty-two per cent of public high schools start before 8.00 a.m., and 43 per cent of public high schools start between 8.00 a.m. and 8.29 a.m. These start times lead adolescents to start their day before they have slept the recommended eight or more hours. Nearly 70 per cent of adolescents report seven or less hours of sleep on an average school night. This nightly 'sleep debt' can contribute to chronic sleep deprivation.
- (3) ________________________________
  Homework, sports, other extra-curricular activities, part-time work, and social commitments may further contribute to late bedtimes.

- (4) ___
  A stimulating environment, such as television, the internet, and computer gaming delay a teenager's bedtime.
- (5) ___
  Light cues the brain to stay awake. In the evening, lights from televisions, mobile phones, and computers can prevent adequate production of melatonin.
- (6) ___
  Insufficient sleep causes a teenager's brain to become more active. An over-aroused brain is less able to fall asleep.
- (7) ___
  In Western culture, keeping active is valued more than sleep.
- (8) ___
  Sleep disorders, such as restless legs syndrome or sleep apnoea, can affect how much sleep a teenager gets.

Tips for a better night's sleep

'Sleep hygiene', a variety of practices that are necessary to have normal quality sleep, is essential to the health of not only adolescents and young adults, but individuals of all ages. The following tips have shown to be effective at improving sleep hygiene for various ages.

- Get up and go to bed at the same time every day.
- Go to bed only when sleepy.
- Develop sleep rituals.
- Optimise your sleep environment (keep the room dark, minimise noises, moderate room temperature).
- Don't take your worries and responsibilities to bed.
- Get up if you can't fall asleep to the point of becoming frustrated. Do something relaxing until you feel sleepy.
- Limit being in bed to times when you are sleeping or sick.
- Do not watch the clock.
- Minimise napping.
- Stay away from caffeine, nicotine, and alcohol at least 4–6 hours before bed.
- Have a light snack before bed.
- Refrain from exercise at least 2 hours before bed.

Text handling

Add the following headings to the report above.

- Leisure activities
- Early school starts
- Vicious cycle
- Social attitudes
- Hectic after-school schedule
- Other sleep-related problems
- Hormonal time shift
- Light exposure

General comprehension

Answer the following questions in complete sentences.

1 Why do teenagers experience a shift in their circadian rhythms? Explain in your own words.

2 How much is known about the influences on sleep among young adults?

Vocabulary

Match the words (1–4) as they are used in the text with their meanings (a–d).

1 physiological	a concerned with our society and culture
2 behavioural	b concerned with or related to the world in which we live
3 sociocultural	c related to the way we act
4 environmental	d the way a person functions

Find words or phrases in the text which match the following meanings.

5 happen at the same time
6 go through a change
7 serious lack of sleep
8 cause teenagers to go to bed late
9 a lively, stimulated brain cannot go to sleep

Grammar in context

In Chapter 3, we learned how to use the imperative to tell people what to do, give advice and instructions. We can also use the imperative to give commands or orders.

In the event of fire, ***close*** *doors and windows,* ***follow*** *the teacher's instructions, and* ***exit*** *the building silently.*

Can you remember how to form a negative imperative?

Find words in the text which match the following meanings.

1 make the very best
2 create
3 reduce
4 avoid
5 restrict

For health professionals: What can be done?
Public health approaches to improve sleep hygiene thus far have ranged from school policy change to informational programmes that aim to increase knowledge about sleep and improve the sleep habits of adolescents and young adults. Evidence for the effectiveness of most interventions is minimal for this emerging issue. Research on interventions involving parents is especially sparse. Descriptions of efforts to improve sleep health follow.

Delayed school start times
Description: Several studies have examined the impact of delayed school start times on sleep and related problems. District-wide changes were implemented, with schools starting approximately one and half hours later in Minnesota and Massachusetts, and one hour later in Kentucky.

Professional – Report

Evaluation: The evaluations suggest that delayed start times is a promising strategy for increasing sleep time and related outcomes. Delayed start times in Minnesota, implemented in 1996, produced encouraging results, including longer sleep times, improved attendance, increase in continuous enrollment, less tardiness, and students making fewer trips to the school nurse. Notably, urban and suburban parents differed in support for the change. Later school start times caused hardship by disrupting transportation and work schedules for urban students and parents, while suburban parents generally supported the change. In Kentucky (1998), delayed school start times appear to have led to a significant decrease in countywide car collision rates among teens. Delayed school start times implemented in Massachusetts in 2004 resulted in longer sleep times, improved academic performance, and reduced tardiness. A 2013 study conducted in eight public schools in Minnesota, Colorado, and Wyoming found that starting school at 8.30 a.m. or later allowed for more than 60 per cent of students to obtain at least eight hours of sleep per school night. Additional results included improved academic performance, reduced tardiness, and improved performance on state and national achievement tests. When schools shifted start times from 7.35 to 8.55 a.m., car accidents among drivers ages 16–18 decreased by 70 per cent.

Sleep education leaflet

Description: This study was conducted among 1209 high school students ages 15–18 from 12 high schools in Croatia. An educational leaflet about healthy sleep was distributed to two intervention groups, one that received pre- and post-tests and one that only received post-tests.

Evaluation: Positive effects on sleep knowledge, as measured by pre- and post-tests, were found in students ages 15–17 but not aged 18. In male students, positive effects of the leaflet intervention were found only in the group that had not been pre-tested, while in female students, positive results were found in both pre-tested and not pre-tested groups.

InShape is a prevention programme to improve physical, mental and spiritual well-being of college students.

InShape

Description: InShape emphasises the positive image benefits of setting goals to increase physical activity, healthy eating, sleep, and stress management, while avoiding alcohol, cigarettes and illicit drugs to maintain a healthy lifestyle. Major programme components include a self-administered behaviour image survey, a brief talk about fitness and health with a designated fitness specialist, and a set of fitness recommendations and goals to improve fitness behaviours and self-image. The programme was administered to over 300 college students (ages 19–22).

Evaluation: Results from a three-month follow up showed an increase in the duration of sleep, along with other health results.

Mindfulness-based stress reduction (MBSR)

Description: Mindfulness-based stress reduction trains individuals to direct their attention to an event or experience, while avoiding evaluative thought or judgement, with the goal of alleviating stress and stress-related outcomes.

MBSR was implemented with adolescents in an outpatient psychiatric programme who had received a psychological diagnosis. Adolescents in the treatment group received MBSR, plus their usual psychiatric care. Controls received their usual psychiatric care.

Evaluation: Results showed that those in the treatment group significantly improved their sleep quality, along with other outcomes.

General comprehension

Answer the following questions in complete sentences.

1 What has been done so far to improve sleep hygiene?
2 Is there sufficient evidence to show how effective these measures are?
3 What were the positive results of delayed school starting times?
4 What were the disadvantages of later school starting times in Minnesota?
5 What country did the sleep education leaflet study take place in?
6 What does InShape recommend avoiding in order to maintain a healthy lifestyle?
7 What did the results of the MBSR study show?

Intercultural activity

To what extent are the ideas in the text on sleep deprivation in adolescents and young adults shared in your culture?

Paper 1 practice task

Do you and your peers have enough sleep each night? Are you wide awake and ready to study when you get to school each morning? Investigate the claims of researchers published on the internet to see what they say, and then compare their comments with your own experience and that of your colleagues.

Write either a blog, an article for the school magazine, or a speech to share the results of your research.

SL students should write 250–400 words. HL students should write 450–600 words.

For tips on how to write a blog, see page 9 of Chapter 1, Identities. For tips on how to write an article, see page 29 of Chapter 1, Identities. For tips on how to write a speech, see page 62 of Chapter 2, Experiences.

Mass media – Article

TABLETS OUT, IMAGINATION IN: THE SCHOOLS THAT SHUN TECHNOLOGY

Parents working in Silicon Valley are sending their children to a school where there's not a computer in sight – and they're not alone.

In the heart of Silicon Valley is a nine-classroom school where employees of tech giants Google, Apple, and Yahoo send their children. But despite its location in America's digital centre, there is not a tablet, smartphone, or screen in sight. Instead, teachers at the Waldorf School of the Peninsula prefer a more hands-on, experiential approach to learning that contrasts sharply with the rush to fill classrooms with the latest electronic devices. The pedagogy emphasises the role of imagination in learning and takes a holistic approach that integrates the intellectual, practical, and creative development of pupils.

But the fact that parents working for pioneering technology companies are questioning the value of computers in education begs the question – is the futuristic dream of high-tech classrooms really in the best interests of the next generation?

A global report by the Organisation for Economic Co-operation and Development (OECD) suggests educational systems that have invested heavily in computers have seen 'no noticeable improvement' in their results for reading, maths, and science in the Programme for International Student Assessment (PISA) tests. The OECD's education director, Andreas Schleicher, says: 'If you look at the best-performing education systems, such as those in East Asia, they've been very cautious about using technology in their classroom.'

Schleicher adds, 'Those students who use tablets and computers very often tend to do worse than those who use them moderately.'

Other reports have raised concerns about the potentially negative impact of social media on young people, and the disruptive behaviour associated with use of mobile phones and tablets in the classroom is being examined in the UK.

Beverly Amico, leader of outreach and development at the Association of Waldorf Schools of North America, explains that their approach uses 'time-tested truths about how children learn best'. Teachers encourage students to learn curriculum subjects by expressing themselves through artistic activities, such as painting and drawing, rather than consuming information downloaded onto a tablet.

For example, a typical lesson for fourth grade students might include learning about Norse mythology by making their own pictures of the stories, acquiring problem-solving and maths skills through knitting, or practising a modern language by playing a game of catch.

Amico insists that this more creative approach to education brings lessons to life and is far more effective than showing students a series of images on a screen.

'Lessons are delivered by a human being who not only cares about the child's education, but also about them as individuals,' she says. 'What do you remember as a child in the classroom? It is usually field trips, getting your hands dirty in a lab or a beautiful story. Those are the things that stay with you 50 years later.'

Waldorf classrooms are also designed to make students feel relaxed and comfortable, with natural wooden desks and plants. The idea is to remove the distraction of media and encourage stronger engagement between teacher and pupils during lessons.

Amico claims that one of the reasons people working in the digital industry are choosing a lo-tech, no-tech education for their children is that it teaches students the innovative thinking skills many employers desire. She adds that students weaned on technology often lack that ability to think creatively and problem solve.

General comprehension

Answer the following questions in complete sentences.

1 In the second paragraph, why do you think the expression 'despite its location' is used?
2 At the Waldorf School of the Peninsula, what approaches do the teachers prefer?

3 In the fourth paragraph, how does the writer describe the behaviour of students who use technical gadgets in the classroom?
4 Why does the writer use the term 'consuming information' to contrast with the Waldorf methodology?
5 Why are the people in the digital industry interested in lo-tech, no-tech education for their children?

State whether the following sentences are true or false. Justify your answers.

6 The school where the Silicon Valley employees prefer to send their children is unusually large.
7 The students bring their own devices into school.
8 In schools in East Asia where academic results are high, schools are careful not to use too much technology in classrooms.
9 Children in Waldorf schools are encouraged to be creative.
10 Waldorf students develop problem-solving and math skills through knitting.
11 Amico believes companies want to employ people with innovative thinking skills.

Vocabulary

Find words or phrases in the text which match the following meanings.

1 reject
2 spent money on
3 education with minimal or no technology
4 brought up with
5 think outside the box

Paper 2 practice task (4.1) – Parent-Teacher Association (PTA) mid-year meeting

You will hear a speech made by the School Director at a mid-year meeting of the Parent-Teacher Association (PTA). Answer the following questions.

1 Which new change will be popular with the older students?
2 What is the name of the social events organiser?
3 How many hours should teenagers sleep each night?
4 What are three challenges facing teenagers which rob them of sleep?
5 When will the new times be introduced?
6 Will staff and teachers be allowed to have mobile phones in school?
7 What should students do if they need to contact someone in an emergency?
8 What do the executives in Silicon Valley not allow?
9 Have any other schools introduced this ban?
10 Do the faculty support the Director on these changes?
11 Will the Director now discuss the changes with parents?

Listen again. State whether the following sentences are true or false.

12 The boys were very active at the Back to School Picnic.
13 The parent-teacher coffee mornings are well attended.
14 Parents are asked to sign up to help with the annual summer fête.
15 The School Director has three changes to introduce.
16 No other schools have banned mobile phones.

Mass media – Webpage

The shanyrak system in Kazakhstan

Schools in Kazakhstan have house groups called 'shanyraks'. The shanyrak is the roof of a yurt, where the framework overlaps in a criss-cross pattern which holds the structure together.

Figure 4.3 A shanyrak

Students in a shanyrak group are often from two different grade levels: one older and one younger. In that way links are formed across the school. Students remain in the same shanyrak group throughout their years in the school and usually with the same teacher-leader.

The older students take responsibility for the younger ones and as they progress up the school strong friendships develop. When the older group finally graduates, a new younger group of students joins the shanyrak and the students who were the youngest become the older ones.

The shanyrak system is focused more on cooperation and mutual support than competition. The students meet almost daily with their teacher-leader and they discuss problems and situations of every kind, with the emphasis strongly on respect and mutual support. They also undertake projects to support others less fortunate than themselves: they may make handicrafts to give or they may organise concerts and invite other students. One very popular activity is for a shanyrak group to plan and carry out a flash mob activity during break times. Suddenly loud music will be heard across the recreation area and a couple of the students from the shanyrak group will lead the way in a series of dance steps in time to the music. Everyone joins in – students and teachers – and everyone has fun and a bit of exercise between classes.

General comprehension

Answer the following questions in complete sentences.

1 What is a shanyrak?
2 In a shanyrak, how are students grouped?
3 What is the main focus of the shanyrak system?

4 What kind of activities do the students undertake?
5 What is a flash mob?

In the text below, a ninth grade student in an international school in Kazakhstan describes what the shanyrak group means to her.

Shanyrak means family to me

by Nazym Musin

Personal – Account

Shanyrak is a small social group of high school and middle school students which aims to improve communication across grade levels and to encourage mutual support and friendship. We often plan special events such as Health Day or Art Festival, and the best event can win the shanyrak group special award or even an excursion to a nearby cultural centre.

Shanyrak hours have always meant more than making friends with new people. It is all about growing in a caring environment where one becomes a brother or sister and the shanyrak tutor is a parent. From the first day I was called to the shanyrak hour, the time has passed by so quickly. It is important to mention how getting accustomed to the new school environment is greatly facilitated through the support of the older students. Being a member of this group itself is as comfortable as being surrounded by relatives because to me shanyrak means family.

The terms *homeroom group* or *advisory group* are used to describe the way students are organised into groups at the beginning of the day when attendance is taken and any bulletins shared. The homeroom/advisory teacher helps and supports the group throughout the school year in many different ways. Students know they can talk to this particular teacher about academic or social/emotional issues.

Discussion task

How does your school's homeroom/advisory group compare with the shanyrak system? Think about the similarities and differences, and then discuss them with a partner.

Mass media – Webpage

Why I love the IB

by Dr Catherine Barber

I love the IB. It's what got me where I am today: a commissioning editor for all things IB. I get to work with passionate authors to create resources that I hope will inspire a new generation.

I was very fortunate to spend my teenage years at an international school in Istanbul. I was plucked from the UK school system at 14 and never looked back. The IB Diploma meant that I took a much broader range of subjects than I would have taken at A Level, which was certainly painful at times (languages were never my forte!), but it allowed me to explore a path I would not have considered otherwise, and made me a much more well-rounded individual. Inspired by a wonderful teacher, I opted to take chemistry at Higher Level. Thanks to the IB, I had kept my options open.

When it came to deciding my university future, I chose to follow my newfound love of chemistry, and in particular, environmental chemistry. I received an offer from the University of Reading, without the need for an interview (unlike most of the friends I later made on my course, who had come via the A level route). Back then, IB was still a novelty, but the way it generates independent thinkers with the skills they need to hit the ground running at university stands strong.

IB prepared me well for university. Through my extended essay and TOK course, I had developed better critical thinking, inquiry, and independent research skills than my UK peers, which stood me in good stead for my final year independent research project in particular. I was much less phased by the mammoth task than my friends were. But most importantly for me, the fact that my IB education had required me to take maths meant that I did not have to take the dreaded 'Maths for Chemists' module, giving me the freedom to choose an extra module to supplement the environmental chemistry route I wanted to go down.

I didn't stop at my undergraduate degree. Spurred on by a thirst for discovery, which I'm certain was the result of my IB experience, my next step was a PhD in atmospheric chemistry. Although I had learned a lot during my undergraduate course, the independence, deadline juggling, and ambition that the IB had drilled into me is what really got me through the long days (and nights) of my PhD. I didn't stay in academia, I did something better. I now work in an industry that allows me to express and build on my love for the IB on a daily basis. I just hope what I do has some part to play in supporting and inspiring the IB spokespeople of the future.

General comprehension

Choose the two true statements according to the text. Give a quote from the text to support your answers.

a The IB requires students to take chemistry.
b The IB Diploma course offered possibilities to experience a wide range of subjects.
c The writer took languages at Higher Level.
d The encouragement to think independently offered by the IB Diploma course was an advantage when applying for a university place.
e The writer studied for the PhD mostly at night.
f The writer thinks the IB is not for everybody.

Text handling

Match the beginnings of the sentences with the most suitable endings.

1 Students taking the IB Diploma
2 Good teachers
3 Before going to university
4 The extended essay and TOK
5 Chemistry students need to

a students often prepare for an interview.
b study mathematics.
c can be inspirational.
d study a variety of subjects.
e prepare you to be analytical.

Zoom in on language

Idiomatic language

In the above text, the writer says '…with the skills they need to hit the ground running at university'. The phrase 'to hit the ground running' is used idiomatically. This means the words in the phrase have a different meaning from those of the individual words. In this case, the idiom means to make immediate and rapid progress. The writer was well prepared for the challenges of university and lost no time in beginning the course.

A second use of idiomatic language in the text is 'research skills…stood me in good stead'. It means that her research skills put her in a good position or place for her future. The word 'stead' originates from an old word for 'a place'.

In addition, 'to be spurred on' is another example of idiomatic language and means to be encouraged to do something. A spur is a piece of metal fixed to a horse rider's boot and when the horse is kicked in the side, it moves forward.

Paper 1 practice task

You have just started a university course of your choice. Write an email to your friend telling them about your first experiences and how the IB has prepared you for your studies. Use ideas from the text above as well as your own thoughts.

Write no more than 400 words.

Paper 2 practice task (4.2) – School announcements

Students are having lunch in the school canteen. You will hear a message for students in the school orchestra over the school loudspeaker system. State whether the following sentences are true or false.

1 This message is only for the choir.
2 The sopranos will practise for 30 minutes at lunchtime tomorrow.
3 The altos will rehearse in the choir room.
4 The tenors will practise after school tomorrow.

Paper 2 practice task (4.3) – School announcements

Students are in the lunchroom. You will hear a message for students in the school orchestra over the school loudspeaker system. Complete the following gaps. Use no more than three words for each gap.

1 As you know, we have a concert next Friday evening so I want to ____________ several important points.
2 They can ____________ the lights and disturb the audience.
3 Also, as you well know, there may be ____________ worn and only very little light make-up please.
4 Be sure your knees are covered when ____________.
5 Now boys, this ____________ for you.

Internal assessment (SL)

Figure 4.4 School: the best time of your life?

Examine the photograph above and consider the following points.

- What do you see in the picture? Describe only what you see. Do not give opinions.
- Reflect on the picture in connection with your experience of school and examinations.
- How important are examinations?
- Consider why adults often say 'school is the best time of your life'.
- What aspects of schools do you think can be considered 'the best time of your life'?
- Consider aspects of school life that are not covered by examinations.

Using the points above, spend 15 minutes preparing a presentation about the photograph. Use the preparation time to organise your ideas and plan the sequence of what you will talk about.

Your presentation should last 3 to 4 minutes, after which your teacher and other students will have the opportunity to comment or ask questions about what you have said. You must engage in a conversation with them. In total, this task should take approximately 15 minutes.

4.2 Community projects

Supporting communities

Life has changed significantly in the past 100 years. In the UK, villages used to be thriving communities, often having their own shop, bakery, post office, and a bus service connecting the village to larger towns and cities. Today you would be hard pressed to find even a post office. People no longer live and work in villages. Cars and supermarkets have made dependence on local amenities a thing of the past.

Mass media – Article

WORKING TOGETHER –volunteers raise money to save communities

Groups of volunteers from communities have been raising money to take over local amenities that might otherwise be lost. This has been facilitated by the Localism Act 2011, which gave local authorities more rights and powers to engage in planning. A network of such groups of people from different communities now exists, as this idea has become very popular. It is said that over 5000 assets have been taken over already and the number is increasing all the time.

One example of this is a small café in a Norfolk village. The café was up for sale and would probably have been turned into private housing, which would have meant there would no longer be a meeting place for local people to relax and chat with a hot drink or snack. A group of local people took the initiative and applied successfully for loans and grants to help buy the café and support fundraising efforts. They are now endeavouring to enable a community-run project.

Similarly, a swimming pool in Leeds was running at a loss and the local council decided they could no longer afford to support it. This meant there was no pool available for local people to learn to swim and keep healthy. A group of local citizens bought the pool and it is now serving the community.

In Oxford, a children's centre was to be closed but a group of residents raised the money to buy it by selling shares in the property to other local people. It is now successfully running and there is a nursery, a café, and a community drop-in centre. All of these facilities for local children and adults would have been lost without the successful plan to buy the property.

More and more residents are uniting to make their local area more attractive by buying up buildings to benefit the community and offer more opportunities for people to meet up and stay in touch with neighbours and friends.

The impact of change on people

Change is inevitable but one of the negative results of change is the impact it can have on all age groups. There is a growing awareness of isolation and loneliness. Many studies have revealed that people have said that to feel lonely and have no contact with other people of their own age and interests is worse than being hungry. The Prince's Countryside Fund is a charity established by His Royal Highness Charles, Prince of Wales. One main purpose of this charity is combating loneliness.

Along with other groups, residents have organised themselves to work together and keep shops and post offices open. The groups are often run by volunteers who are united in their awareness that communities need places to meet together and communicate.

TOK

How might the rights of one group supersede the rights of another? On what basis can moral rights be decided?

General comprehension

State whether the following sentences are true or false. Give a quote from the text to support your answers.

1 The café in Norfolk was bought by the government.
2 The children's centre in Oxford was bought by selling shares of the property.
3 The work of many volunteers is motivated by their belief that people need to meet together to avoid loneliness.

Vocabulary

Find words or phrases in the text which match the following meanings.

Paragraph 1

1 things that make life more comfortable
2 resources

Paragraph 2

3 a sum of money that is borrowed

Paragraph 3

4 when a business spends more than it earns
5 operating

Paragraph 4

6 a place to care for children

Paragraph 5

7 working together
8 help

Paragraph 6

9 condition of being alone
10 fighting

Paragraph 7

11 people who have their home in a place
12 understanding

Discussion task

In groups, talk about loneliness and how it might affect different age groups. Think about the difference between the two words 'isolation' and 'loneliness'. Consider the types of activities that might combat loneliness.

Task

With a partner, create a poster promoting one or more activities to get people together in school. Think about the following points before you begin.

- When? After school or lunchtime?
- Where? In school or outside?
- Who? Which age group is your activity for?
- Why? Give reasons for the activity/club/group.
- Organiser? Who will organise this?

Tips for creating a poster

- Use short sentences in the layout and don't overload your poster with text.
- Include sketches and pictures to attract attention.
- Think about including quotations.
- Don't forget to say where and when your activity is taking place.

WITH YOUR HELP WE CAN SAVE THE POST OFFICE

Greenham's post office is under threat from closure. The post office has served the villagers for over 100 years, providing not only postal services, but also selling fresh and frozen food (with weekly deliveries of eggs from Upton Farms) in addition to a range of stationery, newspapers, and magazines. More significantly, the post office has long been the hub of village life – a place to call in for a chat and catch up on local events or post messages on the noticeboard when somebody wants to sell unwanted household items or is looking for help in the garden. However, following the death of the postmistress in summer, the building is to be sold.

Greenham Community Enterprise was formed by a group of villagers to purchase the post office and run it with a team of volunteers for the benefit of the area. More than £150 000 has been raised so far towards buying the building and reopening the post office. We are close to our target now.

Join us at a meeting in the Village Hall on Saturday, 5th November, 6.00 p.m., to discuss further fundraising ideas. Please come along, get involved, and share your ideas. With your help, we can be successful and make the post office once again part of our community.

General comprehension

Answer the following questions in complete sentences.

1 According to the text, what was the most important service the post office offered?
2 Was the post office run by a man or a woman?
3 If the initiative is successful, who will run the post office?
4 How much money has been raised by the Greenham Community Enterprise to buy the building?

Grammar in context

Many nouns can be formed from verbs. In the above text, the word *closure* is the noun derived from the verb *to close*.

Complete the table with the nouns derived from the verbs in the list.

Verb	Noun
succeed	
discuss	
sell	
deliver	
threaten	

Presentation task

Do some research into rural life in the country you are currently living in. Identify any existing initiatives to revive rural communities.

Collect your information to give a three-minute presentation to the class or small group. Be prepared to answer questions from your audience.

Community concerns

Mass media – Reader's letter

The Middle England Gazette
Letters to the editor

Dear Sir or Madam,

I am writing to express my concern about the serious demise of our village and to ask if you or your readers have any solutions to this problem.

The difficulties are as follows: our village branch of the Post Office closed several months ago. Our local shop is a farm shop selling local produce, but it is only open on Wednesdays and Fridays and for other foodstuffs we need to travel to Bominster. The library bus no longer comes to us, which is also a great loss. In addition, our local bus service has now been radically reduced to one bus per hour on three days a week.

The village is growing in size. We have many young families moving into the village. There are even two kindergartens and I have been informed that both have waiting lists, but the primary school was closed several years ago. Our children have to travel to the nearest town, Bominster, either by taking the school bus each day, or by being driven by their parents.

I am deeply saddened by the loss of community life and spirit in the village. The local church which used to be the place where people met and chatted regularly now only has services once a month and the prayer group has been discontinued. Everyone is always in a hurry, but there is nowhere for people to meet and chat even if they do have time. It is especially hard for older people who are no longer as mobile as they were, which makes travelling by bus very challenging. The village has no heart and the community spirit which used to be alive and well has been lost.

Do other villages suffer from the same problems and if so what can be done to remedy this unhappy situation?

Yours faithfully,
William Goldsmith

General comprehension

Answer the following questions in complete sentences.

1 Which of the problems addressed by the writer affect:
   a the children?
   b the churchgoers?
   c the community generally?
2 What does the writer ask at the end of the letter?

Mass media – Reader's letter

Dear Sir or Madam,

What a sorry tale Mr Goldsmith shared in his letter on 12 April. He is right and this is the trend across the country. The facilities which we took for granted in the past – local shops, a post office, bus services, libraries, and so on – are being reduced at a rapid rate and often simply disappearing.

Our village is similarly badly served but a number of initiatives have been started to address the problems. A group of us who are concerned about these issues have formed a Village Community Group. We have invited people to become active members of the group for a nominal annual fee and we plan to produce a newsletter three times a year where we talk about difficulties and try to find solutions with the help of the villagers. We have also erected a village noticeboard where people can share ideas, advertise items for sale or exchange, and offer car transport.

One idea is for people to get together for shopping trips to the nearest market town. We did this by asking car drivers to let us know when they would be going into town, but that became very complicated, so now we just have a list of people who drive into town on market day and are willing to take a passenger or two. This has had limited success as it depends very much on good will and cooperation from both sides. However, the benefits have been that people are communicating and meeting new people in the village.

Our next step will be to hold a village community meeting, but as yet we have not found a venue for this. One option could be to meet in the kindergarten, but some committee members anticipate problems with the seating as the chairs are all for small children not villagers. This could result in very low attendance, which would not be very helpful.

I would be very pleased to hear from Mr Goldsmith and others who are concerned about the demise of village life, and perhaps we can share ideas and become a force for change.

Yours faithfully,
Mabel Morrison

General comprehension

State whether the following sentences are true or false. Give a quote from the text to support your answers.

1 The writer agrees with Mr Goldsmith.
2 The writer's village also has problems.
3 A community group has been formed but so far they have only discussed solutions.
4 They have a venue for the next meeting.

Mass media – Reader's letter

Dear Sir or Madam,

Inspired by the letters on your page recently about the demise of village life and some solutions, I decided to put pen to paper and add my views from life in our little village. I must note that this is the first time in my very long life when I have felt inspired to write a letter to a newspaper.

In our village, we also have a village group which publishes a quarterly newsletter. One very simple and cheap initiative that we undertook was to locate a couple of chairs in a place that offers a good view of the countryside and invite people to take a seat and relax for a few minutes. This has led to people meeting there: mothers appearing with their children who play on the smooth stretch of car-free road with balls and skateboards, workers who take a walk during their lunch break, and so on. We have been very surprised by the success of this venture.

Another initiative which was not quite so successful was our clean-up day. Here we invited villagers to bring sacks, gardening gloves, and pickers and to walk in and around the village collecting trash.

My daughter lives in a village in Germany which is really similar in nature to ours. They have a lively community group which organises summer fêtes and Christmas markets, and the latest venture is a Living Advent Calendar. For this, each day during Advent a different family hosts a short celebration with Christmas style drinks, usually warm wine and snacks, in their garden. The hosts prepare a few carols to sing together. The hosts for each day display the number of their day prominently so that other villagers can see where the event will take place and when. This is a lovely idea which we could copy, as we have done with Christmas markets in England.

Yours faithfully,
Peter Robinson

General comprehension

State whether the following sentences are true or false. Give a quote from the text to support your answers.

1 The writer is very young.
2 They have found a simple initiative to encourage people to meet and talk.
3 The clean-up day was a massive success.
4 The writer's daughter is German.

Mass media – Editor's letter

A note to readers of the Letters Page from the editor

As the number of responses to this topic has become rather large and we have other themes to cover, please address any further suggestions to the newly founded group:

Villagers for Villages
PO Box 345.

A note to the Villagers for Villages from the kindergarten in Bominster.

Dear organisers,

We, the kindergarten teachers, would welcome you to meet as a group in our facility. The entrance lobby is separate from the rest of the rooms and may be used during the evenings as long as one person takes responsibility for opening and locking the gate and the room. Of course, we request that no food or drinks are brought on to the premises.

We have several adult-sized chairs, but suggest that people bring their own.

We have another suggestion. In our building, we have four full-size bookcases which are not suitable for use with our children. As the lack of a library bus was mentioned in one letter, we would like to suggest that villagers bring books they no longer want and leave them on the shelves for others to borrow. This would only be possible in the afternoons, when fewer children are on the premises, and access would be limited to the entrance area only for security reasons.

I look forward to hearing your views on these two suggestions.

Yours,
Felicity and colleagues

General comprehension

Answer the following questions in complete sentences.

1 Who should the writers now contact to continue this discussion?
2 Why is the kindergarten not an ideal meeting place?
3 What does the kindergarten teacher suggest doing with the four bookcases?
4 What area of the school are the adults allowed to access?

Tips for writing a letter to the editor

In this section of Letters to the Editor, the register and format used are formal. Note the layout of the letters and the opening and closing words.

- The opening paragraphs are short and state briefly the aim of the letter.
- The following paragraphs expand on the aim, but in a concise manner.
- The final sentence in the last short paragraph looks for some kind of support, or a way to solve the problem. It also invites others to contribute.
- As the newspaper editor's name is unknown, the letters begin *Dear Sir or Madam*, and end *Yours faithfully*. If the recipient's name is known, the correct ending is *Yours sincerely*.

Discussion task

Together with a partner, examine the letters and identify examples of language which are more formal.

Mass media – Article

STAY CLOSE TO ME

HOW A MAORI SONG SAVED A SMALL TOWN

New Zealand, Aotearoa – the land of the long white cloud – is an island nation parked in the heart of the South Pacific Ocean. Whereas much of the world's population is said to be connected by six degrees of separation, there is a claim that New Zealanders are separated by just two. Much of New Zealand has a small-town feel while its people maintain a fire in their bellies and a confidence and adaptability that is renowned. Visitors are always taken aback by the abundance of beauty and the laid-back way of life. The endless farms, rivers, lakes, mountains, sheep, and forests are no doubt one reason why Kiwis (as the local people are affectionately known) are as outdoorsy as they are. World-class sports people are born and bred in the smallest and unlikeliest of communities.

Legend teaches that long, long ago Maui and his brothers were out fishing in their *waka* (canoe) one night and together pulled from the depths of the sea a fish so enormous it became what is now called the North Island or Te Ika a Maui – the fish of Maui. So fierce was the battle to entrap the fish that it was left with scars and bumps all over. Those are the mountains, rivers, and lakes today.

Maori language, *Te Reo*, has a growing influence on Kiwi English. Even those with little training comfortably understand *whanau, iwi, maunga,* and *whare* (family, tribe, mountain, and house).

It's a rite of passage for all New Zealand children to learn traditional dance such as *poi* or the *haka*. They are lucky to be nurtured in such a culturally rich society. Global citizenship is right there on their doorstep, in the shops, at the park, around the playground, and on the radio, too.

Patea sits humbly on the west coast of Te Ika a Maui. It is a town with a modern day population of just 1200 souls. Driving through, the less observant might just blink and miss it. Patea is the epitome of a small town: rural, tight knit,

To what extent would you agree that 'global citizenship is right there on their doorstep'? Justify your answers with examples from the text.

When we *entwine* something, we twist it together or around something.

and historically dependent on a single industry. For the people of Patea, their dependency was on the freezing works. With hearts of gold and hands as rough as guts, they got by slaughtering and freezing lamb and beef to eventually ship to the four corners of the world. It was all going well until the early eighties. Families were being fed. People were getting together each day to support each other, as if it wasn't a town but one large *whanau*.

Just 99 years after the formation of the West Coast Meat and Produce Export Company, in 1982 workers hung up their bloody aprons and put down their knives one last time. A decline in the national meat industry led the British-owned Vestey Group to make their decision to close the freezing works. Little regard was shown for the hundreds of livelihoods dependent on those hard-working folk who turned up to the eyesore which was the Patea Freezing Works.

But like a phoenix, the predominantly Maori locals embraced the opportunity to show the world what they were made of – the grit, the community, and the songs. Led by two of New Zealand's national treasures, the self taught and chart-topping musician Maui Dalvanius Prime and the linguist Ngoi Pēwhairangi, a plan was born to retain identity and culture in Patea.

'Poi E' is a pretty, powerful *waiata* (song) that evokes the deep traditional sense of connection shared by Maori and other Polynesian cultures with the rhythmic hip swings. And the words 'Stay close to me', 'draw near', 'don't go astray', 'take care of me', 'be entwined around me', 'our love...binds', say it all.

The song is gorgeous, driven by the force of the woman's chants entwined with rap and computer game type beeps and bops. Performed by the Patea Maori Club, 'Poi E' became the first all-Maori song to make it to the New Zealand charts. It remained there for 22 weeks, including four weeks at number one. Maui's island was captivated by this new traditional sound, the story, the women, the man, the happiness, the rejuvenation of a town, and the affection for Patea was overwhelming. A community was unbeaten, lifted through song.

In 1985, as the Patea Maori Club performed for HRH Queen Elizabeth II at the Royal Gala Performance in London, each woman and man chanting and rapping truly showed the world what they were made of – real community.

Figure 4.5 The Patea Maori Club remains strong and vibrant in its mission for its members to be ambassadors for Patea, New Zealand, and Maori language and customs. This photo is of the renovated hall, which was made possible by sponsors and donors nationwide

General comprehension

Look at a map of New Zealand. Then answer the following questions in complete sentences.

1 What is the connection between New Zealand and a long white cloud?
2 What does the writer claim is special about New Zealanders?
3 What surprises visitors to New Zealand?
4 What is the story of the North Island? Use your own words to tell it.
5 Why does the writer write 'global citizenship is right there on their doorstep'?

State whether the following sentences are true or false. Give a quote from the text to support your answers.

6 The people of Patea work in a supermarket.
7 The people of Patea are like a family.
8 The factory was ugly so the owners closed it.
9 The owners were very concerned about the people who lost their jobs.
10 Two local politicians wrote a song for the people.

Vocabulary

Match the words (1–6) as they are used in the text with their meanings (a–f).

1 laid-back	a a very ugly sight
2 maintain	b plenty of something
3 renowned	c relaxed
4 abundance	d keep or preserve something
5 epitome	e well-known
6 eyesore	f a typical example

4.3 Getting together

Unusual ideas for get-togethers

Mass media – Webpage

The World Cup

London is the often described as the most multicultural city in the world. So with that in mind, we thought it must be possible to meet up with fans from every one of the 32 nations taking part in the 2018 Football World Cup to watch matches together.

We took three weeks off work for the venture with the intention of watching a World Cup match with fans of every nation without ever leaving London. This website is a record of the messages and photos from each of the venues where we met fans of every nationality.

The original idea came about when we tried to plan where we would meet to watch the matches together. We thought it would be fun to contact fans of each game being played, to watch the games together, face to face. To do

Figure 4.6 Football fans watching the World Cup

this each of us contacted fans from different nationalities and arranged where we could watch together.

We met Nigerian fans in a Nigerian barber's shop. We joined Panama fans in a café near the Embassy of Panama. (Did you know there are only about 250 Panamanians in the whole of England?) The noisiest were from Iceland. They sang their national anthem with gusto.

The first match we watched was the opening match, Russia versus Saudi Arabia, with plenty of Russian fans, but we struggled to find any Saudi fans in London. We managed to join up with fans from Egypt, Iran, Portugal, Australia, Iceland, Nigeria, Costa Rica, South Korea, Panama, and Tunisia, to name a few.

We received invitations to watch the games from many quarters. For example, we got invitations from the Korean Cultural Centre and even from an Argentinian family to watch the game in their home.

The venture was three weeks well spent. We met many new friends from different nations, all with a shared interest. We began to learn more about other cultures and intercultural communication.

General comprehension

Answer the following questions in complete sentences.

1 What was the novel idea the writer and his friends had?
2 How did they set about organising this?
3 Who were the noisiest fans they met?
4 Which fans did they have difficulty finding?
5 Who invited them to watch the game in their home?

Mass media – Social media post

IY **A WHITE PARTY**
FRIDAY, 7TH MAY, 6.01 PM

NO PLANS THIS EVENING? JOIN US FOR A WHITE PARTY HOSTED IN THE MIDDLE OF CITY PARK.

Everyone is welcome, as long as you come dressed in white and with everything you need for a fun evening of meeting new people and sharing great conversations and food. No need to sign up or pre-register. This is a spontaneous event and we look forward to seeing you at 8.00 p.m. this evening.

General comprehension

Answer the following questions in complete sentences.

1 Where is the white party being held?
2 Why is it called a white party?
3 Why is the party considered to be spontaneous?

Mass media – Article

HOW MOVING A BOOKSHOP BECAME A SPONTANEOUS EVENT

In Southampton, a city in the south of England, rents on the High Street for shop premises had recently been raised considerably. As a result, a small independent bookshop was forced to look for new premises. A nearby suitable site, with a more reasonable rent, was found further down the High Street. This was important for the book shop owners as they were concerned that moving away from the High Street would mean a loss of trade. On the High Street, people are always walking past. They glance in the windows, then often come in and look around, which leads to sales, so the location is important.

The problem was how to move all of the books from one shop to the other on a pedestrian precinct.

The three employees decided that the only way to do this was by passing the books from hand to hand. It was several hundred metres from one shop to the other, which meant there would be a lot of walking back and forth to do.

They set up their system with one person in the old shop who would take the books from the shelves and walk halfway towards the second person, then hand over the books and go back for the next pile, while the second person carried the books to the third person who would take them into the new shop.

This process attracted a lot of attention and some amusement from shoppers and passers-by on the High Street and within a very short time people were offering to help. Suddenly the whole process was speeded up as more and more people joined in and the books were being handed from one person to the next with minimal walking necessary.

During the course of the morning, people joined the chain, or left as they had shopping to do and other people took their places. By the evening, the books were all in the new shop. What an amazing example of spontaneous social organisation!

Vocabulary

Match the words (1–10) as they are used in the text with their meaning (a–j).

1 rent	a a vehicle-free zone
2 premises	b a series of actions to achieve a particular result
3 suitable	c a quick look
4 glance	d something which is right or appropriate for the purpose
5 location	e the building or land occupied by a business
6 pedestrian precinct	f very small quantity or degree
7 employees	g a place where something happens
8 process	h not planned or arranged
9 minimal	i the money you pay regularly to have or use something
10 spontaneous	j people who work for a company or business

Paper 1 practice task (SL)

The three social groups above are all very different. Which one would you have enjoyed the most? Why?

Imagine that you were part of one of the groups and write a report about it for your school magazine. Write 250–400 words.

Tips for writing a report

- Give the date and type of group you were in.
- Use the past simple tense to write about what happened.
- Give descriptions of people and places.
- Give recommendations to your peers.
- Give personal reflections on the success of the activity.
- End with a positive comment about your participation.

Internal assessment (SL)

Figure 4.7 Learning about each other is an important social skill

Examine the photograph above and consider the following points.

- Begin by describing what you can see in the picture.
- Consider the caption and what it tells you about this situation.
- How important is it to learn about each other's interests and culture?
- What consequences can it have if this is neglected?
- Give examples from your own experience and your school.
- Extend the idea of the value of understanding people to a wider global perspective.

Using the points above, spend 15 minutes preparing a presentation about the photograph. Use the preparation time to organise your ideas and plan the sequence of what you will talk about.

Your presentation should last 3 to 4 minutes, after which your teacher and other students will have the opportunity to comment or ask questions about what you have said. You must engage in a conversation with them. In total, this task should take approximately 15 minutes.

4.4 Clubs and groups

Enjoying time with people who have similar interests

Staying in contact with friends and teachers from secondary school and university can be a great way to find work and build lifelong friendships.

An interview with an Alumni Coordinator

Figure 4.8 Institut Montana Zugerberg

Mass media – Interview

Interviewer: Hi Velia. Thank you so much for taking time to talk to me today. You work with alumni. Some people may not be familiar with the term alumni. Can you explain it briefly for us?

Velia: Of course. Alumni is a Latin term used to refer to former students of a specific college, university, or other school. I'm often asked by fellow alumni if they need to have graduated from Institut Montana in order to be considered 'alumni' and participate in our reunions. Here, being alumni doesn't necessarily mean that the person graduated from the institute. We consider all our ex-students alumni, regardless of the length of their stay and of their graduation at Institut Montana.

Interviewer: And are you the Alumni Coordinator for the school. Is that your correct title?

Velia: My title is Head of Community Relations and my responsibilities can be simplified to three main areas: connecting, activating, and involving our alumni community.

My goal is to build a more lively and interconnected community through the development of new communication tools that will facilitate social exchange and, as a result, create worldwide opportunities within our community.

I'm proud to say that in June we launched a private networking space. Now, wherever we are in the world, we can organise or join events, create and lead interest groups, exchange opportunities (such as jobs and internships, leads, and project works), promote our companies and start-ups, or find Montana partners.

Part of my job is to integrate alumni in the present community for the benefit of current and future students. I'm working at increasing the alumni role in the future development of the school through projects across the generations. I include alumni in the school programme and in enriched activities, such as entrepreneurship as mentors or inspirational role models.

However, my job starts with the current students and the alumni induction programme. It is the development of these students after they leave our school and their connection and attachment to Institut Montana, as well as to the people who supported their growth, that is also part of our future.

Interviewer: What made you want to take up this work?

Velia: I think it was the feeling I have for Institut Montana Zugerberg – the fact that it is my home away from home. I'm an alumni myself and I have a passion to want to see students succeed.

Interviewer: Is there a specific type of training for someone in your position? If not, what was your training?

Velia: Not to my knowledge. I studied Business Management at Bocconi University in Milan and I was very fortunate to be able to receive intensive training in all of the departments of my family's business. This helped me develop comprehensive project development skills. Then I would say my personal experience as a boarding student at Institut Montana, together with my personal motivation to fulfil the position, contributed to my training.

Interviewer: What qualities would you say make you the right person for the job?

Velia: I have very practical organisational skills, such as managing and developing projects. I have a lot of new ideas and I am able to multitask. I also feel I am able to relate well to people of all ages. It is a necessary skill for the job.

Interviewer: What does a typical 'day at the office' look like for you?

Velia: I never have a dull moment, and there is no such thing as a typical day.

Interviewer: I gather you travel quite a lot. What kind of events do you organise?

Velia: I organise alumni reunions at Institut Montana and around the world. I also organise other events, which range from simple class dinners to fundraising dinners. Of course, I organise the highlight of the alumni calendar, the Homecoming. That takes place every two years, and a lot of members of the alumni community join in from all over the world.

Interviewer: Can you tell us a little about the kind of work your alumni are doing now and where some of them are?

Velia: Oh wow, our alumni are a diverse group of passionate people. Let me give you just three examples. My brother, Dr Antonio Tricoli, is a Professor of Nanotechnology at the Australian National University. He and his team have made real progress researching methods to prevent skin cancer and other health problems through breath analysis.

Then, Thomas Hanan has been awarded EY Entrepreneur of the Year. He convinced the jury of his skill as an entrepreneur. He not only has excellent digital instincts, but he is a responsible employer. Webrepublic, his company, is one of the best-known digital agencies, not only in Switzerland but also around the world.

Finally, Marc Forster is a film director, film producer, and screenwriter who I am sure you have heard of. He is best known for directing the films *Monster's Ball*, *Finding Neverland*, *Stranger than Fiction*, *The Kite Runner*, *Quantum of Solace*, and *World War Z*.

Interviewer: And we could include you as another example of alumni who are doing great things. I know you work extremely hard to keep everyone involved in the group and am very aware that you also travel all over the world meeting up with alumni and telling prospective students and their families about your school.

Velia: Yes, thank you for the compliment. I'm lucky to have such a wonderful job.

Interviewer: What excites and inspires you about your position?

Velia: I'm always excited to see the young students arriving at Institut Montana Zugerberg at the beginning of a new school year. They experience for the first time what it really means to be away from home and outside of their comfort zone, as I did. And then later, I really enjoy seeing these young students leave after becoming citizens, logical thinkers, and good problem solvers who are equipped with a moral compass to make a difference in our society.

Interviewer: Have you had any funny or exciting experiences in your work?

Velia: Yes, I have had many different experiences. My favourite was when I led the summer programme with a team that included five recent Montana graduates and a fellow alumna. The atmosphere we created together was wonderful for everyone. We enjoyed four weeks of work and fun, which were unforgettable for everyone involved.

Interviewer: How do you see your role in ten years' time? What do you think you will be doing then and how will it be different?

Velia: In ten years' time, I still see myself working for something that gives me a sense of purpose. I hope to remain involved, directly or indirectly, with Institut Montana. I think that technology will reduce some of today's challenges. Communication will be even easier and hopefully we will overcome the challenges of maintaining our alumni databases.

General comprehension

Answer the following questions in complete sentences.

1 Is it necessary to have completed all your education and have graduated from a school to become an alumni?
2 What are Velia's three main responsibilities as she sees them?
3 In her role, what is Velia aiming to build?
4 What was created in June and why?
5 Why does she want to integrate alumni in the present school?
6 What qualities does someone in Velia's position need?
7 What is the highlight of the alumni calendar?

Vocabulary

Match the words (1–10) as they are used in the text with their meanings (a–m). There are more options than you need.

1 reunion	a continue something
2 facilitate	b a person who employs people
3 integrate	c a very strong emotion
4 mentor	d read aloud
5 passion	e do more than one thing at a time
6 multitask	f feeling or mood of a place
7 diverse	g destroy
8 employer	h make possible
9 experience	i come into contact with
10 atmosphere	j great deal of variety
	k combine to become part of a whole group
	l meeting again after a period of time
	m a person who advises another over a period of time

Paper 1 practice task

You have been offered the role of Alumni Coordinator after you graduate. Decide whether or not this would be an interesting job for you and explain your answer in a formal letter to the Human Resources department of your school. Give a detailed account, including reasons or causes. Consider why they might have thought you would be suitable for this post in your answer.

SL students should write 250–400 words. HL students should write 450–600 words.

For tips on how to write a formal letter, see page 54 of Chapter 2, Experiences.

The organisation parkrun has started running groups based on the simple principles that runners meet weekly to run 5 km together and it is free. Many countries around the world have taken up the idea and established parkrun events which are gaining new followers after every run.

Mass media – Webpage

The growth of parkrun

parkrun organises weekly 5 km runs that are free for anyone to take part in.

The timed runs usually take place in parks and are open to all abilities and ages, everyone is welcome.

parkrun in Dublin, Ireland

The Marlay Park course in Dublin is run on tarmac and gravel paths. The paths can become muddy and waterlogged on rainy days. In this case, signs will be in place to warn runners to be careful.

This course uses shared paths. Therefore it is essential that runners are mindful of other park users. Please do not put other users in danger.

To help reduce our impact on the environment, runners are encouraged to make their way to the event on foot or by public transport. Another option is to car-share, however parking may be limited so try to arrive early.

parkrun in Sydney, Australia

The course in Sydney is in Sydney Park and is run on tar and concrete. The park is on the south side of the city and is made up of 40 hectares of lush grass, landscaped gardens, rolling hills, meandering pathways, and picturesque wetlands. Creeks flow through the park and attract all kinds of birds.

Runners' comments:

Marley (17) from Sydney: I had heard about parkrun but I wasn't sure if I would be fast enough to join in a run. Last year my friend convinced me to try it. That was the best running experience of my life and now I run every week.

Sue (22) from Glebe, a suburb of Sydney: My husband and I have always been long-distance runners, but parkrun gives us that special feeling of community – we often meet the same people on the weekly run and it is simply part of our fitness routine now.

John (19) from Auckland, New Zealand: I run every week back home, so when I knew I would be applying for a study place here, I searched for parkrun. I came here a few months ago and through running I am making new friends.

Siobhan (20) from Dublin: I have only just started running and I love the fact that so many people taking part in the parkrun here in Marlay Park are just like me – slow!

Finbar (35) from Donegal: I am here on holiday and usually run about 20 km a week, so this is a fun run for me and a chance to chat to people.

General comprehension

Answer the following questions in complete sentences.

1 According to the introduction, what groups of people take part in the run?
2 In the description of the Dublin run, which phrase tells you that the runners do not exclusively have the use of the park?
3 In the description of the Sydney run, which word tells you that parts of the park are especially beautiful?

Text handling

Arrange these words from the text into three groups: adjectives, nouns, and verbs. Three words can be both verbs and nouns.

concrete	meandering	lush	path	picturesque
rolling	try	use	users	week

Mass media – Webpage

Lawn bowling – originally considered the most quintessential of British sports

Figure 4.9 People playing lawn bowls

So, what is lawn bowls?

Each player has four weighted bowls – or woods – that are heavier on one side, giving them a bias. The objective is to roll these bowls along a flat grass bowling green, approximately 110–130 ft (34–40 m) long, towards a much smaller white ball, or jack. Points are scored for the bowls closest to the jack.

The British game can be traced back to the 13th century and relies on a mix of precision, patience, and at times, power (when performing a drive to knock an opponent's wood clear of the jack). There is also an indoor version and the appeal is to all age groups.

How popular is the sport?

There are said to be more than 400 000 bowlers in England, while Scotland has nearly 100 000. The annual World Championships usually pull in around 3 million television viewers.

The sport of bowls is played across the world. World Bowls is the recognised international federation for the sport of bowls, which is played from Argentina to Zimbabwe and 53 places in between.

Championships are held every four years. The first one was held in Australia in 1966. Since 2008, the men's and women's events have been held together. Gold, silver, and bronze medals are awarded to the winners, who play in teams of five players. There is also a trophy for the best overall team in the championship: the Leonard Taylor trophy for men and the Taylor trophy for women.

The history of lawn bowling

Historians believe that the game developed from the Egyptians. The sport of lawn bowls is the forerunner of curling, a tremendously popular winter version played in northern countries (including Canada) on ice. The oldest lawn bowls site still played on is in Southampton, England: the Southampton Old Bowling Green which was first used in 1299. It is said to be the world's oldest bowling green.

The legend of Sir Francis Drake at Plymouth and his love of bowling

Legend says that in July 1588, word came that the Spanish Armada had been sighted and so an English force led by Sir Francis Drake left Plymouth to meet it. It is said that when Drake was told of its approach, he simply replied that he had plenty of time to finish his game of bowls before defeating the Spanish! Was it an example of his courage and confidence or just knowledge of the tides and his awareness that his boats could only leave at high tide a couple of hours later? Whatever the reason, generations of British schoolchildren heard this story first at school, and the connection with bowls makes a good story even if it cannot be proved.

Maintaining interest for the sport amongst young people

Lawn bowling is often seen as a sport played by old people. So, changing the appeal of a sport once thought to be the domain of the grey-haired set was an important step towards getting young people interested. The change has come in the form of the introduction of barefoot bowls. The Australians had the idea first, but barefoot bowls is also being embraced by the British. No sign of the white blouses and the long grey trousers that used to remind you of school uniforms – and obviously you don't need the shoes. But knowing that a bowl could weigh up to a kilo, you ought to avoid dropping one on your toes! London has started the movement and barefoot bowls is now being played at Finsbury Park Bowls Club. Accompanied by stands selling street food, with DJs and palm trees to provide distractions for those who aren't taking it too seriously, and expert help at hand for those who are, barefoot bowl is bowling's version of beach volleyball.

Figure 4.10 People playing barefoot bowls

General comprehension

Answer the following questions in complete sentences.

1 When did the game of bowls originate in the United Kingdom?
2 Is the playing of bowls a sport unique to the UK?
3 Why is the paragraph about Sir Francis Drake and the Spanish Armada called a legend?
4 Why do you think barefoot bowls appeals more to young people?

Zoom in on grammar

should* and *ought to

We use *should* and *ought to* to say what is the best thing or the right thing to do. There is no difference in the meaning.

Before you start cooking, you ***should*** *wash your hands.*

We have a vocabulary quiz tomorrow, so I ***ought to*** *study.*

Grammar in context

Find an example of the use of *ought to* in the text about lawn bowling.

Intercultural activity

Is there a sport or social activity which is special for your culture or the culture you live in? Discuss with a partner.

Presentation task

Based on research that you do individually, choose one of the following sports (a sport which you don't play or watch) and prepare a three-minute presentation for your fellow students.

- curling
- ice hockey
- baseball
- cricket
- beach volleyball
- tennis

Be prepared to engage in a discussion with your audience at the end of the presentation and answer any questions. Listen and respond to their own accounts of the sports.

Mass media – Article

TOK

On what basis might some musical instruments be judged as more 'artistic' than others? Can the arts be considered a system of knowledge with a rigid framework for assessment? Is judgement in art purely subjective?

UKULELE REVIVAL

The ukulele is undergoing a revival. It is as popular now as it was 100 years ago when it first became a much-played instrument. It originated in the 19th century as a Hawaiian adaptation of the Portuguese machete, a small guitar-like instrument introduced to Hawaii by Portuguese immigrants mainly from Madeira and the Azores.

This is a reaction from one enthusiastic ukulele player who reports about her experience.

I had never played a ukulele until about three years ago when, during a visit to a good friend of mine, I picked up her ukulele and started strumming it. As I had studied the guitar quite seriously when I was in my twenties, it was relatively easy for me to play. Anyway, she insisted that I join her ukulele group. I soon realised that the two men who were running the group didn't know much about music; they were downloading song sheets from the internet that were full of errors. I could hear this while others couldn't. Sometimes they would struggle with a song and not really understand why it

Figure 4.11 A band of ukulele players

wouldn't work. They also didn't understand rhythm and had a poor sense of timing. So, bit by bit I took over and the two men, who were understandably miffed, left the group. Since then the group has gone from strength to strength and I now have around 20 members, about half of whom I have taught from scratch, and a full diary of appearances.

We call ourselves The Village Green Ukulele Society. The name comes from a song written by Ray Davies of The Kinks in the 1960s. It was originally titled 'The Village Green Preservation Society' but we have adapted the title and re-written the lyrics with a lot of local references and use it as our theme song.

We play at church events, village fêtes, and also in retirement and care homes. Our repertoire is mainly from the 1960s, so the older people love to sing along to the old familiar tunes. This year we are particularly busy in November because of the numerous events being held to mark the centenary of the end of the First World War. We are practising hard for three local gigs at the moment and I have been busy arranging medleys of First World War songs. We also feature in the local pantomime, and Christmas and carol services are just around the corner! As I said, we are fully booked!

About the ukulele

The ukulele is one of the easiest instruments to learn as it has only four strings, and there are a lot of tunes you can play after mastering some basic strumming patterns so you soon feel like a player. In fact, there are a whole lot of tunes you can play with just four chords. It's not an expensive instrument and as the groups are quite big, it is also a social experience. What's not to like? Meet your friends, have fun, and play music together!

Why play the Ukulele?

The ukulele is small, convenient, and relatively inexpensive, and one can often quickly and easily learn the basics to a rewarding level. One can then undertake a world tour with only hand luggage. Some people go so far as to say that playing a tune on a ukulele is a way of identifying good music. If the composition is good, it sounds good on a ukulele; the very limitations of the instrument encourage thinking creatively about music.

General comprehension

Answer the following questions in complete sentences.

1 How was the ukulele introduced into Hawaii?
2 How did the writer come to be the leader of the ukulele group?
3 How is the recent surge in interest for the ukulele explained?
4 What is the connection of the ukulele group to the 1960s?
5 Why is the group particularly busy in November?

5 Sharing the planet

5 Sharing the planet

Research questions

- Why is it important that we take care of the Earth?
- In what ways can we change the negative influences affecting the places we live in?
- How can we work together to share the planet and live responsibly?

Objectives

- To examine issues related to climate change.
- To discuss these issues in a class debate.
- To demonstrate an understanding of the benefits and disadvantages of plastic.
- To outline the role tourism plays in global pollution.
- To look at the role of space exploration.

Language skills objectives

- To practise interactive oral skills in relation to the social organisation theme.
- To revise the use of phrasal verbs.
- To revise the use of the past continuous and passive voice.
- To practise writing formal and informal letters and emails.

TOK

Species extinction appears to be a natural part of the Earth's life cycle. On what basis should it be decided which species are 'saved'? On what basis should emotion be allowed to influence the discussion?

There is an extraordinary diversity of life on planet Earth and it is the responsibility of humanity to protect and care for it. We share the planet with many different species of life – an estimated 8.7 million species. As all life needs an environment in which to develop, we also share responsibility for maintaining healthy habitats and ensuring that planet Earth, already over four and a half billion years old, continues to provide a safe environment for many more years to come. There are still unknown parts of our planet and solar system: the deepest oceans and the outer space surrounding Earth are waiting to be explored. As we observe changes in climate, the effects of pollution, and the disappearance of ecosystems and the species within them, we must all make choices and take responsibility for preserving the planet for future generations.

5.1 Climate change

Protecting the planet

Mass media – Article

A *reservoir* is a natural or artificial lake that is used as a water supply.

WHY FRESH WATER SHORTAGES WILL CAUSE THE NEXT GREAT GLOBAL CRISIS

As reservoirs dry up across the world, a billion people have no access to safe drinking water. Rationing and a battle to control supplies will follow.

Figure 5.1 Dry reservoirs mean water shortages

Water is the driving force of all nature claimed Leonardo da Vinci. For our planet, unfortunately, supplies are now running dry – at an alarming rate. The world's population continues to soar, but that rise in numbers has not been matched by an accompanying increase in supplies of fresh water.

The consequences are proving to be profound. Across the globe, reports reveal huge areas in crisis today as reservoirs and aquifers dry up. More than a billion individuals – one in seven people on the planet – now lack access to safe drinking water.

Recently, in the Brazilian city of São Paulo, home to 20 million people, and once known as the City of Drizzle, the drought became so bad that residents began drilling through basement floors and car parks to try to reach groundwater. At the time, city officials warned that rationing of supplies would soon be likely and that citizens would only have access to water two days a week.

In California, officials have revealed that the state has seen four years of continuous drought. At the same time, per capita water use has continued to rise.

In the Middle East, swathes of countryside have been reduced to desert because of overuse of water. Iran is one of the most severely affected. Heavy overconsumption, coupled with poor rainfall, have ravaged its water resources and devastated its agricultural output. Similarly, the United Arab Emirates is now investing in desalination plants and waste water treatment units because it lacks fresh water. As Crown Prince General Sheikh Mohammed bin Zayed Al-Nahyan admitted: 'For us, water is [now] more important than oil.'

The global nature of the crisis is underlined in similar reports from other regions. About 600 million people live on the 2000 sq km area that extends from eastern Pakistan, across the hot dry plains of northern India and into Bangladesh, and the land is the most intensely irrigated in the world. Up to 75 per cent of farmers rely on pumped groundwater to water their crops and water use is intensifying – all this at the same time that satellite images show water supplies are shrinking at an alarming rate. The world faces a water crisis that will touch every part of the globe.

General comprehension

Answer the following questions in complete sentences.

1 What is the main theme of this text?
2 What do you think Leonardo da Vinci meant when he said, 'Water is the driving force of all nature'?
3 What is rising faster than supplies of fresh water?
4 What countries with water problems are mentioned?
5 Who said that water had become more important than oil? What country is he from?

Vocabulary

1 Find a word in the text that means 'the limiting of water that people have access to'.
2 Find a word in the text that means 'a prolonged period of no rain' and quote the sentences it occurs in.
3 Use your dictionary to find the meaning of the word 'aquifer'. What is the difference between a reservoir and an aquifer?

4 Which of the following words best explains the meaning of 'desalination'?
  a reduction of quantity
  b removal of salt
  c improvement of quality
5 Which word in the text means 'water present beneath the surface'?

Presentation task

In pairs, research the water crisis in some of the countries mentioned in the text or in other countries suffering the same problem. Organise your research into a presentation and find ways to illustrate your results to your class. Think about how you present results in your other subjects such as maths and science.

Your presentation should last 3 to 4 minutes.

Paper 1 practice task

Write a formal letter to the editor of your local paper about the future world water shortage. Introduce yourself first. Use some of the points mentioned in the above text and/or your own research to describe the current and future water situation. Consider the fact that a water shortage may affect different countries in different ways. Explain how you think each individual can contribute to increasing awareness of the problem and saving water in their daily lives. Say why you feel we have a responsibility to do this.

SL students should write 250–400 words. HL students should write 450–600 words.

For tips on how to write a formal letter, see page 54 of Chapter 2, Experiences.

Internal assessment (SL)

Figure 5.2 There are more trees on the planet than people, so why worry when some are cut down?

Examine the photograph above and consider the following points:

- What do you see in the picture? Describe only what you see. Do not give opinions.
- Reflect on the picture in connection with the idea of taking care of our planet.
- Consider the benefits trees have for us and why they are important.
- What are some of the reasons why trees are cut down in different places around the world?
- Make connections to your own learning about the environment.

Using the points above, spend 15 minutes preparing a presentation about the photograph. Use the preparation time to organise your ideas and plan the sequence of what you will talk about.

Your presentation should last 3 to 4 minutes, after which your teacher and other students will have the opportunity to comment or ask questions about what you have said. You must engage in a conversation with them. In total, this task should take approximately 15 minutes.

What is climate change?

Mass media – Webpage

The science is clear. Climate change is real. Climate change is happening now. Climate change requires immediate and ambitious action to prevent the worst effects it can have on people and wildlife all over the world.

We know that the planet has warmed by an average of nearly 1 °C in the past century. If we are to prevent the worst effects it can have on people and wildlife all over the world, there is global agreement that temperature rises need to be kept well below 2 °C from the pre-industrial era, with an ambition to keep it below 1.5 °C. Currently, however, assessments suggest that we are on course for a temperature rise of up to as much as 4 °C or higher.

Recently we have seen a number of unwanted developments.

- Most of the years in this century have been the warmest years on record.
- The current levels of atmospheric concentrations of greenhouse gases are unprecedented in the last 800 000 years
- And recently, scientists have declared a new geological time period: the Anthropocene, in which human activity is said to be the dominant influence on the environment, climate, and ecology of the Earth.

As the planet continues to warm, climate patterns change. Extreme and unpredictable weather will become more common across the world as climate patterns change, with some places being hotter, some places being wetter, and some places being drier. These changes can have (and are already having) a drastic impact on all life on Earth.

TOK How do we know about climate change? Does knowing about climate change make us responsible for action?

General comprehension

Answer the following questions in complete sentences.

1 What, according to the writer, is needed right now?
2 How can we prevent the worst effects of climate change?
3 When did the warmest years on record occur?
4 How does the writer define the new geological time period, the Anthropocene?
5 What will be the further effects of climate change?

Vocabulary

Find words or phrases in the text which match the following meanings.

1 happen right now
2 stop something happening
3 never happened before
4 cannot be expected or planned for
5 effect

Discussion task

The activities of humans are resulting in negative effects on the environment and the climate. One of the causes of this is the amount of carbon dioxide humans produce in daily life. This can be calculated for individuals in the form of a carbon footprint. What is a carbon footprint? It is a tally of all of the carbon dioxide produced as a result of human activity. There are many websites with short quizzes about your daily life which can calculate your personal carbon footprint. Do some research and see how high yours is, and then consider what actions you could take to reduce it. The calculator websites often give advice. Compare your carbon footprint, and the actions you have identified to reduce it, with a partner.

Paper 1 practice task

Write a formal letter to your school newspaper summarising what you learned about your carbon footprint and what your reactions were to the information you gathered. Use this as an opportunity to encourage the readers of the school newspaper to make their own efforts to reduce their carbon footprint. Give reasons why this would be beneficial for the environment.

SL students should write 250–400 words. HL students should write 450–600 words.

Paper 2 practice task (5.1) – A speech about climate change

You will hear a student, Jonah, giving a speech in a school in New Zealand. He wrote the speech himself and delivered it to his whole school in an assembly.

According to Jonah, which of the following statements are true? Give a short extract from the speech to support your decisions.

1 Due to climate change, most coastal cities will be under water in the future.
2 As a result of climate change, many people will be homeless.
3 Greenhouse gases do not affect glaciers.
4 Jonah wants everyone to stop using light bulbs.
5 Trees make our air much cleaner.

Listen again and complete the following gaps. Use no more than three words for each gap.

6 Some people believe their beautiful landscapes ______________ than their bank accounts.
7 I'm definitely not blaming anyone in this room but that ______________ rubbish that 'just fell out of your lunchbox' could eventually kill a turtle or a small fish.

TOK

Climate change is a natural part of the Earth's life cycle. How do we know which changes are caused by human activity?

8 You might not have known this, but greenhouse gases such as carbon dioxide and other fossil fuels ________________ melting of beautiful arctic glaciers and this is causing sea levels to rise.
9 One example is to ________________ the light bulbs in your house with energy-saving ones.
10 In conclusion, climate change is ________________ and it needs to be fixed so we can save our planet.

Mass media – Article

CANADA'S HIGH ARCTIC GLACIERS AT RISK OF DISAPPEARING COMPLETELY, STUDY FINDS

Figure 5.3 Climate change is causing glaciers to melt at unprecedented pace

Hundreds of glaciers in Canada's high Arctic are shrinking and many are at risk of disappearing completely, an unprecedented inventory of glaciers in the country's northernmost island has revealed.

Using satellite imagery, researchers catalogued more than 1700 glaciers in northern Ellesmere Island and traced how they had changed between 1999 and 2015. The results offered a glimpse into how warming temperatures may be affecting ice in the region, from glaciers that sprawl across the land to the 200-metre thick ice shelves, said Adrienne White, a glaciologist at the University of Ottawa.

'It's an area that's very difficult to study,' said White. 'Logistically it's very hard to get to and even with satellite imagery – for the longest time Google Earth didn't even have complete imagery – it was kind of the forgotten place.'

White's study, published in the *Journal of Glaciology*, found that the glaciers had shrunk by more than 1700 sq km over a 16-year period, representing a loss of about 6 per cent. A previous study of glaciers in the region – which used air photos and did not include ice shelves – showed a loss of 927 sq km between 1959 and 2000, hinting that the pace of the loss may be increasing.

Of the 1773 glaciers tracked by White, 1353 were found to have shrunk significantly and a handful had disappeared altogether. 'What we found is a loss of three complete ice shelves,' stated White. 'In terms of glaciers that terminate on land, we've lost three small ice caps.'

None of the glaciers in the study showed any signs of growing. The findings echo the changes White has observed during her years of visiting the island. 'We see a lot more icebergs,' said White. 'Where there was one continuous ice shelf, we now see individual icebergs broken up, we see a lot more crevasses.'

She attributed the findings to an increase in temperatures. Canada's Arctic – one of the world's most glaciated regions – is warming at one of the fastest rates of anywhere on Earth. In northern Ellesmere Island, the annual average temperature in the region increased by 3.6°C between 1948 and 2016.

In particular, 'there seemed to be a shift in the mid-90s,' she said, describing it as a 'sudden increase in warming' that saw temperatures increase at about 0.78°C per decade between 1995 and 2016.

'These increases were greatest in autumn and winter,' added White. 'So what you end up with is a lot more melt.'

While the most direct impact is rising sea levels, the melting ice also risks wiping out the region's unique ecosystems, such as the freshwater lakes that form when the water flowing off a glacier is trapped by a floating ice shelf.

'When these glaciers break away, all of a sudden there's nothing holding back these ecosystems that have been growing and developing for thousands of years,' said White. 'And they're gone before we even have a chance to study them.'

Extrapolating from research done on glaciers from a neighbouring island, White's study suggested that many of the glaciers on northern Ellesmere Island may not be high enough to accumulate enough snow to counter the pace at which they are melting.

TOK

How can cause and effect be established in the natural sciences when experiments cannot be conducted to test the climate change hypothesis?

General comprehension

Answer the following questions in complete sentences.

1 What is the problem with the glaciers in Canada's high Arctic?
2 How did researchers document the glaciers between 1999 and 2015?
3 What did they learn about the glaciers between 1999 and 2015?
4 Why is the area difficult to study?
5 Are any of the glaciers growing?
6 What other differences has White noticed in the icebergs?
7 When was there a change in the rate of temperature increase? What are the direct effects of this?
8 Why does White think the glaciers will not be able to collect more snow?

Vocabulary

Find words or phrases in the text which match the following meanings.

1 a complete list
2 the results reflect
3 a scientist who studies glaciers
4 spread out
5 inferring from other findings
6 difficult to reach
7 made lists of
8 appeared to be a slight change
9 suggesting
10 collect an adequate amount of snow

5.2 Plastic pollution

A life without plastic?

Paper 2 practice task (5.2) – A phone conversation about rubbish

You will hear a phone conversation between Ben and Janet. They are talking about rubbish on a beach. According to the conversation, which of the following statements are true?

a Janet has finished her history essay.
b Ben took a walk on the beach last week.
c Ben prefers the beach in summer.
d Janet says the wind has increased the amount of rubbish on the beach.
e Janet will write the letter to the Town Council.

Listen again complete the following gaps. Use no more than three words for each gap.

1 I'm fine, but still ______________ history essay.
2 You would get an awful shock if ______________ go down today, and not because of the weather.
3 And you wouldn't want to touch ______________ junk either.
4 They say soon there will be more plastic in the sea than fish and ______________ that the fish are eating the plastic and then we eat the fish.
5 But that's awful, someone has to do something, can't the local council ______________? Isn't that their job?
6 They are so busy right now ______________ in the road after such a long hard winter.
7 You are better at getting your ideas ______________ than me.
8 I am so ______________ the history essay.

Figure 5.4 A beach full of rubbish

Mass media – Webpage

Plastics in the 21st century

Everyone who reads a newspaper or watches the news online or on television must be aware of what plastic waste is doing to our planet. Every individual is contributing to tonnes and tonnes of waste every day, but a number of engaged citizens are doing what they can to raise our awareness of this issue.

A Dutchman, Merijn Tinga, a biologist and a visual artist, set out to paddle the length of the River Rhine, 1320 km. The Rhine connects the Alps to the North Sea. It is an important transport link and the boats, laden with oil, coal, cars, and other products, travel up and down the Rhine all day and night. The Rhine provides a major transport connection and is an alternative to the hundreds of lorries which thunder up and down the autobahns.

On the way, Merijn is collecting plastic waste from the river and river banks, which he is sending to the CEOs of the relevant companies to raise

Figure 5.5 Plastics in our waterways

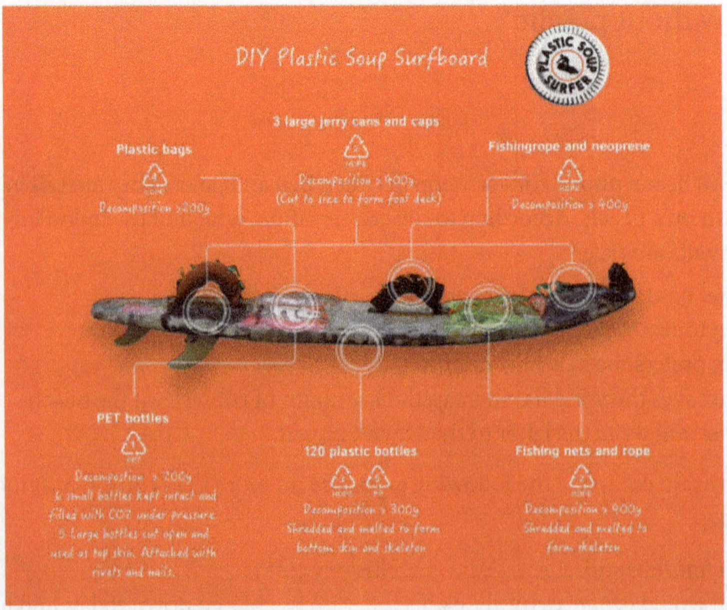

their awareness of the damage their products, or more importantly, the wrappings, are doing to the environment.

He says the process is exhausting, physically and mentally, but it is the achievement not the process which counts. He sleeps each night in a small tent beside the river, but faces many challenges such as finding enough to eat and drink to maintain his strength and his concentration levels. The Rhine is a fast-flowing river which can also be a death trap, as careless swimmers have found in the past.

To see the journey he is taking and hear him talking about it, visit https://plasticsoupsurfer.org.

General comprehension

Answer the following questions in complete sentences.

1 What was Merijn's goal?
2 Was Merijn's goal easy to achieve? Why?
3 What effect did the process have on Merijn?
4 What other problems did he face?
5 Where did he sleep?

Vocabulary

Find words or phrases in the text which match the following meanings.

1 have to know about something
2 people who are actively involved in a project
3 final result
4 keep something up
5 a potentially fatal place

Paper 1 practice task

Write a letter to Merijn expressing your thoughts about what he is doing and suggesting some ways you can support his work. Your letter can be informal, but make sure to explain who you are and why you are interested in what he is doing. Make suggestions to support his venture.

SL students should write 200–400 words. HL students should write 450–600 words.

The following letters show an exchange between a student and the Town Council in her area about the state of the local beach.

Mass media – Public commentary

The Cottage
6 Bluebell Lane
West Easton
20 February

To West Easton Town Council:

Dear Sir or Madam,

My name is Janet and I have lived in West Easton all my life. I am in the middle of preparing to take my final school exams but today, when I took a break from studying and went out to enjoy nature, I had an awful shock which I want to share with you in the hope you will be able to help.

Our beautiful local beach is in a terrible mess. I wonder if you have had time to go down to the beach lately? The sand is littered with rubbish, mostly plastic, which has washed up from the sea. It looks horrible. It's also dangerous: children who play there could injure themselves on it or become infected because everything is so dirty. The gulls were pecking at some of the rubbish and in fact one had its legs tangled in the stuff. It managed to get free but it was a nasty situation for a few minutes. The beach is so disgusting no one will even think about swimming in the summer if nothing is done.

I know you are very busy, but this is really important for the well-being of the whole community and for protecting nature in West Easton. Please let me know what can be done to solve the problem.

With best wishes,
Janet

General comprehension

Answer the following questions in complete sentences.

1 Why did Janet go down to the beach?
2 Why is Janet writing the letter?
3 What happened to the gull?
4 Why does Janet say nobody will want to swim?
5 What does Janet want the Town Council to do?

Mass media – Public commentary

Town Council
West Easton
23 February

Dear Janet,

Thank you for your letter. As soon as I had read your letter, I went down to our beach myself to see how bad it is.

I have to say I was horrified. It is absolutely disgraceful and a real blot on our beautiful landscape. In fact, I started to pick up the rubbish myself, but even after a quarter of an hour of bending down and picking up, I couldn't see any improvement at all.

We really do not have the resources to solve a problem like this. However, recently I read in a newspaper about an initiative in another village to clear the rubbish which had landed on their beaches from the sea. They managed to get the whole community involved. I wonder if this is an idea we could adopt for our village. What do you think?

We from the Town Concil could supply equipment (sacks and pick-up grippers) so that people would not have to use their hands and risk injury or infection, but we would need to get the whole village involved.

It would be helpful if we could talk about this. Maybe you have some friends who would help start the initiative? If we had a group of people wanting to get involved, I think the problem could be solved. We could help with posters, advertising spaces, and an article in the local newspaper.

I look forward to hearing your ideas on how to involve the whole community.

Best wishes,
Colin Smith
Councillor

General comprehension

Answer the following questions in complete sentences.

1 What was the councillor's reaction to the state of the beach?
2 Why can't he help to get the beach cleared?
3 What does he suggest?
4 What steps does he suggest taking to start the initiative?

Vocabulary

Match the following words (1–6) as they are used in the text with their meanings (a–f).

1 horrified	a large bags
2 disgraceful	b very bad
3 a blot	c shocked
4 initiative	d some kind of physical damage
5 sacks	e something that spoils the appearance of something else
6 injury	f a strategy

Mass media – Public commentary

The Cottage
6 Bluebell Lane
West Easton
26 February

Dear Mr Smith,

Thank you for your letter.

I have been talking to my class at school and everyone is interested in getting involved. We have decided to make posters advertising a beach clean-up for the second Saturday in March starting at 10 a.m.

Should we collect the rubbish sacks and pick-up grippers from the Council?

School finishes early on Friday so we could come over then. Our art teacher is really interested in the idea and is letting us use the art room and supplies for the posters, so we can start working on them right away.

Best wishes,
Janet

Task

Create a poster advertising the beach clean-up. Be sure to use persuasive language to encourage people to take part.

Tips for using persuasive language

- Give reasons why a clean-up is a good idea.
- Make use of rhetorical questions, e.g. *Do you want a cleaner beach?*
- Appeal to reason by giving facts and figures about pollution.
- Appeal to emotions by giving examples of the dangers of plastic to wildlife and the role the individual can play.
- Speak directly to the reader, e.g. *We need you to. . .*

Paper 1 practice task

You have taken part in a beach clean-up while on holiday. Write an informal email to one of your classmates telling them about the activity and your experiences. Choose which aspects of the day you want to focus on: the fun element, the environmental concern, your own dismay at the amount of rubbish on the beach, etc. Encourage your friend to join in a similar activity.

SL students should write 250–400 words. HL students should write 450–600 words.

For tips on how to write an informal email, see page 49 of Chapter 2, Experiences.

Mass media – Poster

WE NEED YOU!

When was the last time you went to the beach?
Have you seen it lately?
Our beach is a mess.
It's covered in litter of every kind,
making it dangerous for us, and deadly for fish and birds.

There are plastic bottles, bags, tins, broken bottles, and more!

Come and help us clean it up!

Meeting point: on the beach
When: Sat. 10th March at 10 a.m.! Bring gloves.

We will have rubbish sacks and pick-up grippers.
Let's make a difference and make
our beach beautiful again: clean and safe!

Mass media – Public commentary

7a The High Street
West Easton
5 March

Dear Sir or Madam,

I have to share my enthusiasm for the quite remarkable initiative taken by some young members of our village and I would like to encourage everyone to take part in this very worthwhile venture.

The students are quite right. Our village beach is a disgrace, but it is of course a sign of the times we live in. Our throwaway society has caused this problem and it is not only our beach which is being destroyed. The rubbish can be found on almost every beach around Great Britain and the sea is full of it too.

Newspapers report stories of plastic pollution and the government must act to limit the destruction which is taking place all over the country, in fact all over the world. When will we learn that it is unacceptable and an environmental disaster to continue to produce endless amounts of plastic for wrapping and single-use drink containers – in fact for absolutely everything we use every day?

Take a look at your shopping basket next time and count how many items are wrapped in plastic which is indestructible and steadily ruining our planet. We should all take a stand on this. Cleaning up the beach is an admirable first step, but much more needs to be done. We have to raise awareness of the dangers of plastic in our lives.

I propose that as a village we take the first step and attempt to ban, or at least severely limit, plastic in our lives.

Who will join me in this?

Can we go back to milk sold in bottles, vegetables and fruit sold loose, as in a market, and other products sold with no plastic at all?

I propose a public meeting to be held in the Community Centre to share ideas and I would welcome comments from our community leaders.

Yours respectfully,
George Smith-Jones

General comprehension

Answer the following questions in complete sentences.

1 Why is the writer so enthusiastic about the action of the young members of the community?
2 Why does the writer say it is 'a sign of the times'?
3 What does the writer think the government should do?
4 What does the writer describe as an environmental disaster?
5 The writer admits that cleaning the beach is a first step. What should be done after that?
6 Which concrete ideas does the writer suggest?

Mass media – Webpage

I rely on plastic straws and baby wipes. I'm disabled – I have no choice

by Penny Pepper, a writer and disability rights activist

Figure 5.6 Using straws is not a lifestyle choice for many

I know the environmental damage they cause, but I don't have the luxury of a plastic-free life

I remember the dawning of my green consciousness: the sudden, painful realisation that products were tested on animals. This was in the early 1970s. I was about ten years old. A teacher told me that talcum powder was put in the eyes of cats and dogs to make sure it was safe. She also said that the plastic container would pollute the Earth.

A few years later, as punk sensibility captured my naturally rebellious heart, I immersed myself in the ecological fight. I joined Greenpeace. I wrote letters – even to the pope on his visit to Britain – arguing against the clubbing of baby seals in Canada. This passion has never left me.

Throw into the mix that I've been disabled since the age of 14, however, and environmentalism can start to get tricky. Over the years, I've had to learn that being green does not always sit comfortably with my access needs.

Take the plastic straw debate, and the warning that baby wipes are a major cause of fatbergs. Along with many disabled people, I need both. Not as a lifestyle choice. Not as a luxury. I need straws that bend, ones that can handle all drinks, including medication, and all temperatures. I need straws that aren't too fat, that won't cause me to choke or be difficult for me to keep in my mouth.

This is why news that Seattle has become the first major US city to ban the use of plastic straws causes me some conflict, as do reports that the UK wants to ban them as well.

I've been in this ecological battle for longer than many newcomers have been alive. I get uncomfortable and angry when I see non-disabled people behave as though they know the answer to the dilemma in exchanges that can get heated, if not abusive. Why do we need plastic straws? Won't paper ones do? What about bamboo? Or glass? Metal? These questions are not easy to answer. Paper straws generally don't do well in hot liquids and I've yet to find decent flexible ones. This is important to get the angle right for safe drinking

TOK

On what basis can the needs of the individual be superseded by the needs of other groups?

when you can't hold a cup or even if another person holds it for you. Metal ones are often fat, better used for smoothies and not good if you have a biting issue. I tried silicone straws, which were too soft and fat to be reliably useful.

As for disposable wipes, the issue is mostly cost. Many biodegradable versions are available, but some of the best eco options can cost as much as £4.99, with an equivalent non-biodegradable set 79p. Hard-up parents, disabled people, and those on benefits may be forced to choose the cheaper option. I know I certainly have done over the years.

Disabled people don't want to have to put their own care above the environment – but it seems no one is considering the impact of future legislative changes on our well-being. If there's going to be a ban, let governments and manufacturers come up with decent, affordable green alternatives for us all.

General comprehension

Answer the following questions in complete sentences.

1 Why does the writer not have the luxury of a plastic-free life?
2 When did the writer become environmentally aware and green?
3 What did the writer's teacher tell her then?
4 What are the writer's special needs with regards to straws?
5 Which alternatives to plastic straws are suggested by environmentalists?
6 Why does the writer feel uncomfortable and angry?
7 What is the problem with disposable wipes for people with little money?
8 What does she want the governments and manufacturers to do?

Vocabulary

Find words and phrases in the text which match the following meanings.

1 the awakening of my environmental awareness
2 deeply involved
3 add another argument to the discussion
4 discussions that may become unfriendly
5 something that is broken down naturally
6 a strong emotion for something
7 a large mass of solid waste
8 can be thrown away
9 short of money

Paper 1 practice task

Write either an article for the school magazine, a letter to your local paper, or a blog to explain the problems disabled people face being environmentally aware and proactive. Suggest how people can help solve these problems.

SL students should write 200–400 words. HL students should write 450–600 words.

For tips on how to write an article, see page 29 of Chapter 1, Identities. For tips on how to write a blog, see page 9 of Chapter 1, Identities.

Mass media – Webpage

Is it possible to live comfortably without single-use plastics?

Plastics last for a very long time. It is thought that soon there will be more plastic in the ocean than fish. We need to learn how to live without plastic, but this is not easy as plastic is so practical and convenient.

Here are some tips to help us all reduce the amount of single-use plastic in our lives and save the environment of our planet for future generations.

When you go shopping

- Take your own bag for your shopping. Research says that the amount of plastic waste has already been greatly reduced since shops began charging people for plastic bags. More and more people are using their own bags. Support that trend!
- Take your own containers to the meat, fish, and cheese counters. These products are almost always wrapped in plastic. But check at the counter first as not all shops allow this.
- Use your shopping basket or a separate bag to carry loose fruit and vegetables. Avoid those pre-wrapped tomatoes, apples, and other fruits and vegetables.
- Make your own bag with an old shirt or T-shirt. It's easy!
- Buy bread from the baker's where it will be wrapped in paper.
- Ask the shop owners why plastic bottles are not sold with a deposit which is refunded when they are recycled. This happens in a number of European countries.

If you stop for a snack or a drink

- Tell the café owner why you do not want a plastic straw.
- Have a reusable coffee cup with you.
- Always carry your own reusable water bottle.
- Carry your own snack, wrapped in paper.

At home

In the bathroom

- Use soap bars instead of plastic bottles of shower gel and shampoo.
- Buy a bamboo toothbrush.
- Try to find bars of skin creams and deodorants.
- Buy paper or bamboo cotton buds.

In the kitchen

- Buy milk and juices in glass bottles.
- Buy pasta in cardboard boxes.
- Grow herbs and salad on your window sill or in your garden.

Cleaning materials

- Baking soda and vinegar are as good as many bought cleaning products.
- Buy washing powder in cardboard packs.
- Use refillable bottles for cleaning products.

Discussion task

How many of these tips do you follow already? Think about the impact these tips may have on the environment. Do you have more suggestions? Share them with your class.

Paper 1 practice task

As part of your Community Action and Service, you have decided to share what you have learned about living without plastics. Try to persuade fellow students to act on your advice and make the school environment, and their lives outside of school, plastic-free as far as possible. Write either a blog, an article for the school magazine, or a speech to be given in assembly.

SL students should write 250–400 words. HL students should write 450–600 words.

TOK How do Ways of Knowing influence our understanding of environmental issues?

For tips on how to write a speech, see page 62 of Chapter 2, Experiences.

Mass media – Blog

THE BIGGEST BEACH CLEAN-UP?

Posted on 19 June

Versova Beach is one of Mumbai's most well-known tourist attractions. Some years ago, when I was working in the city, I heard about a group of volunteers who had decided to do something about the rubbish on this popular beach. At first, only a couple of volunteers worked at cleaning up the beach. They would get together and head out to the beach with gloves and bags to pick up trash. They worked hard and were seen on the beach every week over a number of months. They collected tonnes of plastic over the months, working in the filthy sludge, tirelessly filling their bags.

After some months, the volunteers realised that they needed more help. They rallied friends, neighbours and schoolchildren by spending time going from street to street knocking on doors and telling people about the Versova Beach situation. The press also helped spread the word and Sunday afternoons became a popular beach clean-up time. The volunteers worked knee-deep in rotting garbage, sweating under the burning Indian sun. I know this because I was one of those Sunday volunteers.

The people of Mumbai have rallied in vast numbers to fight for a clean natural area in their city and acknowledge that the mess is the result of our poor consumer. It's our mess and we need to clean it up. Until the amount of plastic dumped into the oceans stops, the volunteers' work will never end.

The press has reported that the work of the volunteers is slowly influencing the next generation of Indian leaders. What is especially notable are the loudest voices appealing to the government – schoolchildren. They have been vocal in pushing officials to get involved in clearing up this mess. Let's hope our leaders will make fighting environmental pollution one of their priorities.

General comprehension

Answer the following questions in complete sentences.

1 Which sentences in the blog tell you which country Mumbai is in?
2 How did the first volunteers get people to join them in the clean-up?
3 When did the volunteers work?
4 According to the text, what is the cause of the plastic piling up on the beaches?
5 When do the volunteers feel their work will be finished?

Vocabulary

Answer the following questions.

1 In paragraph 1, which word tells you that the beach was not sandy, but soft, wet mud?
2 Which verb in paragraph 2 means that the volunteers inspired and motivated new volunteers?
3 Which two words in the text are used as synonyms for the thrown-away plastic?
4 Which verb in paragraph 3 means 'to throw something away thoughtlessly'?

Zoom in on grammar

Phrasal verbs

A phrasal verb is a combination of a main verb and a preposition or adverb. Phrasal verbs can sometimes have a meaning that is idiomatic, that is, not the same as the words on their own.

The cricket ball hit the boy's head and ***knocked him out.***

The phrasal verb *to knock (someone) out* means to make someone lose consciousness for a short time.

Grammar in context

In the above text, there are a number of phrasal verbs: *to head out, to pick up, to clean up, to fight for*. Identify their position and usage in the text. Then write your own sentences using the phrasal verbs to show your understanding of their meaning.

Paper 1 practice task

You have read about the work being done by volunteers in Mumbai in a blog about environmental issues. Write an email to the volunteers, telling them what you think about their work in Mumbai. Write a positive response and include details from the text as well as your own knowledge and ideas about the effects of plastic on our environment.

SL students should write 250–400 words. HL students should write 450–600 words.

THE BEACH CLEAN-UP HAS NOW EVEN REACHED OUR YOUNGEST!

In a Scottish kindergarten, children shared pictures from the local newspaper of a dolphin that had eaten plastic rubbish.

The kindergarten places great emphasis on outside learning and nature. The toddlers go outside every day regardless of the weather. They all have wellingtons and raincapes. A little Scottish rain, or even a bit of a downpour, does not deter the children or their teachers. The nearby woods and fields are exciting areas to explore and the beach is just a few hundred metres away for regular sessions.

The toddlers collect natural products which they find on their outings and love to use them to make artistic decorations. They deliberately do not pick flowers as they are very aware that the bees need them more than they do. They are kept very busy on their outings, observing the flowers, counting and drawing them, as well as looking for bees and butterflies.

With the high level of interest in the natural world shared by the children and their teachers, the pictures of the dolphin with plastic in its stomach greatly disturbed them.

The topic was used during the daily Talk Time. The teacher told the children about the problems with plastic waste and encouraged them to avoid single-use plastic and to dispose of any plastic rubbish properly. The children then explored the classroom looking for examples of plastic which they use every day. Sandwich boxes, drinking beakers, painting aprons, raincapes, wellingtons, table covers and more were all piled up on the centre table.

The children then wondered how the dolphin could have eaten the plastic. The teacher explained that not everyone is careful to dispose of plastic correctly, and that a lot of plastic could be found on beaches all over the world. It was clear that the next outdoor activity would have to be to their beach to see how much plastic was there.

The children and the teachers filled a large sack with litter, which mostly comprised plastic drink bottles, wrappers from chocolate bars, ice creams, and sandwiches that had been thoughtlessly dropped. This led to a long discussion with the children, which will continue to be a focus, comparing their usual foraging expeditions where they collect leaves, twigs, berries, stones, etc. with the kind of litter they found on the beach.

The children were keen and ready to repeat the process again the following day, but the teachers persuaded them that it would be much better to involve more adults. A day was planned for the children and their families to begin a thorough clean-up.

General comprehension

Answer the following questions in complete sentences.

1 What is the specialist focus of the kindergarten?
2 What aspect of the rubbish on the beach will the teachers continue to talk about when they are back in school?
3 What did the children collect from the beach?

Text handling

Answer the following questions.

1 Which phrase tells you that the children were not on the beach with their teachers for the first time?
2 Which two words used in the text describe the things thrown away on the beach?
3 Find the word 'toddler' in the text. Read that paragraph. What do you think a 'toddler' is?

Internal assessment (SL)

Figure 5.7 Plastic pollution – no solution?

Examine the photograph above and consider the following points:

- What do you see in the picture? Describe only what you see. Do not give opinions.
- Outline the problem of plastic pollution from your reading of the texts and your own knowledge.
- Present some current actions against pollution that are going on – locally and globally.
- What options are open to individuals in their day-to-day lives if they want to reduce plastic waste?
- Propose suggestions for measures that governments and countries could take.

Using the points above, spend 15 minutes preparing a presentation about the photograph. Use the preparation time to organise your ideas and plan the sequence of what you will talk about.

Your presentation should last 3 to 4 minutes, after which your teacher and other students will have the opportunity to comment or ask questions about what you have said. You must engage in a conversation with them. In total, this task should take approximately 15 minutes.

5.3 Tourism

The impact of tourism

How do you spend your holidays? Do you have a favourite place and favourite activities? Or maybe you have a destination you dream of getting away to.

In the 21st century, the world has become increasingly mobile. More and more people travel and explore the world, but what are the effects on the environment?

Read the article below to find out more about the negative effects of tourism.

Personal – Social media post

IY **IBRAHIM YUSUF**
PUBLISHED ON TUESDAY

TOURISM'S MAIN IMPACT AREAS

Negative impacts from tourism occur when the level of visitor use is greater than the environment's ability to cope with this use within acceptable limits of change. Uncontrolled conventional tourism poses potential threats to many areas around the world. It can put enormous pressure on an area and lead to soil erosion, increased pollution, discharges into the sea, natural habitat loss, increased pressure on endangered species, and heightened vulnerability to forest fires. It often puts a strain on water supplies, and it can force local populations to compete for the use of critical resources.

General comprehension

State whether the following sentences are true or false. Give a quote from the text to support your answers.

1 Tourists can have a negative effect on the environment.
2 Tourism does not lead to increased pollution levels.
3 Where there are tourists, forest fires are more likely.
4 Water supplies are not affected by mass tourism.

Vocabulary

Find words in the text which match the following meanings.

1 happen
2 possible
3 huge
4 effects
5 territory

Mass media – Webpage

Depletion of water resources

Tourism development can put pressure on natural resources when it increases consumption in areas where resources are already scarce.

Water, and especially fresh water, is one of the most critical natural resources. The tourism industry generally overuses water resources for hotels, swimming pools, golf courses, and personal use of water by tourists. This can result in water shortages and degradation of supplies, as well as generating a greater volume of waste water.

In dryer regions, like the Mediterranean, the issue of water scarcity is of particular concern. Because of the hot climate and the tendency to consume more water on holiday, the amount used by the average tourist can run up to 440 litres a day. This is almost double what the inhabitants of an average Spanish city use.

Golf course maintenance can also deplete fresh water resources. In recent years, golf tourism has increased in popularity and the number of golf courses has grown rapidly. Golf courses require an enormous amount of water every day, and as with other causes of excessive extraction of water, this can result in water scarcity. If the water comes from wells, over-pumping can cause saline intrusion into groundwater. Golf resorts are more and more often situated in or near protected areas or areas where resources are limited, exacerbating their impacts.

General comprehension

Answer the following questions in complete sentences.

1 Which three effects on the water supply are the results of tourism?
2 Why is water scarcity an issue in the Mediterranean area?
3 Why do you think tourists use more water when they are on holiday?
4 Why do golf courses present particular problems?
5 What danger is created by over-pumping from wells?

Vocabulary

Find words and phrases in the text which match the following meanings.

1 use too much
2 use up
3 a reason to worry
4 upkeep
5 not enough of something
6 nearly twice as much
7 need
8 too much
9 creating a larger amount
10 the people who live there
11 can amount to
12 quickly
13 worsening the effects

MAASAI HERDERS DRIVEN OFF LAND TO MAKE WAY FOR LUXURY SAFARIS, REPORT SAYS

Tanzanian government accused of putting indigenous people at risk in order to grant foreign tourists access to Serengeti wildlife

The Tanzanian government is putting foreign safari companies ahead of Maasai herding communities as environmental tensions grow on the fringes of the Serengeti national park, according to the investigation.

Hundreds of homes have been burned and tens of thousands of people driven from ancestral land in Loliondo in the Ngorongoro district in recent years to benefit high-end tourists and a Middle Eastern royal family, says the report by the California-based think tank, the Oakland Institute.

Although carried out in the name of conservation, these measures enable wealthy foreigners to watch or hunt lions, zebra, wildebeest, giraffes, and other wildlife, while the authorities exclude local people and their cattle from watering holes and arable land, the institute says.

'Losing the Serengeti: The Maasai Land that was to Run Forever'* uses previously unpublished correspondence, official documents, court testimonies and first-person testimony to examine the impact of two firms: Thomson Safaris based in the United States and Otterlo Business Corporation based in the United Arab Emirates.

It says Thomson's sister company, Tanzania Conservation Limited, is in a court battle with three Maasai villages over the ownership of 12617 acres (5106 hectares) of land in Loliondo which the company uses for safaris.

One Maasai quoted in the report said Thomson had built a camp in the middle of their village, blocking access. 'Imagine, a stranger comes and constructs a big building in the centre of your home,' reads the testimony. 'Our livestock cannot go to the waterhole – there is no other route for the villagers or their livestock.'

The report says villagers have been driven off, assaulted, or arrested by local police, park rangers, or security guards.

The restricted access to land has made the Maasai more vulnerable to famine during drought years, the report says, noting appeals that locals made for the government to change policies because of growing numbers of malnourished children.

Thomson strongly denies these accusations. It says Tanzania Conservation Limited employs 100 per cent Maasai staff, allows cattle on the property to access seasonal water, and works with local communities and the government to conserve the savannah, improve access to water, and formulate a sustainable grazing policy.

Despite past government promises that the Maasai would never be evicted from their land, the report notes Serengeti national park rangers burned 114 bomas (traditional homes) in 2015 and another 185 in August of last year. Along with other demolitions, local media report more than 20000 Maasai were left homeless.

* 'Losing the Serengeti: The Maasai Land that was to Run Forever' is a report published by the Oakland Institute, California, May 2018.

General comprehension

Answer the following questions in complete sentences.

1 Who is being disadvantaged by the Tanzanian government?
2 Why do tourists visit Tanzania?
3 What effect has tourism had on the local people?
4 What is the reason for the court battle between Tanzania Conservation Limited and three Maasai villages?
5 Why is restricted access to land a problem for the Maasai?

Vocabulary

Match the words below (1–10) as they are used in the text with their meanings (a–j).

1 ancestral	a a formal statement
2 indigenous	b weak, without protection
3 think tank	c native
4 testimony	d a group of experts
5 arable land	e owned by previous family members
6 livestock	f save
7 drought	g lack of rain or water
8 famine	h crop growing areas
9 vulnerable	i animals kept on a farm
10 conserve	j shortage of food

Paper 2 practice task (5.3) – Three friends discuss their holiday plans

You will hear a conversation between three friends discussing their holiday plans. State whether the following statements are true or false.

1 All cruise ships are full of old people.
2 A cruise is an not environmentally friendly holiday according to Jenny.
3 Cruise passengers are beneficial to the ports where they stop.
4 A safari holiday is the best choice for them.
5 Travelling by train is most environmentally friendly according to the three friends.
6 Travelling by train is costly for students.
7 The three friends are unable to agree on a holiday.
8 The friends decide to drive to the railway station.

Listen again complete the following gaps. Use no more than three words for each gap.

9 Well, I have to go and see my parents, I guess, but that isn't ______________ holiday, although it is nice enough.
10 A cruise sounds like a really restful holiday, ______________ catch planes, or try to get a good place on the beach or find good places to eat – it is all there on the ship.
11 Some of them aim for the younger set ______________ activities and fun and games.

12 And the other huge disadvantage about cruise ships is they don't ______________ the local economy.
13 And the ______________ – when they land in small ports with very small populations, the ______________ towns with their huge numbers.
14 No way, think of ______________ and the fuel being burned and polluting the air.
15 Well, I heard that travel by train ______________ friendly, isn't it?
16 Yes, and I have heard ______________ they are not too expensive.

Mass media – Article

HOW TO BE A BETTER TOURIST

Crowd-control measures in Venice, anti-tourism protests in Palma de Mallorca, mounting pressure to bring tourism under control in Barcelona: recent years have witnessed a sharp rise in anti-tourist sentiment throughout Europe.

From Amsterdam to Dubrovnik, Hvar to San Sebastian, locals are becoming increasingly vociferous about the impact tourism is having on their environment.

Oversubscribed cities are implementing policies to mitigate the effects of mass tourism, but there are also calls for tourists to take responsibility for the issue as well.

Rochelle Turner, research director at the World Travel & Tourism Council (WTTC) says they have launched a campaign – dubbed 'Is It A Great Deal To Ask?' – to promote sustainable practices amongst travellers.

10 tips on how to be a better tourist

1. Consider going somewhere else

'If you're considering travelling to a very busy place, you might want to think about the alternatives,' said Turner. 'Think about some of the secondary or tertiary cities that may be equally beautiful or equally interesting.' Utrecht instead of Amsterdam, Verona over Venice, for example.

This will likely improve your holiday experience: as well as having fewer visitors, lesser-known destinations also tend to be cheaper.

2. Avoid the 'honeypot' sites

'Whether it's Barcelona or Botswana, there are always going to be a lot of people going to the "honeypot" sites that everyone knows about,' said Richard Hammond, of the Greentraveller Media Group, speaking for WTTC. 'If you do a little research, often you can go and visit a similar site elsewhere, but have a much better experience because there are far fewer people visiting it.'

3. Go in the shoulder season

An obvious way to ease pressure on a destination – and to have a better experience of the place – is to avoid visiting when everyone else is. The weather is often just as good in the period between the peak and off-peak season and most of the shops and restaurants are open. The added bonus? It's usually a bit cheaper.

4. Ditch the guidebook for a day

And leave your phone in the hotel, while you're at it. Just go out there and get lost, follow your nose. There are delights to be found when you are exploring. Say to yourself, 'I want to find five things not in a guidebook.' You will often be surprised how much fun you can have. If more tourists did that, places would be less overcrowded.

5. Stay in locally owned accommodation

Profits made by hotels owned by locals are more likely to go back into the local economy than those from giant multinational ones. That's not to say, however, that you should shun international chains, which tend to occupy larger premises and therefore employ more people (and have higher turnovers).

6. Ask questions

How much of the food served in your hotel is sourced locally? Are your sheets cleaned locally? Were they made locally? What is your hotel doing to reduce its environmental impact? 'It's about asking these questions and making companies realise that these are issues that are important,' said a representative of WTTC. If the hotel appears to be doing little to support the local economy or protect the environment, then it might be worth thinking about taking your money elsewhere.

7. Learn the local language

If you can converse with the locals in their language, it might make them feel more accommodating. The old trick of pointing and talking loudly in English is just likely to annoy them and reinforce the idea that tourists are a nuisance.

8. Buy local

One of the big issues in Venice is the number of local shops that have closed to make way for cheap souvenir shops (it is deemed more profitable to sell tourists cheap reproductions than regional produce). With that in mind, tourists would do well to avoid buying those cheap souvenirs (which have likely been imported from abroad) and instead spend their money on regional products in local shops.

9. Reduce your plastic waste

From the beaches of Goa to the streets of Rome, plastic waste is a blight on the planet. So try not to add to it when you're on holiday. 'Take your own bottle of water that you can refill, rather than buying a new plastic bottle every time,' advised Hammond, who also suggests shorter showers in areas where water is scarce.

10. Be respectful

As well as feeling outnumbered by tourists, people in destinations like Venice are becoming increasingly angry that some tourists are disrespecting their town (holidaymakers have, for example, been seen jumping in the canals). Wherever you go, abide by the local laws, respect the local customs and dress appropriately. Generally speaking, smarten up and don't go sightseeing in shorts and flip-flops. Ultimately, give locals one less thing to complain about.

General comprehension

Answer the following questions in complete sentences.

1 Why has the World Travel and Tourism Council issued ten tips on how to be a better tourist?
2 Do the tips apply to all cities in countries visited by large numbers of tourists?
3 According to the text, what is positive about going sightseeing without your guidebook?
4 What is a possible negative effect when multinational chains have hotels in cities popular with tourists?

Vocabulary

Answer the following questions.

1 In the first sentence, which word has the same meaning as 'increasing'?
2 In the first paragraph, the writer says, 'locals are becoming increasingly vociferous'. What does this mean?
   a Local people are actively protesting more.
   b Local people are angrier but do not complain.
   c Local people are expressing their opinions more loudly and forcefully.

3 In paragraph 3, which word has the same meaning as 'to lessen'?
4 Tip 2 is 'Avoid the "honeypot" sites'. What do you think 'honeypot' means?
5 Which verb in the tip headings means 'to throw away'?

Paper 1 practice task

Your art class has planned a summer trip to Barcelona. You are concerned about the impact 20 students will have on the overcrowded tourist destination. After speaking to your fellow students, they agree with you. Write a proposal to your art teacher for an alternative destination and give your reasons for choosing it. Explain that this is a concern shared by the majority of students. Use arguments from the above text as well as your own ideas.

SL students should write 250–400 words. HL students should write 450–600 words.

Discussion task

Figure 5.8–11 Forms of holiday transport

When we go on holiday, we can benefit or harm the local community and the people living there. Often, there are consequences for the environment.

In groups, look at the photos and discuss the following question in groups.

- Which of these forms of transport are environmentally friendly?
- Which of these forms of transport are the best/the worst for local communities?

Mass media – Article

OVER-TOURISM IN JAPAN

Japanese complain of 'tourist pollution' as number of sightseers skyrockets

Japan's traditional sense of *omotenashi*, meaning to wholeheartedly look after guests, is wearing decidedly thin as residents of many of the nation's must-see tourist spots increasingly express their frustration at loud and disrespectful foreigners, crowded public transport, and poor etiquette among visitors. The problem has become so bad in some towns, such as the ancient capitals of Kyoto and Kamakura, that local people are complaining to their local authorities about 'tourism pollution'.

Japan's tourism agency is frantically encouraging tourists to get off the

'Golden Route' that links Tokyo with Kyoto and Osaka and to explore more remote parts of the country.

That campaign appears to be having some impact, but most travellers – especially first-time visitors – still want to experience the skyscrapers and bright lights of the present capital, the cultural and historic delights of Kyoto, and the cuisine, entertainment and shopping opportunities that abound in Osaka.

While hotels and businesses that rely on the tourist trade have welcomed the influx of foreigners, local residents are less enamoured with so many outsiders in their towns.

Kyoto has seen an upsurge in complaints linked to the rise in tourist numbers. Locals say it is difficult to get on buses that go near the most famous sights in the city, while demand for accommodation has encouraged unscrupulous landlords to lease out unlicensed properties.

Foreign tourists are also often unaware of local customs – such as meticulously separating rubbish before it is collected – which has added to the friction with local people.

The city's tourism authorities say they are aware of the problems and are taking measures to reduce discord between locals and visitors.

'Undoubtedly the increase in tourists has had an influence on the daily lives of the citizens of Kyoto', said Shuhei Akahoshi, head of the city's Department of Conventions & Tourism. 'But we have several ongoing advertising campaigns that promote better manners among tourists.'

Travel authorities are also encouraging people to visit outside of the peak season or to see sights at less popular times of the day.

General comprehension

Answer the following questions in complete sentences.

1 What are three complaints that local people have about the problems caused by increased numbers of tourists?
2 What are the four cities mentioned as being popular tourist destinations?
3 What campaign has Japan's tourism agency started?

Vocabulary

Choose the option (**a**, **b**, or **c**) that is closest in meaning to the words in the text.

1 skyrocket
- **a** fly
- **b** change in numbers
- **c** increase rapidly

2 frantically
- **a** angrily
- **b** desperately
- **c** unhappily

3 cuisine
- **a** restaurants
- **b** a style of architecture
- **c** a style of cooking

4 enamoured
- **a** pleased
- **b** angry
- **c** disappointed

5 unscrupulous
- **a** dirty
- **b** unpopular
- **c** dishonest

Internal assessment (SL)

Figure 5.12 The tourist industry generates billions of dollars but is everyone happy about it?

Examine the photograph above and consider the following points:

- What do you see in the picture? Describe only what you see. Do not give opinions.
- Reflect on the picture in connection with the following theme: Tourism's impact on cities and their inhabitants.
- Who benefits the most?
- What options are open to someone who wants to be a more responsible tourist?
- Make connections to your own experience and the experiences of people you know.

Using the points above, spend 15 minutes preparing a presentation about the photograph. Use the preparation time to organise your ideas and plan the sequence of what you will talk about.

Your presentation should last 3 to 4 minutes, after which your teacher and other students will have the opportunity to comment or ask questions about what you have said. You must engage in a conversation with them. In total, this task should take approximately 15 minutes.

Speaking practice: a class debate

'Tourism is positive for the economy of the country involved.'

All students prepare for a class debate. Your teacher will divide the class into two groups. One group will prepare arguments in favour of tourism and one group will prepare arguments against it.

Both groups should research information about the effects of tourists and tourism and consider countries around the world in both developed and developing countries.

The debate takes place in two stages. In the first stage, half the class make a circle of chairs: equal numbers for and against. The rest of the class listen, observe, and take notes in an outer circle.

The inner group begins the discussion, and the observers note down the use of language to introduce points into the discussion, and the arguments and how well they are supported.

After a prearranged time, the discussion stops and the outer circle give their feedback. The groups switch and continue as before.

Finally, the whole class takes a vote on which side most efficiently and convincingly puts their case.

Language and phrases for a discussion or debate

Agreement

- *I agree with what you said.*
- *I follow your argument and agree with you.*
- *That is a very interesting point, I would like to add...*

Disagreement

- *I'm sorry, but I disagree with what you said.*
- *Although I understand what you're saying, I cannot agree with you...*
- *It is really unacceptable to state...*
- *I find the argument lacks strength.*

Interrupting

- *I'm sorry, I really must stop you there...*
- *Excuse me, I think you are repeating yourself.*

5.4 Taking action

Going vegan

Mass media – Webpage

Veganism

What is veganism?

Veganism is a way of living which seeks to exclude, as far as is possible and practicable, all forms of exploitation of, and cruelty to, animals for food, clothing, or any other purpose.

One thing all vegans have in common is a plant-based diet avoiding all animal foods such as meat (including fish, shellfish, and insects), dairy, eggs, and honey, as well as avoiding animal-derived materials, products tested on animals and places that use animals for entertainment.

Reasons to become a vegan

For the animals

Preventing the exploitation of animals is not the only reason for becoming vegan, but for many it remains the key factor in their decision to go vegan and stay vegan. Having emotional attachments with animals may form part of that reason, while many believe that all sentient creatures have a right to life and freedom.

For your health

Well-planned vegan diets follow healthy eating guidelines, and contain all the nutrients that our bodies need. Both the British Diabetic Association and the American Academy of Nutrition and Dietetics recognise that vegan diets are suitable for every age and stage of life. Some research has linked vegan diets with lower blood pressure and cholesterol, and lower rates of heart disease, Type 2 diabetes, and some types of cancer.

Going vegan is a great opportunity to learn more about nutrition and cooking, and improve your diet. Getting your nutrients from plant foods allows more room in your diet for health-promoting options like whole grains, fruit, nuts, seeds, and vegetables, which are packed full of beneficial fibre, vitamins, and minerals.

For the environment

From recycling our household rubbish to cycling to work, we're all aware of ways to live a greener life. One of the most effective things an individual can do to lower their carbon footprint is to avoid all animal products.

General comprehension

State whether the following sentences are true or false. Give a quote from the text to support your answers.

1 Veganism is not only about not eating meat.
2 Vegans believe that it is acceptable to wear leather clothes.
3 Vegan diets may lessen the risk of heart disease.
4 Minerals and vitamins, vital for a healthy diet, can be found in grains and nuts.

Mass media – Webpage

Reducing the burden on the environment

Why is meat and dairy so bad for the environment?

The production of meat and other animal products places a heavy burden on the environment – from crops and water required to feed the animals, to the transport and other processes involved from farm to fork. The vast amount of grain feed required for meat production is a significant contributor to deforestation, habitat loss, and species extinction. In Brazil alone, the equivalent of 5.6 million acres of land is used to grow soya beans for animals in Europe. This land contributes to developing world malnutrition by driving impoverished populations to grow cash crops for animal feed, rather than food for themselves. On the other hand, considerably lower quantities of crops and water are required to sustain a vegan diet, making the switch to veganism one of the easiest, most enjoyable, and most effective ways to reduce our impact on the environment.

For people

Just as veganism is the sustainable option when it comes to looking after our planet, plant-based living is also a more sustainable way of feeding the human family. A plant-based diet requires only one third of the land needed to support a meat and dairy diet. With rising global food and water insecurity due to a myriad of environmental and socio-economic problems, there's never been a better time to adopt a more sustainable way of living.

So what do vegans eat?

A great deal – you'll soon find a whole new world of exciting foods and flavours opening up to you. A vegan diet is richly diverse and comprises all kinds of fruits, vegetables, nuts, grains, seeds, beans, and pulses – all of which can be prepared in endless combinations that will ensure you're never bored. From curry to cake, pasties to pizzas, all your favourite things can be suitable for a vegan diet if they're made with plant-based ingredients.

General comprehension

Answer the following questions in complete sentences.

1 According to the text, how does switching to veganism reduce the burden on the environment?

2 Apart from fruit and vegetables, what do vegans eat?

3 What crop is grown in Brazil to feed animals in Europe?

Vocabulary

Choose the option (**a, b,** or **c**) that is closest in meaning to the words in the text.

1 deforestation
- a selling trees
- b planting trees
- c removing trees

2 malnutrition
- a a lack of nutrients in the diet
- b not eating
- c eating too much meat

3 myriad
- a important
- b problematic
- c large number

4 sustainable
- a replaced
- b maintained
- c rebuilt

Internal assessment (SL)

Figure 5.13 Veganism: just a passing phase – or something more?

Examine the photograph above and consider the following points:

- What do you see in the picture? Describe only what you see. Do not give opinions.
- Reflect on the picture in connection with the theme of sharing the planet.
- What is a vegan?
- Consider why veganism is growing and include ethical arguments.
- Make connections to your own experience and the experiences of others you know.
- Make connections to global issues of land, water, and population.

Using the points above, spend 15 minutes preparing a presentation about the photograph. Use the preparation time to organise your ideas and plan the sequence of what you will talk about.

Your presentation should last 3 to 4 minutes, after which your teacher and other students will have the opportunity to comment or ask questions about what you have said. You must engage in a conversation with them. In total, this task should take approximately 15 minutes.

The importance of insects

Mass media – Article

A FRIEND TO THE BEES: MIKAILA ULMER

This 12-year-old entrepreneur seeks to help support the declining bee population with her family's lemonade recipe.

It all started when Me & the Bees Lemonade founder Mikaila Ulmer was four. She was brainstorming product ideas to enter a competition in Austin, Texas, USA, for Lemonade Day when she was stung by a bee – twice. Although she was scared, Mikaila was also curious: What purpose did bees play in the world?

Mikaila learned how important bees are for our ecosystem. In fact, honeybees are responsible for pollinating three-fourths of the foods we eat, like nuts, vegetables, herbs, and fruits. The rapidly declining bee population has spurred quick action from the scientific community to investigate, finding a leading cause linking to the pesticides, fungicides, and a new class of pesticide called neonicotinoids humans use to keep plant-damaging pests at bay.

As Mikaila, now 12, began to learn more about bees, an idea came to her: If she opted to sweeten her great-grandmother's flaxseed lemonade with local honey, she could share the profits

TOK

Bees, pandas, polar bears, wolves, elephants, whales, and dolphins all elicit sympathy when their populations are endangered. To what extent do emotions help or hinder knowledge creation in the natural sciences?

with organisations working to save declining honeybee populations. Her award-winning Me & the Bees Lemonade can now be found in natural markets nationwide, along with a growing number of restaurants, food trucks, and natural-food-delivery companies.

General comprehension

Answer the following questions in complete sentences.

1 What event made Mikaila want to learn more about bees?
2 According to the text, what role do bees play in our ecosystem?
3 What does the scientific community believe is causing a decline in the bee population?
4 What was the idea that Mikaila had to help the bees?
5 What sentence from the text shows Mikaila won a prize for her idea?

Zoom in on grammar

The past continuous

The past continuous tense is used to show that at a time in the past someone was in the middle of an action. It is often followed by a verb which shows what interrupted the continuous action.

*She **was brainstorming** product ideas, when she was stung by a bee.*

The passive voice

The passive voice is often used to describe what happened rather than who did an action. The person doing the action is called the agent. As the passive voice focuses on what happened (the action), it is sometimes considered impersonal and formal.

*Mikaila **was stung** by a bee.* (In this case the agent is *a bee* and is mentioned to add clarity because other insects can sting.)

*Me & the Bees Lemonade **can** now **be found** in natural markets...* (In this case the agent – *the customer* – is not mentioned.)

Mass media – Article

WHERE HAVE ALL OUR INSECTS GONE?

There is a crisis in the countryside – and a massive decline in insect numbers could have significant consequences for the environment.

When Simon Leather was a student in the 1970s, he took a summer job as a postman and delivered mail (1) ______ the villages of Kirk Hammerton and Green Hammerton in North Yorkshire. He recalls his early morning walks through its lanes, (2) ______ the porches of houses on his round. At virtually every home, he saw the same picture: windows plastered (3) ______ tiger moths that had been attracted by lights the previous night and were still clinging to the glass. 'It was quite a sight,' says Leather, who is now a professor of entomology (4) ______ Harper Adams University in Shropshire.

But it is not a vision that he has experienced in recent years. Those tiger moths have almost disappeared, 'You hardly see any, although there used to be thousands in summer and that was just a couple of villages.'

It is an intriguing story and it is likely to be repeated (5) ______ the next few weeks. The start of summer is the time of year when the nation's insects should make their presence known by coating countryside windows with their fluttering presence, and splattering themselves on car windscreens. But they are spectacularly failing to do so. Instead, they are making themselves newsworthy through their absence. Britain's insects, it seems, are disappearing.

This point was underlined last week when tweets from the naturalist and TV presenter Chris Packham went viral after he commented on the absence of insects during a weekend at his home in the New Forest. Packham said he had not seen a single butterfly in his garden, and added that he sleeps with his windows open but rarely finds craneflies or moths in his room in the morning. By contrast they were commonplace when he was a boy. 'Our generation is presiding over an ecological apocalypse and we've somehow or other normalised it,' he later said.

Certainly, the statistics are grim. Native ladybird populations are crashing; three-quarters of butterfly species – such as the painted lady and the Granville fritillary – have dropped significantly in numbers; while bees, of which there are more than 250 species in the UK, are also suffering major plunges in populations, with great yellow bumble bees, solitary potter flower bees and other species declining steeply in recent years.

As for moths, some of the most beautiful visitors to our homes and gardens, the picture is particularly alarming. Apart from the tiger moth, which was once widespread in the UK, the V-moth recorded a 99 per cent fall in numbers between 1968 and 2007 and is now threatened with extinction. And it is a decline that could have crucial consequences. Our creepy crawlies may have unsettling looks but they lie at the foot of a wildlife food chain that makes them vitally important to the make-up and nature of the countryside. They are 'the little things that run the world', according to the distinguished biologist Edward O Wilson, who once observed: 'If all humankind were to disappear, the world would regenerate back to the rich state of equilibrium that existed 10 000 years ago. If insects were to vanish, the environment would collapse into chaos.'

The best illustration of the ecological importance of insects is provided by our wildlife. Without insects, hundreds of species face starvation and some ornithologists believe this lack of food is already causing serious declines in bird numbers, a point stressed by the naturalist and wildlife author Michael McCarthy. 'Britain's farmland birds have more than halved in number since 1970,' he points out. 'Some declines have been catastrophic.'

Text handling

Complete paragraphs 1 and 2 of the text with the following words.

at	over	past	to	with

General comprehension

Answer the following questions in complete sentences.

1 Why does the writer say insects are making themselves newsworthy?
2 What does the writer mean when he says Packham's tweets 'went viral'?
3 What does Packham mean when he states that the ecological apocalypse 'has been normalised'?
4 What does the phrase 'threatened with extinction' mean?
5 What are 'creepy crawlies'?
6 What are 'the little things that run the world'?
7 What did Edward O Wilson say would happen to the world if all humankind disappeared?
8 And what will happen to the world, according to Wilson, if all insects disappear?

State whether the following sentences are true or false. Give a quote from the text to support your answers.

9 These days, everyone's windscreens are always covered in dead insects.
10 Packham only saw one butterfly in his garden.
11 As a boy, Packham frequently had moths in his bedroom in the mornings.
12 Ladybird numbers are declining slowly.
13 There are more than 300 species of bees in the UK.
14 Creepy crawlies are essential to life on the planet.
15 Without humans the world would return to how it was 1000 years ago.
16 Birds are dying from hunger because there are not enough plants to eat.

Mass media – Article

WARNING OF 'ECOLOGICAL ARMAGEDDON' AFTER DRAMATIC PLUNGE IN INSECT NUMBERS

Three-quarters of flying insects in nature reserves across Germany have vanished in 25 years, with serious implications for all life on Earth, scientists say.

The abundance of flying insects has plunged by three-quarters over the past 25 years according to a new study that has shocked scientists.

Insects are an integral part of life on Earth as both pollinators and prey for other wildlife and it was known that some species such as butterflies were declining. But the newly revealed scale of the losses to all insects has prompted warning that the world is 'on course for ecological Armageddon', with profound impacts on human society.

The new data was gathered in nature reserves across Germany but has implications for all landscapes dominated by agriculture, the researchers said.

The cause of the huge decline is as yet unclear, although the destruction of wild areas and widespread use of pesticides are the most likely factors and climate may play a role. The scientists were able to rule out weather and changes to landscape in the reserves as causes, but data on pesticide levels has not been collected.

'The fact that the number of flying insects is decreasing at such a high rate in such a large area is an alarming discovery,' said Hans de Kroon, at Radbound University in the Netherlands who led the research.

The research, published in the journal *Plos One*, is based on the work of dozens of amateur entomologists across Germany who began using strictly standardised ways of collecting insects in 1989. Special tents called malaise traps were used to capture more than 1500 samples of all flying insects at 63 different nature reserves.

The amateur entomologists also collected detailed weather measurements and recorded changes to the landscape or plant species in the reserves, but this could not explain the loss of the insects. 'The weather might explain many of the fluctuations within the season and between the years, but it doesn't explain the rapid downward trend,' said Martin Sorg from the Krefeld Entomological Society in Germany, who led the amateur entomologists.

General comprehension

Answer the following questions in complete sentences.

1 Which two European countries were involved in the research?
2 Where was the information collected?
3 Who led the research?
4 Who undertook the research?
5 How did the researchers gather their information?
6 What other information did they gather?

Vocabulary

Find words or phrases in the text which match the following meanings.

1 large amounts of something
2 victims
3 not professional
4 ruled by
5 discount an idea
6 catch
7 variations

The cost of fashion

Intercultural activity

The following is a text from an Australian newspaper which uses some Australian terms – an 'op shop' is an opportunity shop. What do you think an opportunity shop could mean?
The word 'daggy' means 'untidy' or 'dishevelled'. Do you know any other words with similar meanings?

Mass media – Article

SUSTAINABLE FASHION

Shop less, mend more: making more sustainable fashion choices

Every day, most of us dress ourselves in items churned out by what is arguably the world's second-most polluting industry. Reportedly topped only by oil, the fashion industry is contributing to major environmental destruction – mainly because consumers insist on buying so many clothes at such cheap prices.

Water is a significant part of the problem. Textile manufacturing uses huge amounts of water, much of which gets flushed into waterways laden with contaminants such as bleaches, acids, inks, and dyes. Horrifyingly, farmers in parts of China and India are reportedly predicting fashion's next biggest hues by the colour of rivers tainted by textile industry runoff. Fast fashion has terrible impacts on people too, with workers in developing nations often paid a pittance to labour in unsafe conditions.

Alternatives do exist. The solution lies in buying less and choosing better quality items that are made as ethically as possible. But how to tell good brands from bad? Our guide to ethical fashion navigates the conundrum.

(1) ______________________________

Step one is choosing brands that consider the planet and their workers. The desire to wear cheap new looks daily has led to offshore manufacturing in often deplorable circumstances – buying local, well-made pieces can sidestep all that.

(2) ______________________________

Think beyond where or how clothing is made, to exactly what each piece is made from. Where possible, skip petroleum-based synthetics such as polyester and nylon, which are actually plastics that take forever to breakdown once tossed. Each time fabrics are washed, they shed thousands of microfibers that end up polluting rivers and oceans. (Guppy Friend filter bags, developed in Berlin, are a solution to trapping microfibers in laundries.)

Natural fabrics must also be selected with care. About half the world's clothes and textiles are made from cotton, usually grown with pesticides and requiring mammoth water inputs. Bamboo has been touted as a more ethical option, but while the plant is farmed sustainably, toxic chemicals are often used to turn bamboo into fabric.

Organic cotton and bamboo linen are better, as is hemp, linen, silk, and wool. Lyocell, made from natural cellulose found in wood pulp, harvested from sustainably farmed forest plantations, also rates fairly well. Some brands are even recycling waste into fabric: Melbourne's Bombshell Bay Swimwear range incorporates polyester made from recycled ocean plastics. While Byron Bay's Salt Gypsy surf wear uses Econyl yarn spun from pre- and post-consumer waste.

'Choosing better fabrics is essential to us transforming this industry for the better,' says Clara Vuletich, a Sydney-based sustainability strategist who works with Australian fashion brands. 'If you consciously decide to purchase a garment made using recycled material or an exciting new fibre, such as cruelty-free leather made in a lab, you are supporting start-up companies creating new markets and avoiding the toxic impacts associated with conventional textiles.'

(3) ______________________________

Once clothing becomes tired and hole-ridden, don't rush straight to the bin: try mending instead. Call a local clothing repairer or, better yet, join the #visiblemendingprogramme, which encourages entirely obvious and colourful hand-sewn repairs.

'Most clothing problems are easily mendable: missing buttons and loose stitching, for example. But mending is also an opportunity to make your clothes better than new. Visible mending allows you to be creative and celebrate the life of your clothes,' says Erin Lewis-Fitzgerald, who runs a Visible Mending Project in Melbourne. 'One creatively mended garment might not save the planet, but it might inspire three other people to start mending and become more aware.'

Those with more time and skills can join the slow clothing movement and sew garments from scratch. Look out for Sydney's 'Sewing with Kate' and 'In the Folds' for tips and inspiration, or look at Jane Milburn's 'Sew It Again' 365-day eco-clothing project.

(4) ______________________________

A guaranteed way to reduce the fashion industry's impact is to avoid buying new stuff in the first place. Second-hand stores are the ultimate clothing recyclers – and thrift shop fashion definitely doesn't have to be daggy. Hannah Klose is proof. The Brisbane founder of Never Pay Retail has amassed a huge Instagram following through daily style posts featuring entirely op-shopped clothes.

'I've found so many amazing pieces, some brand new with the tags still attached, for sometimes less than 5 per cent of the retail value – like a Gucci bag for $6, a Carla Zampatti top for $4.50, which would have retailed for over $400, and a Karen Walker skirt for $5,' Klose says. 'Collectively, thrifters are helping to divert 300 000 tonnes of textiles from landfill each year. It's a step in the right direction.'

But a word of caution when it comes to donating clothes. The ABC's War on Waste survey of 36 700 people found 82 per cent of respondents had donated clothes, yet only 53 per cent had ever purchased second-hand clothing. With supply outstripping demand, and charities overwhelmed by mountains of fast fashion items that can never be on-sold, non-profits have essentially become our dumping ground. Yet another reason to support second-hand stores while winding back our fast fashion addiction.

Switching to more ethical fashion options does take forethought, but the health of the planet and the safety of workers in developing nations depends on it.

Text handling

Add the following headings to the article above.

- Avoid fabrics made using petroleum and chemicals
- Reduce your consumption by hitting the op shops
- Extend your wardrobe's lifespan by mending
- Buy clothes made locally by ethical labels

Without referring to or re-reading the text, complete the following paragraph.

But a word of caution (1) ______________ it comes to donating clothes. The ABC's War (2) ______________ Waste survey of 36 700 people found 82 per cent (3) ______________ respondents had donated clothes, (4) ______________ only 53 per cent had ever purchased second-hand clothing. (5) ______________ supply outstripping demand, and charities overwhelmed (6) ______________ mountains of fast fashion items that can never be (7) ______________ , non-profits have essentially become our dumping ground. Yet another reason to support second-hand stores (8) ______________ winding (9) ______________ our fashion addiction.

General comprehension

Answer the following questions in complete sentences.

1 According to the writer, what is arguably the second most polluting industry?
2 Which industry is the worst cause of pollution?
3 What happens to much of the water used in the fashion industry? Why is that a problem?
4 What does the writer suggest are the alternatives to the problem?
5 What are the problems presented by petroleum-based synthetics?
6 Why is the answer to simply buy natural fibres not really a solution?
7 What does the writer suggest should be done if your clothes are old and worn?
8 What is the best way to reduce the negative effects of clothing production?
9 What is the role of second-hand stores?

Vocabulary

Find words or phrases in the text which match the following meanings.

1 rapidly, thoughtlessly produced
2 harmful substances
3 a very low wage
4 a challenge or puzzle
5 thrown away
6 throw something away without thinking
7 creating something from the very beginning
8 keep away from
9 a short warning
10 reducing

Personal – Letter

The Old Mill
White Lane
Oldwold
19 March

Dear Claire,

I do hope you are well as I missed you at the last coffee morning. It was a very enjoyable morning with several new club members too. An idea was presented to the members which I think you will really like.

As we all know, producing the fabrics, making the clothes, washing them, and then disposing of them when we no longer want to wear them, all contributes to environmental pollution. Young people in particular seem to buy an awful lot of new clothes. I often see them in the town with their paper carrier bags and know that a lot of what they have bought has been produced by workers in a less than healthy environment under less than fair conditions. On top of that, the clothes are often of poor quality fabric and so badly made that they will only be worn a few times. These cheap clothes all land in the recycling boxes or dustbins and contribute even more to the pollution which is damaging our planet – the only one we have!

The idea was put forward to have an exchange of our old but much loved clothing. Everyone was asked to contribute a few articles of good quality clothing which they no longer wear. We were all told to take a critical look at our wardrobes and do some sorting! The clothes must, of course, be clean and well presented, and the club committee members are willing to come and pick items up from our homes, if we should prefer that.

Then on the sales day, we can all go along to see if there are any items which would suit us and liven up our wardrobes. Doesn't that sound like an excellent idea and a lot of fun too? There will of course be coffee and refreshments provided for a minimal fee.

Basically, the idea is firstly to help reduce waste, secondly to help us clear out our wardrobes, and thirdly to give us a thrill of something new for a minimal price. It is a win-win situation! I do hope you will join in.

The date is the second Tuesday of next month, at 10 a.m. at the Chair's house.

I do hope to see you there so that we can have a good chat and find some new clothes.

With very best wishes,
Veronica

General comprehension

Answer the following questions in complete sentences.

1 What is the idea the club are presenting?
2 According to Veronica, which age group buys the most clothes?
3 Veronica thinks that young people buying so many cheap clothes is wrong. What three reasons does she give?
4 What should the club members provide?
5 What should the club members do?
6 Which extra service will the committee members provide, if necessary?
7 What are the benefits of this clothes exchange?
8 What does Veronica mean when she says this is a 'win-win situation'?

Vocabulary

Find words or phrases in the text which match the following meanings.

1 to get rid of something
2 add to
3 changing an old product to something new
4 suggested
5 a swap
6 close examination of something
7 very small
8 feeling of excitement
9 make less

Paper 1 practice task

You have decided to organise a clothes exchange. Decide who will be involved, how it will be organised, and when it will take place. Write either an article for the school newsletter, a blog, or a flyer to advertise the event. Clearly inform participants what they need to do. Be enthusiastic and encouraging so that people will want to join in.

SL students should write 200–400 words. HL students should write 450–600 words.

For tips on how to create a flyer, see page 130 of Chapter 3, Human ingenuity.

5.5 Sharing our space

Space exploration

Can you name an astronaut? Maybe you can name the first man who travelled into space. It was Yuri Gagarin, the Russian astronaut, in 1961. Or can you name one of the scientists who became the first men on the Moon in 1969? Three Americans: Neil Armstrong, Buzz Aldrin, and Michael Collins were the first human beings to make a lunar landing and walk on the Moon. They travelled to the Moon in the rocket Apollo 11 and made history. Since then we have become used to rockets being launched and experiments being carried out in the process of exploring space. But how important is space exploration to us today?

The achievements of the first men on the Moon inspired a whole generation to grow up wanting to be astronauts, engineers, and rocket scientists. In addition, space research programmes have been responsible for many new developments in our lives. Much of the environmental work done today on air quality, climate change, and alternative energy was inspired by NASA (National Aeronautics and Space Administration) and its scientists. Space research has enabled work on the possibilities of discovering other natural resources, as the concern for the future of fossil fuels here on earth grows.

So, what has space research led to? The spin-off has created new markets and economies that have changed our lives. Just to mention a few: LED lights, the development of artificial limbs, improved car tyres, fire-resistant materials, and the purification of water.

Can you find more space exploration spin-offs?

The following text is from ESA, the European Space Agency.

TOK On what basis can scientific achievement be measured? How do we know what has been a scientific advancement?

Mass media – Webpage

Would you like to be an astronaut?

You do not have to be superman or superwoman to fly in space. Many men and women, from many different countries, have become astronauts. ESA, for example, now has 14 astronauts from eight different countries.

If you want to be one of the few people to experience the thrill of lift-off, see the Earth from on high and float in a spacecraft, then how do you go about it?

Here are five tips on how to become an astronaut
First: You must really want to become an astronaut as it takes many years of study and work before you even begin your training. Most astronauts begin when they are between 27 and 37.

Second: You need to be clever enough to attend a university to study engineering, medicine, or one of the sciences. Many astronauts also learn to be pilots in their country's air force.

Third: Astronauts come from many different countries in Europe, and may share missions with astronauts from the USA, Russia, and Japan. They need to speak English and Russian so that they can all talk to one another.

Fourth: You must be healthy, since astronaut training and spaceflights can be very tiring.

Lastly: On a spacecraft, astronauts live and work in a very small space so you need to be good at getting on with people.

Are you still interested? If so, maybe you will become one of the men and women who orbits the Earth in a spacecraft, walks in space, or visits the Moon. See you in space!

Training at the European Astronaut Centre

If a human space mission is to be a success, astronauts (and mission teams on the ground) have to be familiar with every aspect of spacecraft operations. Training in Europe is based mainly at the European Astronaut Centre (EAC) in Cologne, Germany. Today, the EAC is the home base of ESA's 14 astronauts.

Led by astronaut Frank De Winne, the EAC team is made up of ESA staff, as well as people from the German Aerospace Centre (DLR), the French space agency CNES, and European industry. The EAC prepares European astronauts for many different types of mission.

One way in which this is done is by rehearsing in-orbit activities in a huge water tank that contains mock up spacecraft modules. Space-suited astronauts use the tank to practise spacewalks in 'neutral buoyancy', similar to weightlessness. The uplift of the water offsets the pull of gravity, so the astronauts can train in near-real conditions.

The EAC also contains full size mock-ups of space modules, including the ATV supply ferry and the Columbus science lab, as well as simulators and other hands-on equipment. It enables astronauts from countries such as the USA, Russia, and Japan to learn about the European parts of the International Space Station.

Modern computer technology also enables astronauts to practise by using a virtual reality system. Wearing a special headset, they can move around or through the space station as if they were really there.

The EAC also provides medical support to the astronauts and their families when they are sent to the USA, Russia, and Japan. Dozens of space missions involving astronauts from ESA and its Member States have been supported by the EAC since it was created in 1990.

General comprehension

Choose the best ending for the following sentences (1–3) from the list (a–h) below.

1 In order to communicate with others in the team, ___.
2 Cologne, Germany, is the home base for ___.
3 Practising being on a space station is ___.

a the astronauts must speak one European language well
b the 14 astronauts currently training at ESA

c enabled by a virtual reality headset
d the astronauts need to be able to speak English and Russian
e the astronauts need to be good with computer technology
f the most important part of training
g the research into rocket design
h the result of years of training

Students give their opinions about space exploration

One teacher asked her tenth grade class their opinions about space exploration. Here are some of their responses:

Personal – Opinion

1. We need to explore space to finally find out if there is anyone else out there. I mean there are so many planets, we can't be the only inhabited one. So much literature has looked at this question. — Timur

2. I'm not sure. There is so much that needs to be done here on Earth. Last summer I joined a group from our school working in Romania to help build houses for poor people. I don't think they cared much about space exploration. They just wanted a roof over their heads and an indoor toilet. — Yutaro

3. Well, I definitely believe space exploration is a waste of time and money. The TV is full of appeals for people to donate to charities that are helping people in need all around the world. So there is obviously a shortage of funding for that. — Polina

4. Well, we really need to think about this. It's a complex subject. Space exploration is not just about space. It's about research and finding out new possibilities for our lives here on earth too. — Stella

General comprehension

Answer the following questions in complete sentences.

1 Which response draws attention to the positive results that space exploration has for people on Earth?
2 Where does Polina think money spent on space exploration can be put to better use?
3 What does Yutaro's response say about people too poor to have their own house?

Paper 1 practice task

Do we need space exploration? Present an argument for or against space exploration and give reasons for your choice. You may write a speech to the school body, an essay, or an article for the school newspaper.

SL students should write 250–400 words. HL students should write 450–600 words.

Mass media – Press release

UK SPACE AGENCY'S SATELLIFE COMPETITION
– a national competition for young people to present their ideas for innovative uses for satellites

Press release

GPS* wristband for surfers among winning ideas from young space entrepreneurs. The winners of the SatelLife competition, aged between 13 and 21, will go on to pitch their ideas to a panel of 'dragons'† from the space sector.

From: UK Space Agency, Department for Business, Energy & Industrial Strategy, and Sam Gyimah MP

(1) ____________________

A group of school children from Cornwall and a student from Wiltshire have won a competition for ideas on how satellites could improve life on Earth, Science Minister Sam Gyimah announced today (Friday, 13 April). Ellie Jones, Jessica Knight, both 15, Summer Jeffery, and Emily Haddrell, both 14, from Truro, scooped £7500 for the best group entry in the UK Space Agency competition with their Surf Safe concept. Ieuan Higgs, from Chippenham, received £7500 for the best individual entry for his Infrastructure Planning and Development Analysis Tool.

Figure 5.14 How could satellites improve life on Earth?

(2) ____________________

The SatelLife Challenge supports the development of science, data handling and technological skills, complementing the Government's Year of Engineering campaign which is championing careers in science, technology, engineering and mathematics to the next generation.

Science Minister Sam Gyimah said: 'The UK leads the world in building satellites and we want to encourage young people like those entering this competition to get involved in every part of our thriving space sector.

'The creative use of data from space can solve many challenges and help establish successful businesses. It's a vital part of the Government's Industrial Strategy to back the entrepreneurs of tomorrow as we build an economy that's fit for the future.'

(3) ____________________

Ellie, Jessica, Summer, and Emily's idea was for a wristband that uses satellite location data and communications services to identify the locations of swimmers and surfers in the sea.

Ellie Jones said: 'It was so exciting, finding out about the competition. We had never done anything at all like this before. As students living in Cornwall, the sea has always been important to us and from the very start we knew we wanted to do something involving the beach. It was such a surprise to find out we had won and everyone was so happy

* GPS: Global Positioning System is a satellite-based radio navigation system operated by the United States government.

† 'Dragons' is a reference to the BBC television programme *Dragon's Den* where budding entrepreneurs get three minutes to pitch their business idea to a group of multi-millionaires who are willing to invest their own cash to give support to starting up those businesses.

when we got the email that for a long time, it didn't seem real.

'This whole experience has been amazing, we really enjoyed having the opportunity to do something like this. It has definitely given us the confidence to pursue STEM careers (STEM: Science, Technology, Engineering, Mathematics).'

(4) ______________________________

When combined with tidal and rip tide data, this could provide real time tracking and identification of people approaching known danger areas, and provide coast guards or the Royal National Lifeboat Institution (RNLI) with potentially life-saving information. Jon Oxenham, RNLI's Community Safety Manager, said: 'It's great to see young people thinking about water safety and creating new ideas which could save lives at sea. At the RNLI we are always trying to find new ways to save lives through innovation, data analysis, and new technology.'

(5) ______________________________

Ieuan Higgs' winning idea was for a tool that would map change in urban areas using satellites and algorithms, identifying where building is taking place and potential sites for development.

Ieuan, who is studying Computer Science at the University of Reading, said: 'I thought it would be an exciting opportunity to do a project on a topic I am very passionate about. I came up with my idea after combining my knowledge of current space technology with my areas of interest in computer science – using both to form a realistic business solution I thought would be both useful and achievable. It came as a massive shock to see that I was one of the winners, but it was certainly a welcome one! This unexpected result has given me the confidence to continue researching and working on my ideas in my spare time.'

(6) ______________________________

The competition is split into three age groups: 11–16; 16–18; 18–22, and a further seven entries from across the age categories were awarded £5000. The judging panel was made up of experts from the UK Space Agency, the European Space Agency, the Satellite Applications Catapult in Harwell, and industry. All nine winning entries will be able to pitch their ideas to a panel of 'dragons' from the space sector.

Text handling

Add the following headings to the press release above.

- What it means to the competitors
- Town planning
- Who took part?
- Get involved!
- The next steps
- A contribution to saving lives

General comprehension

Answer the following questions in complete sentences.

1 What prizes were awarded to the winners of the competition?
2 Which national rescue agency praised the idea put forward by Ellie, Jessica, Summer and Emily? Why?
3 Who were the judges who decided the winners?

Vocabulary

Find words in the text which match the following meanings.

1 present an idea to a panel of judges
2 developing successfully and getting better all the time
3 relating to or describing city or town areas

Mass media – Webpage

Space exploration

For centuries, people dreamed about leaving Earth and travelling to other worlds. Then, in 1957, the Soviet Union made the first small step into space by launching a small satellite, called Sputnik. The Space Age had begun.

Early space activities were dominated by the United States and the Soviet Union. However, as time went by, Europe and Japan built their own satellites and rockets. Today, countries such as China, India, South Korea, Israel, and Brazil are developing their own space industries.

Figure 5.15 A rover on Mars

During the last 60 years, unmanned probes have been sent towards all of the planets in the Solar System, as well as many satellites, asteroids, and comets. Spacecraft have soft-landed on half a dozen worlds, while rovers have driven over the surfaces of the Moon and Mars. The Sun has also been explored in great detail by a fleet of spacecraft.

Many space observatories, such as the Hubble Space Telescope, have been launched to look at the distant universe. They have sent back some amazing pictures taken in visible light. But they can also observe stars and galaxies at wavelengths that are invisible to human eyes – radio, infrared, ultraviolet, X-rays, and gamma rays. The flood of discoveries has changed the way we look at the universe.

More than 500 people have flown in space since Yuri Gagarin paved the way in 1961. Twenty people have travelled to the Moon and 12 of them have walked on the Moon. Space stations have been built, and astronauts have learned to live and work in space for many months, or even years.

General comprehension

Answer the following questions in complete sentences.

1 What are the five wavelengths mentioned in the text?
2 How long can astronauts stay in space?

Look at the table of numbers that appear in the text and write a sentence stating what each number represents.

Number	What it represents
60	
500	
1957	
1961	
20	
12	

Vocabulary

1 Find a phrase in the text that means 'rockets travelling in space without an astronaut'.
2 Find a phrase in the text that means the number six.

Internal assessment (SL)

Figure 5.16 Astronauts working inside the space station

Examine the image above and consider the following points:

- What do you see in the picture? Describe only what you see. Do not give opinions.
- Summarise some of the history of space exploration.
- What benefits can space exploration bring us?
- Consider some of the problems that space exploration can bring.
- What is your view of tourism in space as an idea for the future?

Using the points above, spend 15 minutes preparing a presentation about the photograph. Use the preparation time to organise your ideas and plan the sequence of what you will talk about.

Your presentation should last 3 to 4 minutes, after which your teacher and other students will have the opportunity to comment or ask questions about what you have said. You must engage in a conversation with them. In total, this task should take approximately 15 minutes.

Are we alone?

Mass media – Webpage

Life beyond Earth

Figure 5.17 Reull Vallis – a valley on Mars

Mars was once warmer and wetter than it is today. Pictures sent back by ESA's Mars Express and other spacecraft show huge channels that look like dry river beds. Where did the water go?

A small amount is locked up in the polar ice caps. Some escaped into space. But much of it is frozen into the soil and rock.

It is possible that life began on Mars billions of years ago when it was warm and wet. Today, the surface is too cold and dry to support life. However, some scientists think that simple life, such as bacteria, may still exist deep underground.

Figure 5.18 Configuration of the ExoMars rover

ESA is planning to send a rover to search for Martian life. This will be followed by a mission to return rock and soil for scientific study.

Apart from Mars, life may exist in ice-covered oceans on some of the moons of Jupiter.

General comprehension

Answer the following questions in complete sentences.

1 What kind of life do scientists think may exist on other planets?
2 Is it possible to find complex life on the surface of Mars? Why?
3 According to the text, what kind of object could be used to collect material and samples from distant planets?

Research and presentation practice

Examining the literature of space travel and life in space

There have been many novels written about life in space or on other planets. Do some research and collect your findings into an ordered account. Use the information to give a three-minute presentation about your research, focusing either on one novel, or two or three novels.

Consider whether illustrations would improve your presentation.

Reading and HL literature recommendations

Reading is the single most successful way towards language acquisition.

The greatest incentive to read is the enjoyment level experienced by the reader. There is also a correlation between reading and writing. Reading widely improves vocabulary and writing style. Here we have listed suggested titles for free reading or class study. The titles are organised according to the five themes in the book and are considered to have content relating in some way to the overall theme. Enjoy!

Identities

The Book Thief by Markus Zusak

The Australian writer, Markus Zusak, was inspired to write this book after listening to accounts about life in Germany and Austria during the Second World War, which he heard from his parents and grandparents. The novel tells the story of a young German girl, Liesel, and her experiences of the war in a small village. When Liesel's brother dies in the early part of the story, the reader is introduced to Death, the surprisingly compassionate narrator who collects the souls of those who have died. It is also the moment where Liesel finds a book in the snow, *The Gravedigger's Handbook*. During the dark years of the war, books were scarce and Liesel had a strong desire to read. The title gives the reader an idea of what Liesel's involvement with books might be. It is a novel that shows the reader the best and the worst of our fellow humanity, but it is the enduring echo of the goodness that remains.

Salt to the Sea by Ruta Sepetys

Ruta Sepetys is an internationally acclaimed author of historical fiction and winner of several literary awards. Her works have been published in over 50 countries and in 36 languages. She is Lithuanian-American and lives in the United States.

Salt to the Sea tells the stories of three young people in the year 1945 as they try to escape the war-torn countries they are from. From three different countries – Lithuania, Poland, and East Prussia – they have one aim: to survive. It is the story of how it feels to be a refugee and have survival as your main focus in life. The refugees find a ship to take them to safety, but that ship is the *Wilhelm Gustloff* and it will never reach its destination.

Noughts and Crosses by Malorie Blackman

Noughts and Crosses has been voted Britain's best-loved teen story. It is a love story, but not a straightforward one. Not only are the boy and girl from different ethnic backgrounds, but they also live in a world set in the future where white European people are slaves and Africans are technologically better organised and economically strong. Black people are 'the crosses' and white people are 'the noughts'. The two young lovers, Callum and Sephy, are the narrators and the story unfolds through their narration. The story moves quickly and the reader is forever in suspense wondering if Callum and Sephy will ever be able to find happiness. The novel is full of powerful ideas and provides much inspiration for discussion.

The Girl Who Saw Lions by Berlie Doherty

Abela is a young girl living happily in Tanzania, but when her mother dies as a result of AIDS, her life changes. She is sent to Europe, to live with her uncle in London. London is a strange and different world for Abela. In Africa she knew about the danger of lions, but she realises that lions exist in London too, in the shape of her cold, hard uncle and his bitter wife. She is kept in a dark room and has to clean and cook in the household. Her story is told in parallel to the story of Rosa, living some streets away, whose life is also sent into turmoil when her mother announces she wants to adopt a child. Berlie Doherty beautifully weaves the stories of Abela and Rosa together to show the reader hope and the meaning of family.

Beyond the Bright Sea by Lauren Wolk

Beyond the Bright Sea is a story about finding your identity. Crow lives on a beautiful island but there are few people there: Osh, the old man who found her as a baby when she was washed up on the beach from a shipwrecked boat, and Miss Maggie, their neighbour. It is the outbreak of a fire that symbolically lights Crow's desire to find out who she is and where she is from. It leads to the discovery of buried treasure and is a heart-warming tale.

Experiences

To My Sons by Bear Grylls (non-fiction)

Bear Grylls is a mountain climber, world-record holder, and internationally known television personality. The British adventurer and explorer has led a very out-of-the-ordinary life. At the age of 23, he became one of the youngest climbers to conquer Mount Everest. This book is dedicated to his three sons and is full of humour and anecdotes. It encourages the reader to live a life that values not only knowledge and learning, but also risks and setbacks. The writing draws on the personal experiences of Bear Grylls and gives an insight into what drives this unusual character.

A Walk in the Woods by Bill Bryson (non-fiction)

Bill Bryson has been called the world's funniest travel writer. His books certainly give the reader plenty of laughs, but they are more than simply 'funny books'. They are superbly written with a wealth of descriptive passages that give insightful observations of people and places. In this book, he documents his progress as he walks one of the world's longest footpaths: the Appalachian Trail along the east coast of the United States of America. It is a 2200-mile (3500 km) trail through remote areas of beautiful scenery that is also home to insects, poisonous snakes, bobcats, moose, and bears. Bryson only managed to complete about 800 miles of the trail, but this does not make the book any less interesting.

Bone Talk by Candy Gourlay

The story is set in 1899, at the beginning of the colonial era, in the highlands of the Philippines. This is a time in history when the Western world knew very little about the Philippines and it was visited only by a small number of anthropologists. The story centres on the young Filipino boy, Samkad, who lives with his tribe in a remote area. He is concerned with the rituals of his village and the interactions with other tribes. His life changes when the country is invaded by the Americans. The reader is drawn into the story, observing the changes, threats, and new knowledge affecting Samkad's life as he encounters people from outside his country for the first time. It is both a gripping adventure story and a wonderful piece of historical fiction.

Metamorphosis by Franz Kafka

The word metamorphosis means 'a biological process of change', such as the change from a tadpole to a frog, or a caterpillar to a butterfly. In Franz Kafka's story the protagonist, Gregor Samsa, wakes up one morning to find he has changed into a gigantic beetle. The short story was originally written in German, Franz Kafka's native language. In this humorous but terrifying story, Kafka explores what it is like to be an outsider, the person who does not fit in. It is a great classic of its time.

Human ingenuity

The Mortal Instruments 1: City of Bones by Cassandra Clare

The Mortal Instruments is a tremendously popular series of stories (ten so far). Set in New York City, it is a splendid fantasy of witches, werewolves, fairies, and shadowhunters. Clare makes an unreal world of magic seem surprisingly real, creating a parallel world of weird happenings and excitement. *City of Bones* centres on Clary, a girl who is able to see what all the others around her cannot see: the shadowhunters. But why can she see them when no one else can? As the story unfolds, we are drawn into the secret world of demons and their hunters. You won't be able to put this story down, as you turn the pages, racing along with the shadowhunters after their enemies.

The Da Vinci Code (the young adult adaptation) by Dan Brown

The best code-breaking story has now been adapted for young adults. Robert Langdon, American professor of religious symbology, is in the Louvre Museum, Paris, to meet the curator. However, the meeting never takes place because the curator has been murdered. Mysterious symbols are left around the body and together with Sophie, a French cryptologist (code-breaking expert), they set out to solve the code and find the murderer before they become victims themselves.

Virtuosity by Jessica Martinez

Carmen has been playing the violin in her home country, the United States, since she was four years old. Now, at 17, she is preparing for a music competition, the Guarneri, and desperately wants to win. Then along comes Jeremy, a British boy, and it seems he is seriously good at playing the violin and therefore a challenge to Carmen. But who wants Carmen's success more than she does herself? It is her mother who puts pressure on Carmen. There is no need to know a lot about classical music to enjoy this compelling story where we learn of the contrast between the beauty of the music and the suffering and heartache the young virtuosos endure.

Silver Skin by Joan Lennon

Skara Brae is a village on the Orkney island of Mainland at the most northerly part of the British Isles. When Rab arrives here, he has become lost in a time loop and has travelled back in time from his life in the future to Skara Brae in the Neolithic period. He is wearing a silver coloured suit and his Neolithic ancestors think he is something magical. The writer not only beautifully describes the scenery and life on Skara Brae, but also the amazing technology of the future. As the reader is drawn into the story, we see life through Rab's eyes. It is a fascinating mix of future and past – and both are credible.

Social organisation

Animal Farm by George Orwell

This novel is considered to be a classic and no list of top books is complete without it. Pick it up and see what you think. Orwell's writing is clear and easy to understand, even though the ideas behind this story are complex and inform our understanding of how societies work. The interactions of the animals on the farm reflect developments in society during the period in history leading up to the Russian Revolution of 1917.

Lord of the Flies by William Golding

A group of boys shipwrecked on an island start to organise themselves. The story starts quite gently, but quickly moves to a frightening climax as the boys group together to survive when they realise they are on an uninhabited island. At the start of the novel, the boys are identifiable as a group of English schoolboys, but by the end the reader is confronted by a group of wild and fearful savages. It is society in the making: the workers, the thinkers, the leaders, and the followers. Written in 1954, it remains a classic novel that provokes discussion about social organisation and the roles that individuals play.

The Fun They Had by Isaac Asimov (short story)

The Fun They Had is a science fiction short story depicting school in the future. Written in 1954, the story is set in the year 2155 when children no longer go to school but are taught at home by computers. Two children, Margie and Tommy, find a book. This is a rare thing in itself, but the book is also an account of school in the past, when children were taught by teachers and all sat in one room together. The story ends with the children daydreaming about such a wonderful place and the fun those children must have had.

Wolf Hollow by Lauren Wolk

A gripping novel about bullying by the successful and award-winning novelist, Lauren Wolk. The novel focuses on one young girl's confrontation with this ugly form of behaviour. Annabelle meets Betty who is 'dark-hearted' and a violent bully. Annabelle is afraid of her, but when an old man becomes the target of Betty's bullying, Annabelle has to make difficult decisions.

No Fixed Address by Susin Nielsen

This is a story of poverty in a modern, Western city. We meet Felix and his mother, who have no fixed address and live in a van. This fact has to be kept a secret when Felix starts a new school. The novel is based on the reality of the lives of people who fall through the cracks of our carefully organised society which is based on home, work, and school. Susin Nielsen magnificently portrays a life of secrets, hopes, and the power of friendship and compassion to change lives.

Sharing the planet

See You in the Cosmos by Jack Cheng

Jack Cheng, who was born in Shanghai and grew up in Michigan, USA, has written a captivating novel about Alex Petroski, a young boy who is fascinated by rockets, space, and anything to do with space travel. His aim is to emulate the idea of Carl Sagan who was responsible for the 'Golden Record': a phonograph recording of sounds and images to be included on board the Voyager spacecraft on its journey into space in 1977. It was a recording reflecting life on Earth for those who might be living on other planets. So Alex sets out on a journey through the United States of America with his iPod, to record today's sights and sounds. The story is a road trip: a journey of discovery for Alex as he finds out more than he expected about himself, his family, and the people he meets along the way.

A Long Walk to Water (based on a true story) by Linda Sue Park

In this story of conflict and survival set in the Sudan, focusing on the lives of two children, the unifying theme is water. Without water there can be no survival. Though the book is easy to read, it portrays the horrors of war, the struggle for survival, and the hope of finding a safe place to live.

Stormy Seas: Stories of Young Boat Refugees by Mary Beth Leatherdale

This book tells the stories of refugees who voyage across the seas in the hope of finding a better place to live. It is a non-fiction resource for class and group discussion on refugees. The reader is presented with five true stories, ranging in time from 1939 to the present. This is a book you must read. It is powerfully written and gives you insights into young lives and lifestyles you have probably never experienced.

The Islands at the End of the World by Austin Aslan

This is a fascinating story set in Hawaii. After a world-wide electronics failure, the world is plunged into a situation where all people become isolated from their usual contacts. The novel has been described as an affirmation of the beauty of those things in the universe waiting to be discovered. The author has a degree in tropical conservation biology and the novel is a cornucopia of information about Hawaii and the surrounding islands. The book is part of the new emerging genre of climate fiction.

Teen Titles – A book review magazine for teenagers

Teen Titles is stuffed with book reviews written by teenagers themselves. It gives an honest, unedited, unbiased view of the newest young adult fiction and non-fiction books. Teenagers all over the UK read *Teen Titles*.

Readers can join in by sending in their own book reviews to the Readers Write section.

Teen Titles aims to promote reading in a fun way that will appeal to young people.

For librarians, it is a great ordering tool for the newest young adult titles.

Answers

1 Identities

What it means to be American

General comprehension

1 The writer describes being American as being one, but being diverse within that oneness. She thinks it must be more to do with actions, beliefs, and values than ethnicity.
2 The writer thinks being American is about actions, beliefs, and values.
3 In general, Americans are talkative and friendly.
4 The writer feels Americans value the ideals of freedom and believe that people create their own destiny.
5 The writer thinks American identity can be described as in a constant state of evolution because the country is young compared with the rest of the world.

Vocabulary

1 c   2 e   3 d   4 f   5 b   6 a

What it means to be Kazakh

General comprehension

1 The citizens of Kazakhstan are very patriotic and proud of their country.
2 Two features of Kazakh duty are knowing their family tree and their country's traditions.
3 In Kazakh families, a guest is made to feel like a privileged person and is embraced.
4 Young people are taught values such as belief in religion, respect for the individual, and social justice.

Vocabulary

1 c   2 e   3 a   4 b   5 d

What it means to be Scottish

General comprehension

1 The writer left Scotland for further education and work.
2 He mentions Scottish customs, music and regional dialects.
3 He loves the landscapes.
4 'People make Glasgow' is the slogan.

Vocabulary

1 a   2 c   3 e   4 g   5 j
6 i   7 h   8 g   9 d   10 b

Zoom in on grammar

Phrasal verbs used in text: *talk about, born into, grow up, come from.*

Grammar in context

1 about
2 after
3 up
4 over
5 on

What it means to be English

General comprehension

1 The views and smells / treks with family, sitting behind stone walls, eating boiled egg and cheese sandwiches trigger the writer's memories.
2 'In the oral tradition' refers to songs that were passed down from generation to generation by singing them together.
3 A moor is windswept, treeless, and beautiful.

Vocabulary

1 a burning issue
2 multiple
3 dreadlocks
4 aisle
5 daft

Paper 2 practice task (1.1) – Alumni Speech Day

1 unimaginable
2 completely lacking (in)
3 have been enough
4 much good at
5 not my strength
6 Martin took a gap year to travel to Africa to work as a volunteer. Then he took a job at an agricultural firm.
7 Any three of the following: shy, physically weak, rather overweight, completely lacking in self-confidence, no real friends, bullied.
8 He went for long walks.
9 His self-confidence grew.
10 To take opportunities
11 b
12 c
13 b

Children given philosophy lessons to face challenges of the future

General comprehension

1 Researchers believe learning to think about thinking will help children face future problems.
2 If a ship goes on a long voyage in which every part of the ship is repaired or replaced, will the ship be the same ship at the end of the voyage?
3 They thought changing the model was like destroying it.
4 Later they decided the model had the same function, so it was the same thing.
5 False: 'Students in a south London primary school were involved in the pilot scheme.'
6 False: '... they all seemed to enjoy it.'
7 False: 'The preliminary results of the project were presented at a conference of the Royal College of Psychiatrists.'
8 True: 'Plutarch... asked a similar question.'

Identity and our roots

General comprehension

1 He first travelled abroad in his early adulthood.
2 People in the Gulf are often asked, 'Where are you from?'
3 At first, the students gave predictable answers.
4 The discussion itself was the most interesting.
5 Parents want their children to have a clear idea of their home identity.

The four true statements are: a, e, f, h.

Vocabulary

1 c	2 g	3 i	4 b	5 e
6 h	7 j	8 a	9 f	10 d

Text handling

1 'Gidday, Welcome home'
2 missed the 'Giddays'
3 the discussion was more interesting than the answer, or answers

Belonging everywhere and nowhere; living, working, and raising children abroad

General comprehension

1 For people who live nomadic lives, there is an inability to provide children with a home in the traditional sense of the word.
2 The writer's home is in the southwestern United States.
3 They lived into the house room by room.
4 The house was secluded and surrounded by hills and stunning scenery.
5 It was maybe the last trip because the parents had rented the house out and the purpose of the trip was to clear the house.
6 The family decided to move because the house was heated by wood or pellet stoves / it was on a steep slope sometimes impassable in winter / it had a septic tank / the paths between the buildings were uneven / the house was challenging to live in. (Accept any two reasons.)
7 She is concerned that her children do not and will not have such a place in their childhoods.
8 Having relationships, family, communities, friendship, and shared experiences.
9 False: 'I did have a home.'
10 False: 'where so much of who I am was shaped and nurtured.'
11 True: 'It grew slowly and lovingly over decades.'
12 True: 'things I had, at one point in may life, felt were important enough to save…'
13 True: '… home doesn't have to be a physical space.' / 'And is anywhere and everywhere that we are loved.'

Vocabulary

1 d	2 e	3 a	4 b	5 f
6 c	7 i	8 g	9 h	10 j

Text handling

1 Students' own answers.
2 Students' own answers.
3 Students' own answers.

Who are you?

General comprehension

1 The student reflects on the question when he is extremely exhausted or depressed.
2 It tells us that the student doesn't see himself as very important. (Accept any reasonable answer.)
3 His lofty ambition is to be an ordinary person with nondescript looks. He calls it 'lofty' as a joke because it is a simple ambition, not a lofty one.
4 He/she was 13 years old.
5 The student feels like his/her life is suspended.

Text handling

1 Students' own answers.
2 Students' own answers.

The only way you can change anything is in small increments

General comprehension

1 The elixir of a good life for Cerys is music, food, and good company.
2 Students' own answers. (Suggested answer: This is an idiomatic phrase used to talk about someone who is important but only within a limited area of influence.)
3 Cerys has started cycling and running, and she cooks fresh food every day.

Vocabulary

1 It means that you are realistic.
2 It means hoping to live longer.
3 It means life is what it is / it is difficult to change things.

The ten essential rules for slowing down and enjoying life more

Text handling

1 breath
2 enjoyment
3 connection
4 appreciation
5 suggestion
6 contemplation

Reader's letter **(page 30)**

General comprehension

1 He believes dictionaries are very important and help improve writing skills, but that dictionary publishers need to change with the times.
2 He believes that words that reflect technological progress need to be included in dictionaries.
3 Dictionaries must reflect our changing identity in a changing world. Also, children will not stop being interested in nature just because some nature words are removed from the dictionary.

Vocabulary

1 e 2 c 3 g 4 h 5 f

'Cull' by Anna Coburn

General comprehension

1 Anna feels children are starting to lack contact with nature because they are busy in their rooms staring at the screens of their electronic devices.
2 We will be able to find them in ancient books of natural law; old poems, tales and ditties; and in books of ancient customs.

The Lost Words

General comprehension

1 In response to a children's dictionary's intention to remove some nature words from the new edition.
2 The book forces the reader to 'ask ourselves how well we can experience things we cannot name'.
3 The focus was routes around the British Isles to discover places where nature can still be enjoyed in all its untamed glory.
4 The adjectives used were exquisite, hand-painted, sensitive, meticulous, warm, vivid, golden.
5 The diminishing of nature is really happening/Nature is being replaced with industrial and technological advancements.
6 True: The review says that Morris is clearly a great observer of nature and her illustrations are meticulous in detail.
7 False: The book is a combination of poems and illustrations.
8 False: The reviewer says that it is a book to dip into.

Paper 2 practice task (1.2) – Reflection on nature

1 April / spring
2 cowslips
3 Her father told her the names on their walks when she was little.
4 A small place far from big towns.
5 Finn and Heather
6 a butterfly, a baby sparrow, and next door's cat

The six true statements are: b, e, f, g, i, j.

Paper 2 practice task (1.3) – Changing attitudes to language

1 a minority group
2 has been driven
3 speak their language
4 focuses on
5 Bilingual and multilingual
6 c
7 b
8 c

How have traditional gender roles changed in the 21st century?

General comprehension

1 A breadwinner is the person who earns money to support a family.
2 In the past, women spent their days taking care of the family by doing the washing, cooking, and cleaning.
3 Many wives now go out to work and some earn more than their husbands.
4 Some people still believe that husbands should earn more.
5 Women might under-report their income to save embarrassing their husbands.
6 Good husbands must be seen to support their families as the chief breadwinner and wives should stay at home and take care of the family.

Breathing new life into printed books

General comprehension

1 Students' own answers. Suggested answer: Many libraries are closing because they cost too much money to run.
2 Students have participated in the protests and have designed and displayed posters.
3 They carry the memories of a city, embody a city's heritage, and affect a city's ambiance.
4 They plan to subsidise the bookshops and have one in every district of the city. They also want to incorporate public libraries in the bookshops and for bookshops to stay open longer.

Grammar in context

1 'That' refers to reading books being a popular hobby for young and old before the advent of television and the internet.
2 'This' refers to the market for books having been taken over by the internet.
3 'This' refers to the negative outcomes of people reading on devices.
4 'They' refers to the city authorities.

Reader's letter **(page 40)**

General comprehension

1 An article about falling standards in the behaviour of theatre audiences.
2 Students' answers will vary. The idiom means to get something exactly correct.
3 A young woman paying more attention to her phone than the performance on stage.
4 No. Even the usher did not help.
5 Students' answers will vary. Suggested answer: The actor didn't stop pretending to be his character.
6 Students' answers will vary. Suggested answer: I will answer that phone to stop it from interrupting me.
7 People following a football match on their phone when at the theatre.

Answers

Vocabulary

1 inconsiderate
2 intolerable
3 considerable
4 unimaginable
5 Students' own answers. 'Abysmal' means something that is extremely bad.
6 Students' own answers. An 'aisle' is a row between seats in a building.
7 Students' own answers. An 'abomination' is something you strongly disapprove of.
8 Students' own answers. 'Provincial' means relating to the province of a country.
9 Students' own answers. A 'province' is area that a country is divided into.

Reader's letter **(page 42)**

General comprehension

1 His complaint is that audience members were clapping after individual movements of a symphony.
2 It interrupts the music, which should be heard as one piece, and breaks the concentration of the audience.
3 The audience should wait until the conductor and orchestra members give a clear signal that the piece has finished.
4 The conductor relaxes and often places his baton on his pulpit.

Reader's letter **(page 43)**

General comprehension

1 The letter is written in a joking, humorous tone.
2 He thinks they are lucky because they do not have to clap for every performer individually.
3 Jazz fans are obliged to clap for every solo and when they are called upon to respond to each band member.

2 Experiences

Being a teenager is not always easy

General comprehension

1 Being a teenager in the 21st century is challenging because social media has made teenagers' lives more complicated.
2 Three typical problems are: feeling left out, suffering FOMO, cyber-bullying.
3 The problems are very personal and emotional and parents often have little time.
4 A counsellor needs to be independent, trustworthy, qualified; able to listen and offer advice.
5 Students' own answers. Suggested answer: It means to force yourself to stop feeling upset or sad.

Paper 2 practice task (2.1) – An interview with a counsellor

1 Social Emotional Counsellor
2 She felt lost and confused.
3 She studied psychology with counselling skills.
4 A Social Emotional Counsellor needs to be empathetic and open-minded.
5 To see the difference and the progress in her clients; when students tell her how helpful it has been; when students recommend her to their friends.
6 a difficult childhood
7 as my major
8 torn between their

New app for student counselling ready to provide support

General comprehension

1 The name of the app is Spill.
2 It allows people to talk to a qualified counsellor, anonymously and confidentially.
3 The counsellors are registered with the British Association for Counselling and Psychotherapy.
4 People who do not have friends or family to talk to will benefit most from the service.
5 They will recommend that the person talks to their doctor or to another health specialist.
6 Friends can provide support by making an effort to involve those who seem down in activities and social groups; monitoring unkind comments, real or online; doing their best to listen to those who need support.

Vocabulary

1 c	2 j	3 g	4 e	5 h
6 i	7 d	8 f	9 b	10 a

20 March: International Day of Happiness

General comprehension

1 The International Day of Happiness is on 20 March.
2 It tells us which countries have the happiest people.
3 The index focuses on income, health and life expectancy, social support, freedom, trust and generosity.
4 The wealth is not evenly distributed.
5 For the USA, poor health and life expectancy had a negative effect on the happiness results.
6 The priorities a government has may not be the same as those of the population.

Vocabulary

1 d	2 b	3 c	4 f
5 e	6 g	7 a	8 h

Pleasure and happiness: the great mix-up

General comprehension

1 We often confuse pleasure with happiness.
2 The author means that pleasure doesn't last.
3 The example the writer uses is about eating cakes. Students' own answers. Suggested answer: Happiness is a prolonged experience, and with eating cake, the pleasure is over as soon as we finish it.
4 The writer suggests listening to a Bach prelude endlessly could lead to boredom.
5 The author says that you can experience pleasure at the expense of others. He then gives examples of a businessman rejoicing in the ruin of a competitor, a thief revelling in his booty, a spectator at a bullfight exulting in the bull's death.

Text handling

1 Students' own answers.
2 Students' own answers.

Verb	Noun	Adjective
repeat	repetition	repetitive
lose	*loss*	*lost*
confuse	confusion	*confusing*
exhaust	exhaustion	*exhausting*
receive	*receipt*	receptive

Paper 2 practice task (2.2) – Learning to be happy

1 Rosemary
2 Psychology and the Good Life
3 The course is about happiness and how to achieve it.
4 Bill
5 It would do him good. / He could learn to be happy.
6 Before going to sleep each night for a week, write down five things you are grateful for.
7 Write a letter of thanks to someone who did something important for you.
8 are talking about
9 catch up with
10 write that down

Supporting students in Tanzania

General comprehension

1 It offered the international school students glimpses into lives that are harder than their own.
2 The visit changes them.
3 Ben and Mike wanted the chaperone to sponsor them.
4 They depend on rain.
5 When the students returned home, they appreciated a continuous, reliable supply of fresh water and electricity always being available.
6 The contact was not very regular.
7 A parent from the international school met with one of the sponsored students some years later.
8 He invests time and money in the education of Tanzanian students.
9 Mike is a lawyer and Ben is a teacher.
10 The weather has not changed. The possibility for young Tanzanians to be educated and in a position to drive the country forward needs to change.

Vocabulary

1 a	2 b	3 c
4 a	5 a	6 c
7 c	8 b	9 a

Find the perfect adventure holiday for your family

General comprehension

Witches and wizards

1 Stonehenge is the tourist attraction near Salisbury.
2 He feels the stone-slate roofs, twisted chimney stacks, and mullioned windows make the attraction a magical place.

The urban jungle

3 Trainers, a bottle of water, and a mobile phone are essential for the tourist in New York.
4 A schooner is a sailing boat because it has sails and takes the tourists along the coast.

The mountain trekking experience

5 The Incas are the people who built Machu Picchu.
6 The word quirky means unusual in an interesting way.

Water worlds

7 Surfing is a popular sport because it is exciting, gets you fit, and you can make new friends.
8 In the log books from Captain Cook's trips, surfing is mentioned. The activity originated in the Pacific region.

Aim higher, achieve more

General comprehension

1 It is directed at teachers / activity leaders.
2 The three main aims are to motivate, build confidence, and encourage development.
3 The activities are located in the UK, France, and Spain.
4 They learn to sail a variety of dinghies and paddle a kayak.
5 They offer visits to water parks, sightseeing, and shopping.
6 They can learn teamwork, cooperation, leadership. Through challenging themselves students can discover their own possibilities in these area and also increase self-confidence.

Paper 2 practice task (2.3) – School trip adventures

General comprehension

1 two (a fortnight = two weeks)
2 a handbag
3 She had studied the work of the architect Gaudí in art class.
4 c
5 b

The five true statements are: b, e, g, h, i.

A bilingual opera singer

General comprehension

1 It is helpful as English and German are common languages in opera oratorio and songs, and being a native speaker helps add nuance to performances.
2 She first had singing lessons in her early teens.
3 After high school, she continued her studies at the Royal Conservatoire of Scotland.
4 Having peers and colleagues going through the same journey helped her.
5 She is motivated by the desire to make music and help others do the same.
6 In a recording there is more time pressure to get things just right.
7 In the summer months, she sings at weddings and festivals.
8 Her first piece of advice is to be punctual and prepared.
9 Her second piece of advice is to learn to take criticism well.

Vocabulary

1 aspects
2 niceties / refinements
3 (great) love
4 strenuous
5 think I am
6 understanding / lenient
7 error
8 personality / appeal
9 waiting (to take your place)
10 be organised and efficient

Interview with a librarian

General comprehension

1 He loved working with people and helping them.
2 He loved to read biographies and cookery writing.
3 In the last 30 years, libraries have become more focused on people and the sharing of ideas.
4 Magazines and books can now be downloaded and read electronically, and accounts can be managed with smartphones.

5 The aim of the Summer Reading Challenge is to read and review six books.
6 He enjoyed the wry humour and social commentary.
7 We know for certain the main characters are girls in *The Lie Tree* and *After the Fire*.

Vocabulary

1 f	2 i	3 d	4 a
1 b	2 a	3 c	4 b

Grammar in context

1 would visit
2 would try
3 would go

Student's own answers for 4–6. Suggested answers:

4 he would eat meat
5 would climb the trees in our garden/would read books about dinosaurs
6 would write letters to their friends.

The success of book clubs

General comprehension

1 It's difficult to calculate because the groups meet informally in each other's houses.
2 We know the people are older because the writer says they are 'retired'.
3 The job of the leader is to keep notes about what books they have read and collect suggestions for future reads.
4 Four people walked the trail with her.
5 It means the topics of books are varied.
6 The writer's favourite book is *Wild* because he/she has walked this trail and understands the challenges.

Vocabulary

1 multiple	2 venue	3 designated
4 a log	5 highlighted	6 ongoing

Personal experiences

General comprehension

1 She didn't know anyone and had no idea which relatives were still living in the village.
2 She found more information on a website and was contacted by a cousin of her father's.
3 They saw a piper and he was wearing full highland dress.
4 After Edinburgh, they travelled to Inverness.
5 Even though they were in Inverness / Scotland, she still didn't have the feeling of 'coming home'.
6 False: 'My father always wanted to visit Scotland. . .but he could never afford it. . .'
7 False: '. . . the aunt she heard of was, in fact, my grandmother, Alice.'
8 True: 'Neither of us have ever been to Europe. . .'
9 True: 'The journey took just over three hours. . .'

Vocabulary

1 birthplace
2 emigrate
3 it's now or never

Diary **(page 80)**

General comprehension

25th June

1 They are researching her family not his, so he may be bored.

26th June

2 Culloden was not as exciting as she expected.
3 They should have read about Culloden first.
4 The village was small and quiet and not as exciting as the writer expected.

27th June

5 The café owner had told Susan about them.
6 She did not know who put her grandmother's name and dates on her gravestone.
7 It was not useful as the vicar is only there every third Sunday and they would have left by then.

28th June

8 They had to pay to get in, it was expensive, and they did not learn anything new.
9 An unknown woman greeted them by name.
10 The accents were challenging and familiar words were used differently.
11 They would know where the dolphins would be seen by looking for a crowd.

Vocabulary

25th June

1 avoid
2 explore
3 escaped
4 defeated

26th June

5 scramble
6 read up on it

27th June

7 get your head around
8 family tree
9 walked us there

28th June

10 we all piled into the car
11 greeted us by name
12 eyes glued to the water

That last TOK journal – ever

General comprehension

1 He learned never to just ask yes or no questions.
2 TOK has become part of his life.
3 He has learned to always ask, 'How do we know?'
4 During the course, the level of language in the textbook presented difficulties.
5 He ends the article with a question because asking questions is the essence of TOK.

A pinch of salt

General comprehension

1 The reader knows people in the village helped each other with the work and cooking because everyone shared everything / the old ladies picked the walnuts / they swapped and shared.
2 Baharat is a spice made with allspice berries, cloves, nutmeg, and dried cherry seeds (mahelp).
3 Her memories are of her family's village in Cyprus, the hot weather, and sitting outside talking.
4 She woke up to the smell of onions because her father ran a café downstairs and started cooking early in the day.
5 They grew citrus fruits, olives, strawberries, watermelons, aubergines, and tomatoes.

Vocabulary
1 ingredients
2 vast amounts

3 Human ingenuity

An extremely brief world history of music and musical instruments

General comprehension
1 The human voice is special because it can be used in many ways / every voice is unique. When we breathe out, the air is pushed from our lungs and causes the vocal chords to vibrate.
2 The sound of our voice can be affected by damage to the vocal chords.

Vocabulary
Students' own answers.

Grammar in context
Examples of the present simple passive voice are: *the air from our lungs is pushed upwards; the sound is produced; which are hollowed-out; African drums are sometimes called 'the heartbeat' of Africa; and are used not just for entertainment; It is plucked or strummed; which are plucked or strummed.*
Examples of the present perfect passive voice are: *Devices have been created; Flutes have been discovered.*

The musical human

General comprehension
Paragraph 1: Early years
Paragraph 2: Musical ability
Paragraph 3: The human brain
Paragraph 4: Music as a social activity

1 False: 'My family contained no active musicians…'
2 False: 'We later acquired an old piano, which I taught myself to play as a young teenager.'
3 True: 'The head of the music department heard me practising and insisted that I switch from English to music as my choice of principal subject.'
4 True: '… I didn't have the background of formal instruction that my student peers had.'
5 False: 'Natural ability in music, and many other activities, depends upon the way in which the brain is configured.'
6 True: 'Many people are therefore skilled in different activities at various levels.'
7 True: 'From a scientific point of view, music simply consists of sound waves, or bumpy air.'
8 False: 'Music-making is an enjoyable social activity.'

Vocabulary

Paragraph 1
1 acquired
2 switch
3 principal subject

Paragraph 2
4 fruition

Paragraph 3
5 joy
6 nostalgia

Paragraph 4
7 ensembles

From our arts correspondent

General comprehension

1 The band used their tablets instead of sheet music.
2 The reporter says it was a 'thrilling evening'.
3 The reporter describes the audience as 'enthralled' and 'surprised'.
4 The pianist was the first band member on stage.
5 The bundles of paper notes were missing as the band appeared on stage.

Vocabulary

1 i   2 e   3 g   4 b   5 h   6 d

Reader's letter (page 96)

Grammar in context

1 while   2 during   3 during   4 during   5 while

Interview with Rosie Street, Marketing Manager

General comprehension

1 The Glasgow Science Centre has existed since 2001.
2 The aim was to attract young people to study science, technology, engineering, and maths, and to engage the public with science in a fun and engaging way.
3 No. The Marketing Manager says people who work there are a wide range of ages.
4 The main industry was shipbuilding.
5 After the Second World War, the shipbuilding industry went into decline.
6 The science centre is busiest with general visitors during the school holidays. It is busiest with education visitors in June.
7 The Marketing Manager helps to market everything about the science centre and informs people about what is happening and when.
8 She most enjoys working with an incredible team of people / where people care about what they're doing.

Vocabulary

1 awarded   2 toddler   3 decline   4 fluctuate

Paulina's blog: my week

General comprehension

1 Paulina is a 17-year-old about to start her final year at school who hopes to study English literature and work in the publishing industry.
2 She was surprised as she is a humanities student, not a science student.
3 Sharon had shared a similar experience to Paulina, trying to find a career path with English.
4 She was set a PR taster task and some admin tasks.
5 She feels she has gained real knowledge about the workplace, has grown as a person (becoming more confident), and has broadened her mind.

Peter's visit – guest blog

General comprehension

1 The Science Centre is exciting for Peter because he says it never gets boring and there are many activities.
2 The queuing is never boring because there are so many interesting facts to read as you queue.
3 He usually goes to the illusion and special effects rooms first because they're cool.
4 The best feature of the planetarium is that it can show the sky in 3D.
5 The activity that cheers people up is the dance floor.
6 He uses the word 'yucky' to talk about watching scientists cut up organs.

7 The museum offers autism-friendly hours when it's much quieter, the music is turned down, and the lights get dimmed. There are also quiet areas which have sensory boxes.
8 Some of the positive words he uses are: *amazing, interesting, cool, funny, brilliant, fantastic.*

Grammar in context
1 go to the third floor.
2 post it on the 'Think-It' ideas wall for the scientists to read.
3 You can watch nature documentaries and movies in 3D

The River Clyde in Glasgow

General comprehension
1 It was the lowest fordable point on the River Clyde in Glasgow.
2 In the 18th and 19th century, bridges were built because there was a need for better communications.
3 The bridges nurtured the growth of the city.

Vocabulary
1 f 2 e 3 g 4 h 5 d 6 b 7 a 8 c

Text handling

Verb	Noun	Adjective
balance	*balance*	balanced
communicate	*communication*	*communicated*
contribute	*contribution*	contributed
exhibit	*exhibition*	*exhibited*
reflect	reflection	*reflected*
suspend	suspension	*suspended*

Top tips for new escape gamers

Vocabulary
Students' own answers. Suggested answers:
1 win the game in the time given
2 padlocks are difficult to get open
3 your time is running out
4 it is likely (that)
5 great fun

Norwich escape rooms

General comprehension
1 The Merchants' Vaults
2 Archived Alive!
3 Body of Evidence

Vocabulary
1 d 2 f 3 h 4 a 5 i 6 c

Paper 2 practice task (3.1) – Escape rooms

1 b
The five true statements are: b, d, f, h, j.

Secondary schools are introducing new bans on mobile phones

General comprehension
1 The mobile phone ban applies to pupils aged 11–16.
2 The positive effects of the ban are that more children spend time playing outside, attending clubs and societies, and socialising with each other.
3 Students' own words. Suggested answer: Her attitude is positive as she sees the ban as an opportunity for students to do other things and take a break from social media.

France to impose ban on mobile phones in schools

General comprehension

1 Some parents think children must be able to 'live in their own time'.
2 The two main concerns are that students will use their mobile phones for text messaging and receiving calls.

Text handling

1 on
2 from
3 over
4 at
5 of

Formal letter (page 115)

General comprehension

1 The principal wrote the letter at the start of the new school year.
2 The main reason for banning mobile phones is to create the optimum learning environment.
3 This means that phones are widespread and are seen in all aspects of daily life.
4 Banning phones in schools jumped from 0 to 50 per cent between 2001 and 2007.
5 The principal says that in a test using phones and pen and paper, using the latter was more productive.

The history of the telephone

General comprehension

1 Alexander Graham Bell, Philip Reis, Meucci, Elisha Gray
2 Sir Giles Gilbert Scott
3 silvery green
4 Red was finally chosen because it was considered more noticeable.

Text handling

1 b 2 e 3 a 4 c 5 d

Grammar in context

1 had given
2 had tidied / cleaned up
3 had finished

Public commentary (page 120)

General comprehension

1 VCDs are revolutionising our homes, but there can be disadvantages such as losing the value of being polite.
2 She thinks a solution would be to add a new subject to the curriculum called 'Being polite'.
3 The writer who agrees with her is Molly Garner.

Text handling

Verb	Noun
revolutionise	*revolution*
function	*function*
imply	*implication*
introduce	*introduction*
recommend	*recommendation*
agree	*agreement*

Answers

Grammar in context

1 Don't open	2 inform / tell / ask	3 Heat
4 Close	4 Don't eat / Don't buy	

Nebra

General comprehension

1 Nebra is in the east of Germany.
2 The area is famous for winemaking.
3 No, they did not have permission. They were acting illegally.
4 They also found two swords, two hatchets, a chisel, and some pieces of spiral bracelets.
5 They decided not to hand them over as they hoped to make money from their find.
6 They sold them to other dealers.
7 No, those dealers were dishonest and unscrupulous.
8 An archaeologist was offered the treasures and recognised their value.
9 The dealers who had the treasures at that time were arrested by the police.
10 The original thieves were finally identified and given suspended jail sentences.
11 False: It's a small German town.
12 True
13 False: It was first found in 1999.
14 True
15 False: The two men were illegally searching for treasure using metal detectors.
16 True
17 True
18 False: The police caught some of the criminals in a hotel in Switzerland.
19 False: The original thieves were eventually identified and given suspended jail sentences.
20 False: It's made of bronze.

Paper 2 practice task (3.2) – Nebra Ark audio guide

1 True	6 in its prominent
2 False	7 look forward to
3 True	8 vital fixed points
4 False	9 oldest known visual
5 False	10 explain it all

Stonehenge

General comprehension

1 The writer speculates that Stonehenge might have been used for a cremation ground, a sun worship site, or an alien landing pad.
2 The two reasons are: a new visitor centre and new finds and interpretations.
3 Stonehenge is located on Salisbury Plain, to the north of the A303.
4 Entrance is free at the winter and summer solstices.

Vocabulary

Paragraph 1

1 b	2 d	3 c

Paragraph 2

4 h	5 i	6 g

Paragraph 6

7 m	8 o	9 n

Seahenge

General comprehension

1 The media gave the construction the name Seahenge.
2 It is not known what the purpose of Seahenge was. There is only speculation.

3 The henge can currently be seen in the museum in King's Lynn.
4 Some people wanted to keep the henge in its original location because it had been there for decades before archaeologists discovered it.
5 False: Seahenge is made of wood and Stonehenge is made of stone.
6 False: It was constructed 4000 years ago when that area was inland / before the sea eroded the land.
7 False: Locals had known of its existence for decades.
8 True: It was put in the museum to prevent it from deterioration.
9 True: The word 'henge' is used by archaeologists to describe a circular or oval construction of stones or timber.

4 Social organisation

Sleep deprivation in adolescents and young adults?

General comprehension

1 Two-thirds of adolescents reported insufficient sleep.
2 Lack of sleep causes adolescents to be sleepy during the daytime and have negative moods, increased likelihood of stimulant use, higher levels of risk-taking behaviours, poor school performance, and increased risk of unintentional injury.
3 Over a quarter of students admit to falling asleep in class at least once a week.
4 The growing evidence about the importance of sleep and the negative impact of sleep deprivation has brought this to the attention of public health professionals.
5 Healthy People 2020 has objectives to increase the proportion of students in grades 9–12 and adults who get sufficient sleep.

Vocabulary

1 essential
2 insufficient
3 deprivation
4 irregular
5 unintentional

How many hours are 'sufficient' for adolescents and young adults

Vocabulary

1 memory impairment
2 moodiness and aggression
3 clumsiness
4 truancy
5 mentally 'drifting off' in class / shortened attention span

Why don't teenagers and young adults regularly get enough sleep?

Text handling

Heading 1: Hormonal time shifts
Heading 2: Early start times
Heading 3: Hectic after-school schedule
Heading 4: Leisure activities
Heading 5: Light exposure
Heading 6: Vicious cycle
Heading 7: Social attitudes
Heading 8: Sleep disorder

General comprehension

1 Students' own answers. Suggested answer: Teenagers experience a shift in their circadian rhythms because their hormones change and affect their sleep patterns. Early school start times in adolescence also affect the sleep patterns of teens.
2 Little is known about the influences on sleep among young adults.

Vocabulary

1 d
2 c
3 a
4 b
5 occur simultaneously
6 experience a shift
7 chronic sleep deprivation
8 delay a teenager's bedtime
9 an over-aroused brain is less able to fall asleep

Grammar in context

1 optimise 2 develop 3 minimise 4 refrain from 5 limit

For health professionals: what can be done?

General comprehension

1 There have been a number of measures including school policy change and informational programmes to increase knowledge about sleep and improve sleep habits.
2 No, the evidence is minimal so far.
3 Students had longer sleep times, attendance improved, there was an increase in continuous enrollment, less tardiness, and less students making visits to the nurse.
4 Hardship was caused by disruption to transportation and work times for urban students.
5 The sleep education leaflet study took place in Croatia.
6 InShape recommends avoiding alcohol, cigarettes and illicit drugs to maintain a healthy lifestyle.
7 The results showed that those in the MBSR treatment group significantly improved their sleep quality.

Tablets out, imagination in: the schools that shun technology

General comprehension

1 The expression is used because although the school is located in the heart of the tech industry, no technology is used in the classrooms.
2 The teachers at the Waldorf School of the Peninsula prefer hands-on, experiential learning.
3 The writer describes it as disruptive.
4 The writer uses the term because the Waldorf method encourages students to learn creatively, rather than just passively taking in information.
5 They are interested in lo-tech, no-tech education for their children because they want to encourage innovative thinking skills.
6 False: It is a 'nine-classroom school'.
7 False: 'There is not a tablet, smartphone, or screen in sight.'
8 True: 'If you look at the best-performing education systems, such as those in East Asia, they've been very cautious about using technology in their classroom.'
9 True: 'Teachers encourage students to learn curriculum subjects by expressing themselves through artistic activities, such as painting and drawing.'
10 True: The text states that students acquire 'problem-solving maths skills through knitting'.
11 True: The text states that 'choosing a lo-tech, no-tech education for their children is that it teaches students the innovative thinking skills many employers desire'.

Vocabulary

1 shun
2 invested
3 lo-tech, no-tech
4 weaned on
5 think creatively

Paper 2 practice task (4.1) – Parent-Teacher Association (PTA) mid-year meeting

1 Jamie
2 The later start to the school day.
3 At least nine hours.
4 Social media, Snapchat, etc; fear of missing out (FOMO); their diet.
5 From the start of the new term in January.
6 No, there will be no mobile phones in school at all.
7 They should contact the school secretaries.
8 They do not allow their children to have mobile phones in school.
9 Yes, they have. Mobile phones are banned in all French schools.
10 Yes, they do.
11 No, he says there will be no discussion.
12 False.
13 True.
14 True.
15 False.
16 False.

The shanyrak system in Kazakhstan

General comprehension

1 A shanyrak is the roof of a yurt, where the framework overlaps in a criss-cross pattern and holds it all together.
2 In each group, there are students from two different grade levels.
3 The main focus of the shanyrak system is cooperation and mutual support.
4 The students undertake social projects but also fun activities like the flash mobs.
5 A flash mob is usually a spontaneous gathering of people for a fun activity.

Why I love the IB

General comprehension

True statements:

b – 'The IB Diploma meant that I took a much broader range of subjects than I would have taken at A level.'

d – 'IB was still a novelty, but the way it generates independent thinkers with the skills they need to hit the ground running at university stands strong.'

Text handling

1 d 2 c 3 a 4 e 5 b

Paper 2 practice task (4.2) – School announcements

1 True 2 False 3 True 4 True

Paper 2 practice task (4.3) – School announcements

General comprehension

1 remind you of
2 be reflected by
3 no nail varnish
4 you sit down
5 should be simpler

Working together

1 False: 'A group of local people took the initiative and applied successfully for loans and grants to help buy the café and support fundraising efforts.'
2 True: In Oxford, a children's centre was to be closed but a group of residents raised the money to buy it by selling shares in the property to other local people.
3 True: 'The groups are often run by volunteers who are united in their awareness that communities need places to meet together and communicate.'

Vocabulary

Paragraph 1

1 amenities
2 assets

Paragraph 2

3 loan

Paragraph 3

4 loss
5 running

Paragraph 4

6 nursery

Paragraph 5

7 uniting
8 benefit

Paragraph 6

9 isolation
10 combating

Paragraph 7

11 residents

With your help we can save the post office

General comprehension

1 The post office provided a place for villagers to socialise.
2 The post office was run by a woman. The word 'postmistress' is the female form of the word 'postmaster'.
3 If the initiative is successful, volunteers will run the post office.
4 Greenham Community Enterprise has raised £150 000.

Grammar in context

Verb	Noun
succeed	*success*
discuss	*discussion*
sell	*sale*
deliver	*delivery*
threaten	*threat*

Reader's letter (page 152)

General comprehension

1 a The primary school has closed, so children must travel to the nearest town.
b The churchgoers are affected by the fact that the church services only take place once a month and the prayer group has been discontinued.
c The community generally is affected by the lack of a Post Office, local shopping facilities, and the library bus; by the fact that the local bus service has been reduced to one bus per hour; and there is nowhere for people to meet and chat, which means the village has lost its community spirit.

2 He asks if other villages have the same problem and what ideas people have to make the situation better.

Reader's letter (page 153)

General comprehension

1 True: 'He is right and this is the trend across the country.'
2 True: 'Our village is similarly badly served…'
3 False: The community has taken several actions: they have formed a community committee, erected a noticeboard, and people offer transport to the nearest market town.
4 False: 'Our next step will be to hold a village community meeting, but as yet we have not found a venue for this.'

Reader's letter (page 154)

General comprehension

1 False: 'I must note that this is the first time in my very long life when I have felt inspired to write a letter to a newspaper.' The writer also states that he has a daughter in Germany so he cannot be 'very young'.
2 True: 'One very simple and cheap initiative which we undertook was to place a couple of chairs in a place which offers a good view of the countryside and invite people to take a seat and relax for a few minutes.'
3 False: 'Another initiative which was not quite so successful was our clean-up day.'
4 False: The writer states he has a daughter in Germany, but they are not German.

Editor's letter (page 156)

General comprehension

1 The writers should now contact the newly founded group, Villagers for Villages.
2 The kindergarten is not the ideal meeting place as there may not be enough chairs for adults and people would have to bring their own.
3 The kindergarten teacher suggests that villagers bring their used books and leave them on the bookshelves for others to borrow.
4 They are allowed to access the entrance area only.

Discussion task – Formal letters

Examples of formal language in the letters:

- initiative (first step)
- to address (to look at a problem)
- nominal (small)
- use of *would* – *I would be very pleased to hear from…*
- facility (school building)
- access (the way in)
- *I look forward to…* – use of the simple present rather than the continuous form – *I am looking forward to…*

Stay close to me

General comprehension

1 The islands look like two long white clouds from above or on a map.
2 The writer claims that many New Zealanders are related, the people are adaptable and confident, and they are outdoorsy.
3 Visitors are surprised by the laid-back way of life and the beauty of the islands.
4 Students' own answers. Suggested answer: The north island was an enormous fish and the mountains and valleys are the bumps it suffered when it was caught.
5 Children are surrounded by a culturally rich environment of Maori people with their own language, culture, and traditions and New Zealanders who speak English.
6 False: The people of Patea were meat packers / slaughtered and froze lamb.
7 True: The writer states that the people of Patea were not 'a town but one large *whanau* (family)'.

8 False: The national meat industry was losing money and the company that owned the West Coast Meat and Produce Export Company decided to close the business.
9 False: The writer states that 'little regard was shown for the hundreds of livelihoods dependent on those hard-working folk who turned up to the eyesore which was the Patea Freezing Works'.
10 False: The writer states that 'chart-topping musician Maui Dalvanius Prime and the linguist Ngoi Pewhairangi wrote the song'.

Vocabulary

1 c 2 d 3 e 4 b 5 f 6 a

The World Cup

General comprehension

1 They wanted to meet up with fans from every one of the nations in the World Cup and watch matches together.
2 For each game, they contacted fans from the different nationalities and arranged where they could watch together.
3 The Icelandic fans were the noisiest.
4 They had difficulty finding Saudi fans.
5 An Argentinian family invited them to watch the game in their home.

A white party

General comprehension

1 It is being held in the middle of City Park.
2 It is called a white party because everyone is asked to wear white.
3 It is considered to be spontaneous because the event starts at 8.00 p.m. and was only announced at 6.01 p.m. It also hasn't been planned well in advance and there is no need to commit to going beforehand.

How moving a bookshop became a spontaneous event

Vocabulary

1 i 2 e 3 d 4 c 5 g 6 a 7 j 8 b 9 f 10 h

An interview with an Alumni Coordinator

General comprehension

1 No, it isn't. Anyone who is an ex-student is considered an alumni.
2 Her main responsibilities are connecting, activating, and involving the alumni community.
3 She's aiming to build a more lively and interconnected community.
4 In June, the school created private networking space to organise or join events, create and lead interest groups, exchange opportunities, promote companies and start-ups, and find Montana partners.
5 She wants to integrate alumni in the present school in order to benefit current and future students.
6 Someone in Velia's position needs good organisational skills, lots of ideas, the ability to multitask, and the ability to relate to people of all ages.
7 The highlight of the alumni calendar is the Homecoming.

Vocabulary

1 l 2 h 3 k 4 m 5 c 6 e 7 j 8 b 9 i 10 f

The growth of parkrun

General comprehension

1 Everyone can take part.
2 The phrase is 'This course uses shared paths'.
3 The word 'picturesque' tells us that parts of the park are especially beautiful.

Text handling

Adjectives: lush, meandering, picturesque, rolling
Nouns: concrete, week, users, path, try, use
Verbs: try, use, concrete

Lawn bowling

General comprehension

1 In the United Kingdom, the game of bowls originated in the 13th century.
2 No, it is not. It is played in over 50 countries.
3 It is called a legend because it cannot be proved to be true.
4 Barefoot bowls appeals more to young people because there isn't a strict dress code, there is accompanying entertainment, and it is fun playing without shoes.

Ukulele revival

General comprehension

1 The ukulele was introduced to Hawaii by Portuguese immigrants.
2 Bit by bit, the writer took over and the men soon left the group.
3 The ukulele is easy to learn, you meet new people, and it is fun.
4 The name of the group is taken from a song performed by a 1960s group called The Kinks.
5 The group are taking part in numerous events being held to mark the centenary of the end of the First World War. They are also taking part in a local pantomime and carol service soon.

5 Sharing the planet

Why fresh water shortages will cause the next great global crisis

General comprehension

1 The main theme of the text is that water shortages are causing / will cause a global water problem.
2 He meant that without water there can be no nature / nature needs water to survive.
3 The world's population is rising faster than supplies of water.
4 The countries mentioned are: Brazil, the United States of America, Iran, the United Arab Emirates, Pakistan, India, and Bangladesh.
5 General Sheikh Mohammed bin Zayed Al-Nahyan said that water had become more important than oil. He was referring to the United Arab Emirates.

Vocabulary

1 rationing
2 drought: 'One year. . .drought got so bad. . .' and 'In California, officials have revealed that the state has seen four years of continuous drought.'
3 Students' own answers. Suggested answer: A 'reservoir' is a man-made or natural lake used for collecting water. An 'aquifer' is underground rock which contains water.
4 b
5 groundwater

What is climate change?

General comprehension

1 Immediate and ambitious action is needed right now to prevent the effects of climate change.
2 We need to keep the rise in temperature well below 2°C from the pre-industrial era.
3 The warmest years on record occurred in this century / in the 21st century.

4 The writer defines the Anthropocene as the time period in which human activity is the dominant influence on the Earth.
5 The further effects of climate change will be more extreme and unpredictable weather.

Vocabulary

1 immediate
2 prevent
3 unprecedented
4 unpredictable
5 impact

Paper 2 practice task (5.1) – A speech about climate change

1 True: '... most coastal cities could be underwater in the not too distant future.'
2 True: 'There will likely be an increase in the number of homeless people...'
3 False: '... greenhouse gases such as carbon dioxide and other fossil fuels contribute to the melting of beautiful Arctic glaciers...'
4 False: 'if all the homes in America replaced one light bulb...'
5 True: '... trees "breathe" in carbon dioxide and "breathe" out oxygen. This makes our air much cleaner...'
6 are less important
7 little piece of
8 contribute to the
9 replace all of
10 a huge problem

Canada's high Arctic glaciers at risk of disappearing completely

General comprehension

1 They are shrinking and many are at risk of disappearing completely.
2 They used satellite imagery.
3 They learned that warming temperatures may be affecting ice in the region.
4 It is hard to get to and was a kind of forgotten place as Google Earth did not have complete imagery.
5 No, none of the glaciers showed signs of growing.
6 She has noticed a lot more icebergs, as the ice shelves have broken up, and there are also more crevasses in the ice.
7 There was a sudden increase in warming in the mid-90s. The direct effects of this are that sea levels are rising and there is a risk the region's unique ecosystems will be wiped out.
8 The glaciers will not be able to collect more snow because they may not be high enough.

Vocabulary

1 inventory
2 the findings echo
3 glaciologist
4 sprawl
5 extrapolating from research
6 hard to get to
7 catalogued
8 seemed to be a shift
9 hinting
10 accumulate enough snow

Paper 2 practice task (5.2) – A phone conversation about rubbish

General comprehension

The true statements are: c, e.

1 struggling with that
2 you were to
3 any of the
4 on top of

5 clean it up
6 repairing the holes
7 down on paper
8 tied up with

Plastics in the 21st century

General comprehension

1 His goal was to paddle the Rhine, collect plastic waste, and send to the CEOs of the relevant companies.
2 No, it was an extremely difficult thing to do because the Rhine is a busy, fast-flowing river.
3 It was exhausting physically and mentally.
4 He had to find enough to eat and drink to maintain his strength and concentration levels.
5 He slept in a small tent beside the river.

Vocabulary

1 must be aware of it
2 engaged citizens
3 achievement
4 maintain
5 a death trap

Public commentary (page 183)

General comprehension

1 She went to the beach to take a break from studying and enjoy nature.
2 She is writing the letter because she is shocked by the amount of plastic rubbish on the beach.
3 It had its legs tangled in the plastic.
4 She says nobody will want to swim because the beach is so dirty.
5 She wants the Town Council to let her know what can be done about this situation.

Public commentary (page 184)

General comprehension

1 He was horrified.
2 He can't help because the council doesn't have the resources.
3 He suggests a village community initiative could help clear the beach.
4 He would like to talk to Janet about it and get some people involved.

Vocabulary

1 c 2 b 3 e 4 f 5 a 6 d

Public commentary (page 186)

General comprehension

1 He is enthusiastic because they thought of the action themselves and it is very necessary.
2 He says it is 'a sign of the times' because he believes we live in a throwaway society and rubbish is everywhere.
3 He thinks the government should act to limit the destruction of the environment.
4 He thinks it is an environmental disaster to continue to produce endless amounts of plastic.
5 People should be made more aware of the dangers of plastic in their lives and the village should take the first step by banning plastic.
6 He suggests a return to milk being sold in bottles, fruit and vegetables being sold loose, other products being sold with no plastic at all, holding a public meeting to share ideas.

I rely on plastic straws and baby wipes

General comprehension

1 She does not have the luxury of a plastic-free life because she is disabled.
2 She became environmentally aware and green when she was about ten years old.
3 She told the class that talcum powder is tested on cats and dogs by putting it in their eyes to see if it is safe and that plastic would pollute the Earth.

4 She needs straws that bend, can handle all temperatures, aren't too fat, and are easy to use.
5 They suggest paper, bamboo, glass, or metal straws as alternatives to plastic ones.
6 She feels uncomfortable and angry because non-disabled people think they know the answers, but they do not fully understand the challenges facing disabled people.
7 Biodegradable wipes are too expensive.
8 She wants the government to come up with decent, affordable green alternatives for us all.

Vocabulary

1 the dawning of my green consciousness
2 immersed (myself)
3 throw into the mix
4 exchanges that can get heated
5 biodegradable
6 passion
7 a fatberg
8 disposable
9 hard-up

The biggest beach clean-up?

General comprehension

1 The volunteers worked knee-deep in rotting garbage, sweating under the burning Indian sun. The press has reported that the work of the volunteers is slowly influencing the next generation of Indian leaders.
2 They asked friends, neighbours and schoolchildren to go from street to street knocking on doors and telling people about the Versova Beach situation. The press also helped spread the information.
3 The volunteers worked on Sundays / Sunday afternoons.
4 Human consumer habits are the direct cause.
5 Their work will not be finished until the amount of plastic people throw into the oceans stops.

Vocabulary

1 sludge
2 rallied
3 trash and garbage
4 to dump

The beach clean-up has now even reached our youngest!

General comprehension

1 The school focuses on outdoor learning and forest school.
2 They will talk about the difference between man-made and natural objects.
3 The children collected litter – mainly bottles and food wrappers.

Text handling

1 '. . .the beach is just a few hundred metres away for regular sessions'.
2 litter and rubbish
3 children who are two to five years old

Tourism's main impact areas

General comprehension

1 True: 'Negative impacts from tourism occur when the level of visitor use is greater than the environment's ability to cope. . .'
2 False: 'It can put enourmous pressure on an areas and lead to soil erosion, increased pollution. . .'
3 True: '. . .heightened vulnerability to forest fires'.
4 False: 'It often puts a strain on water supplies. . .'

Vocabulary

1 occur
2 potential
3 enormous
4 impacts
5 habitat

Depletion of water resources

General comprehension

1 The three effects are water shortages, degradation of supplies, and generating a greater volume of waste water.
2 It is a hot, dry region
3 Students' own answers. Suggested answer: Tourists use more water because they use swimming pools and golf courses. Tourists also tend to use more water for personal use when on holiday.
4 The number of golf courses has increased and they need an enormous amount of water daily to maintain.
5 It can cause saline or salts to enter the groundwater.

Vocabulary

1 overuse
2 consume
3 of particular concern
4 maintenance
5 scarcity
6 almost double
7 require
8 excessive
9 generating a greater volume
10 inhabitants
11 can run up to
12 rapidly
13 exacerbating their impacts

Maasai herders driven off land to make way for luxury safaris

General comprehension

1 The Maasai herding communities.
2 Tourists visit Tanzania to watch or hunt the wild animals in their habitat.
3 They have lost their land, their way of life, and their farming has been affected.
4 The court battle is over ownership of the land.
5 Their animals need be able to reach the waterholes.

Vocabulary

1 e	2 c	3 d	4 a	5 h
6 i	7 g	8 j	9 b	10 f

Paper 2 practice task (5.3) – Three friends discuss their holiday plans

1 False	2 True	3 False	4 False
5 True	6 False	7 False	8 False

9 really a proper
10 no need to
11 with loads of
12 contribute anything to
13 other thing is, passengers overwhelm the
14 your carbon footprint
15 is pretty environmentally
16 that for students

How to be a better tourist

General comprehension

1 The Council has issued the tips as a way to counter anti-tourism feelings which have been observed in European cities.
2 No, only to the well-known destinations. Lesser-known destinations do not have the same problems yet.
3 Tourists are likely to find interesting places that are not as well known while still having a pleasurable experience.
4 One possible negative effect is that there are fewer benefits to the local economy as much of the profit does not stay in the country.

Vocabulary

1 mounting
2 c
3 mitigate
4 A 'honeypot' site is a place that attracts a large number of tourists.
5 ditch (Tip 4)

Over-tourism in Japan

General comprehension

1 The three complaints are: tourists are unaware of local customs; they make public transport overcrowded; they show poor etiquette, i.e. forms of inappropriate behaviour.
2 The four cities are Kyoto, Kamakura, Tokyo, and Osaka.
3 A campaign to encourage tourists to explore more remote parts of the country.

Vocabulary

1 c 2 b 3 c 4 a 5 c

Veganism

General comprehension

1 True: 'Veganism… seeks to exclude… all forms of exploitation of, and cruelty to, animals…'
2 False: '… as well as avoiding animal-derived materials…'
3 True: 'Some research has linked vegan diets with… lower rates of heart disease…'
4 True: '… whole grains, fruit, nuts… are packed full of beneficial fibre, vitamins and minerals'.

Reducing the burden on the environment

General comprehension

1 It reduces the burden on the environment by using less water and land.
2 Apart from fruits and vegetables, vegans eat nuts, grains, seeds, beans and pulses.
3 Soya beans are grown in Brazil to feed animals in Europe.

Vocabulary

1 c 2 a 3 c 4 b

A Friend to the Bees: Mikaila Ulmer

General comprehension

1 When she was four years old, she was stung twice by bees.
2 Bees pollinate the foods we eat.
3 The use of pesticides and fungicides on crops.
4 Her idea was to sweeten her grandmother's lemonade with local honey and use the profits from sales to help groups fighting to protect the decline of bees.
5 'Her award-winning Me & the Bees Lemonade.'

Where have all our insects gone?

Text handling

1 to 2 past 3 with 4 at 5 over

General comprehension

1 Insects are newsworthy because are disappearing very fast / there are not many insects left.
2 His tweets were shared rapidly.
3 Although it is an ecological disaster, people are finding it almost normal and not reacting.
4 It means that something is likely to become extinct.
5 Insects that creep and/or crawl.
6 The 'little things that run the world' are insects.
7 He said that the world would revert to the rich state of equilibrium of 10 000 years ago.
8 'The environment would collapse into chaos.'
9 False: 'But they are spectacularly failing to do so.'
10 False: '. . . he had not seen a single butterfly. . .'
11 True: '. . . they were commonplace when he was a boy'.
12 False: 'Native ladybird populations are crashing;'
13 False: '. . . while bees, of which there are more than 250 species in the UK. . .'
14 True: 'Our creepy crawlies may have unsettling looks. . .'
15 False: 'If all humankind were to disappear, the world would regenerate back to the rich state of equilibrium that existed 10 000 years ago.'
16 True: '. . . lack of food is already causing serious declines in bird numbers. . .'

Warning of 'ecological Armageddon' after dramatic plunge in insect numbers

General comprehension

1 Germany and the Netherlands were involved in the research.
2 The information was collected on nature reserves across Germany.
3 Hans de Kroon led the research.
4 They were helped by dozens of amateur entomologists across Germany.
5 They used special tents (called malaise traps) to capture and count the insects.
6 Weather measurements and changes to the landscape or plant species in the reserves were also gathered.

Vocabulary

1 abundance 2 prey 3 amateur 4 dominated by
5 rule out 6 capture 7 fluctuations

Sustainable fashion

Text handling

Paragraph 1: Buy clothes made locally by ethical labels
Paragraph 2: Avoid fabrics made using petroleum and chemicals
Paragraph 3: Extend your wardrobe's lifespan by mending
Paragraph 4: Reduce your consumption by hitting the op shops

1 when 2 on 3 of
4 yet 5 With 6 by
7 on-sold 8 while 9 back

General comprehension

1 The fashion industry is arguably the second most polluting industry.
2 The oil industry is the worst cause of pollution.

3 It is washed into waterways. It's a problem because the water from manufacturing is full of contaminants such as bleaches, acids, inks, and dyes.
4 The writer suggests buying less and choosing better quality items that are made as ethically as possible.
5 They are plastic and take forever to breakdown and each time they are washed they shed microfibers that pollute rivers and oceans.
6 Cotton is usually grown with pesticides and requires huge water supplies. Toxic chemicals are required to turn bamboo into fabric.
7 The writer suggests mending those clothes, or having someone mend them for us.
8 The best way is to avoid buying new clothes.
9 They recycle clothing.

Vocabulary

1 churned (out) 2 contaminants
3 a pittance 4 a conundrum
5 tossed 6 rush straight to the bin
7 from scratch 8 avoid
9 a word of caution 10 winding back

Personal letter (page 214)

General comprehension

1 The idea is for members to exchange their old but much-loved clothes.
2 Young people buy the most clothes.
3 The clothes are produced by those working in a less than healthy environment under less than fair conditions. The clothes are often of poor quality fabric. The clothes are often very badly made.
4 They should provide a few articles of good quality clothing which they no longer wear.
5 The club members should take a critical look at their wardrobes and do some sorting.
6 They will collect the clothes from the members' homes.
7 The clothes exchange will reduce waste, clear out wardrobes, and offer new clothes at a low price.
8 Everyone involved profits from the action. There are no losers.

Vocabulary

1 dispose of 2 contribute to 3 recycling
4 put forward 5 an exchange 6 critical look
7 minimal 8 thrill 9 reduce

Would you like to be an astronaut?

General comprehension

1 d 2 b 3 c

Students give their opinions about space exploration

General comprehension

1 Response number 4 draws attention to the positive results.
2 She thinks the money can be spent on charities helping needy people on earth.
3 Having no roof over your head means your attention is focused on basic human provisions and that need is greater than thoughts about exploring space.

UK Space Agency's SatelLife Competition

Text handling

Heading 1: Who took part?
Heading 2: Get involved!
Heading 3: What it means to the competitors

Heading 4: A contribution to saving lives
Heading 5: Town planning
Heading 6: The next steps

General comprehension

1 Money prizes were awarded to the winners of the competition.
2 The girls were praised by the Royal National Lifeboat Institution because the idea could help identify the position of swimmers in difficulties when swimming and potentially save lives.
3 A panel of experts from space agencies and industry.

Vocabulary

1 pitch 2 thriving 3 urban

Space exploration

General comprehension

1 The wavelengths are radio, infrared, ultraviolet, X-rays, gamma rays.
2 Astronauts stay in space for many months, even years.

Students' own answers. Possible answers include:

Number	What it represents
60	The number of years unmanned probes have been sent to planets in our Solar System.
500	More than 500 people have flown in space since Yuri Gagarin paved the way.
1957	The year that the Space Age began.
1961	The year that Yuri Gagarin went into space.
20	The number of people that have travelled to the Moon.
12	The number of people that have walked on the Moon.

Vocabulary

1 unmanned probes
2 half a dozen

Life beyond earth

General comprehension

1 Scientists think that bacteria may exist on other planets.
2 No, the surface is too cold and dry.
3 A rover could be used to collect material and samples from distant planets.

Index

Index

Z

Text type index

Notes

Notes